"I've spent the last thirty years of my life as a certified appraiser and expert in the field of classic and collectible cars. Buying, collecting and restoring these old vehicles is born of passion, not need. *Zen and the Art of Collecting Old Cars* perfectly captures this passion in a way that strikes a tender chord with those of us so afflicted. The stories in this book candidly illustrate the very significant sacrifices collectors willingly make in pursuit of their car dreams, and the outsized rewards sometimes realized in those exchanges."

— **Steve Linden**, Certified Appraiser, Author of *Car Collecting: Everything You Need To Know*

"Bruce Valley's car stories, and his perspective on life, are informed by a deep appreciation for not just the machines, but for the people who make them come alive. Our old Lamborghini is made more special for having Bruce as its caretaker for so many years. Without such a caring owner, and the good doctor who passed the car on to him, #0517 would never have sailed through the decades with such panache, or been spared the indignities suffered by many of its contemporaries. I have been privileged to carry the torch. Yet I reflect often on the fortuitous phone call that set things in motion more than two decades ago. If old Lamborghinis seem almost fast enough to fly, regrettably, so does the time we have with them."

— **Robert Ross**, restorer and current owner of the 1966 Lamborghini 400GT #0517

"I've followed Bruce Valley's journey since 1954, when we were together in 4th grade. As with his earlier books, his emphasis on the past's helpful lessons and his dedication to standards, is found throughout *Zen and the Art of Collecting Old Cars*, even between the lines, as is his lifelong love of the American automobile. The strength of his views stands out clearly against today's muted embrace of American culture, values, and style. Like any good book, this fine literary effort teaches us through parable about collecting old cars, but much more about living.

— **Roger Byam Nold**, Architect, Noldesign & Chronicler of American Style

"*Zen and the Art of Collecting Old Cars* personifies the passion of a man with the love, patience, and perseverance to oversee the restoration of classic cars over many decades. These included a historically-significant 1929 Packard Sport Phaeton found in Portugal, which exemplifies the high styling and robust engineering of bygone days, when the automobile was only a few years removed from the horse and buggy era. This enlightening book about collecting and restoring classic cars will allow our current generation to better understand the luminous memories of their parents' and grandparents' early lives, generations doubtless fascinated by the advent of the automobile, and its uncommon style and practicality. How they must have marveled as the automobile propelled mankind into the modern transportation era."

> — **Carl Manofsky**, restorer and current owner of the
> 1929 Packard Model 640 Sport Phaeton

"I really enjoyed reading Bruce Valley's *Zen and the Art of Collecting Old Cars*, a well-written and well-told account of growing up in New England as a car guy in the golden era of muscle cars, then spending a lifetime reliving his memories by collecting and restoring his favorites. This book brought a great many fond memories back to me. It's a 'must-read' for those of us who truly love the automobile."

> — **Jay Leno**, *Jay Leno's Garage*, Automotive Hall of Fame
> Inductee, 2020

"Compelling, almost magical, stories of one man's lifelong love affair with the automobile, and an inspiration to those seeking entry into a fascinating hobby. *Zen and the Art of Collecting Old Cars* is truly memorable, one of my most satisfying reads in many years.

> — **Byron Dieckman**, Vietnam Combat Rescue Pilot & Seeker
> of Old Cars

ZEN and the ART of Collecting Old Cars

Adventures in Toyland

Bruce Valley

Bruce Valley

Great Life Press
2020

Print book ISBN: 978-1-938394-47-8
Ebook ISBN: 978-1-938394-48-5
Library of Congress Control Number: 2020909499

published by
Great Life Press
Rye, New Hampshire 03870
www.greatlifepress.com

Please visit the author's website at:
www.brucevalley.com

Remembrance

For Nancy
Spirit having flown
Homeward bound
Sententamente

This book is dedicated to Mike "Oakie" Stansel

Mike Stansel and I have been best friends for almost fifty years. In that time, I cannot recall an argument or disagreement between us. We met in graduate school. Mike was a graduate of the Navy's "Top Gun" fighter weapons school, and a veteran of Vietnam. I was a rescue helicopter pilot in that conflict. We'd both experienced the crucible of war.

Our long friendship and its countless reflective conversations covered many topics. But the focus was always our mutual interest in the automobile. When living near each other, car-related activities sometimes took over our lives. Now in retirement, and on opposite coasts, we are often in touch, and manage weeklong visits twice yearly. When together we wander rural back roads, and through small towns, in search of illusive cars, bookstores and antique shops. We revel in America's past.

Engaged in questing for old cars since my college years, I'm certain that, without Mike's peerless mechanical gifts and encyclopedic automobile knowledge, the list of cars I've found and restored over the decades would have been much shorter, the successes far fewer.

As individuals, Mike and I lacked the skills needed to bring those cars and trucks back to life. Working together, our synergy proved the sum of our assets greater than its parts.

Thank you for your friendship, Mike, and for playing a central role in one of my life's best journeys, a fascinating ride down the automobile's Memory Lane.

Contents

Introduction:
The Zen of Old Car Collecting

Zen begins at the point where there is nothing further to seek.

This book is not about Zen. Nevertheless, Zen pervades its pages. Anecdotally, it's about the hunt for and occasional capture of unique motorcars by one man over a period of six decades. He often won but sometimes lost to the challenges found in each new project. This book details a lifetime of searching, finding, buying, transporting, restoring, enjoying, and eventually selling the products of a hobby gone wild.

This is where Zen enters the picture, assuming a vital but reserved role in the car stories you will read. Zen has been a leitmotif in my life, etching itself into my heart and soul over the decades.

Zen is a concept that words cannot adequately define. It has great power, but is inherently imprecise in language, like the perfect horse in J.D. Salinger's short story, *A Great Day For Bananafish*. Unlike merely superb horses, Salinger's perfect horse "raised no dust and left no tracks, a fleeting thing, as evanescent as thin air."

Zen concentrates on meditation. The philosophy originated in China during the Tang Dynasty and later flourished in Japan. The word Zen comes from an earlier Sanskrit root, meaning "thought," "absorption," or "meditation." The philosophy emphasizes focus, self-control, insight, and intuition.

A Zen state is one of calm attentiveness, where actions are guided more by intuition than conscious effort. In the hobby of car collecting, for example, Zen allows the collector to become lost in the rhythm of the project's tasks, eventually becoming one with the car. I know what you're thinking. It sounds like mumbo-jumbo. But it isn't. Not at all.

Robert M. Pirsig, who died recently in nearby South Berwick, Maine, wrote the cult classic *Zen and the Art of Motorcycle Maintenance: An Inquiry into Values* in 1974. On the surface, it was a road story of a man, his teenage son, and another couple, driving their motorcycles west on America's blue highways, through myriad small towns, to the Pacific coast. Beneath the surface, however, there were references, and sometimes lectures, about the need for caring in our lives, and for a commitment to quality in carrying out life's tasks, including, of course, the maintenance of motorcycles. By creating his transcendent odyssey, Pirsig was able to ask fundamental questions about how we live our lives.

"Peace of mind," he wrote, "isn't at all superficiality. It's the whole thing. That which produces it is good maintenance; that which disturbs it is poor maintenance. The ultimate test is always your own serenity. If you don't have this when you start, and maintain it while you're working, you're likely to build your own personal problems right into the machine."

It wasn't an accident that my book's title mimics Pirsig's. I took his book seriously when I read it in the 1970s, and when re-reading it at least once each decade since. The book seems chaotic and confusing, but is deep in its thoughts and prescriptions. Its secrets are there to be found, as millions of readers have learned. The book's principles have informed my life for half a century, in no part more than my car-collecting hobby.

As you will learn reading these stories, car collecting has been my essential laboratory for learning the ways of Zen. The journey hasn't been linear nor always positive. Mistakes were made. Learning was required. Course corrections were necessary. Often, the result was two steps forward and three backward. But Pirsig's dedication to quality, and his loyalty to a deep caring about how we should do our work, always informed my path.

Pirsig had a few choice words on that subject. "Let's talk about caring." he wrote. "I *care* about my old moldy gloves. I smile at them because they've been with me for so many years, and are so old and tired and rotten there is something kind of humorous about them. They cost three dollars, and have been restitched so many times it's getting impossible to repair them. Yet I take a lot of time and pains to do it anyway. Because I can't imagine a new pair taking their place. That is impractical, of course. But practicality isn't the whole thing with gloves — or with anything else."

Specific rules for Zen do not exist. But, over time, application of its undefined but powerful concepts produces unexpected results. Being in the moment, and surrendering to, rather than struggling against, the swirl of life around us, bore fruit beyond my imagining. Parts or repair issues for vehicle restorations resolved by relaxing instead of stressing. Restored collector cars often sold themselves. Unexpected business or family needs were met by an unanticipated purchase offer for an unadvertised car.

These were not consistent occurrences, and couldn't be relied on with confidence. But they happened often enough through the decades to be gratefully accepted as unusual and special. Something unnamed and unknown played a role in those events, increasing an awareness of the unseen influences in our lives. My commitment to live with an awareness of the power inherent in trusting intuition was established, as I found answers and solved intractable problems.

Somewhere in these car-collecting passages of mind, body, and metal, I realized that I could choose a simpler, less complicated life, and bring mindfulness and a certain passivity to every activity. In consequence, I found a heretofore unknown calmness. These experiences evolved over time into principles for living which aided in daily tasks. I found these principles especially useful facing the unpredictable challenges of bringing an old vehicle back to useful life.

A few of the Zen-like tenets that have been beneficial in my car-collecting journey are:

1. to consider what is necessary in life and work. Live simply. Rid life of as many unnecessary and unessential things as possible to better focus on the essential. By actively determining what's most important, room is made for these matters by eliminating less essential things.

2. to do one task at a time, as slowly and deliberately as possible, and completely. Focus on optimizing quality. Care so much about process and result, that the mind actually unites with the task and its object.

3. to schedule activities so that adequate time and energy are allotted to each task. Allowing space between tasks, time is always available to meet quality standards. Do less if necessary to ensure tasks are done completely, with concentration and conviction.

4. to make a ritual of cleaning up after completing a task, working deliberately and correctly.

5. to escape oneself as often as possible, to that vastly interesting world beyond ourselves.

Reading these true stories of one man's lifelong car-collecting avocation, you'll find the journey seldom follows the anticipated path. As with life itself, there are sudden turns, frequent stops, and frustrating conditions, events, and outcomes. It's probably better to recognize these through others' experiences, rather than stumbling into the pitfalls and darker elements of car collecting on your own and without preparation. As I did.

After you've read the car stories, and had an opportunity to observe mistakes made, and the adverse results that often follow, the book's concluding chapter will offer lessons learned across a car-collecting lifetime. Take heed. These lessons could help prevent similar mistakes in your own collecting pursuits. Who knows, they might even save you from yourself.

Looking back, I wish I'd found something similar sixty years ago to better prepare for the hobby's rigors. Many wasted hours and dollars might have been saved. Above all, these stories should illustrate the difference between learning as you go — flying by the seat of your pants — or gaining information and knowledge before stepping into the rewarding, but also daunting, hobby of collecting old cars. Take the lesson.

1

Life in a Small Town: A Hobby's Origins

As long as one thinks about listening, one cannot hear clearly. And as long as one thinks about trying to let go of oneself, one cannot let go.

How is it that lifelong interests are discovered, then become established, in our callow, youthful selves? It's a commonplace that influences of home, school, church, and community shape the adult who emerges from the youth. But from what source spring our hobby interests?

In my eighth decade of fixation with the automobile, and my sixth of seeking, acquiring, restoring, and enjoying vintage cars and trucks, and studying their histories, mechanical and aesthetic singularities, unique features and handling characteristics, I've come to appreciate the significance of a hobby as an enjoyable pastime exclusive of one's profession. Mine has provided a door into a century's industrial evolution, its underpinning in our country's progress, and, foremost, its creative drive to build beautiful and useful automobiles.

My interest was always tied to another question. Why do certain marques and models live on indefinitely, prized and preserved by collectors, while the great mass of automobiles, tens of millions of them, are rudely stripped of valuable components then, junkyard-bound, crushed for their metal content and forgotten?

Reflecting upon this lifelong interest in the automobile, always a strong and constant factor in my life, I am led back to my boyhood in a small New England town on the Atlantic coastline. There, in memories of growing up in Rye, New Hampshire, I recall events that shaped and sharpened this fascination.

My love of automobiles began when I was young, in first or second grade. Although the advent of my addiction can be traced to one cathartic event, there were other influences. These served to deepen my interest in any object moving about on four wheels under its own power.

That initial event, however, snuck up on me.

* * *

It was the summer of 1951. I was seven years old. Teresa Brewer was singing *Music, Music, Music* on the radio, often echoed by Patti Page with her hit *The Tennessee Waltz*. In small-town New England, as elsewhere throughout the country, the breath-releasing sense of relief at having survived the Great Depression in the 1930s, and global war in the 1940s, was still palpable. Having returned from WWII, our fathers had jobs. As children, we had both parents in the home. When not in school or on weekends, mothers sent their children out to play after breakfast, a peanut butter and jelly sandwich wrapped in wax paper shoved into a back pocket, and told us to be at the dinner table as our fathers came home from work. And not before.

Even with forest, streams, ponds, and fields to explore, not to mention the Atlantic's fascinating shoreline, time often hung heavily upon us in those pre-digital years. So it was that several boys, bored enough to see the arrival of Mr. Bean's postal delivery station wagon on Cable Road as an interesting event, were happy to hear his news.

"Boys," Mr. Bean said, "You don't want to miss seeing some antique cars drive by on Ocean Boulevard in about an hour." He told us that the Glidden Tour, a wandering cavalcade of pre-WWI autos, would be driving from York, Maine, to Cape Ann, Massachusetts, on Route 1 and 1A. He advised us to walk there right away and find a vantage point before the old cars arrived. We hurried down Cable Road to Ocean Boulevard, Route 1A, which ran parallel to nearby Jenness Beach, and climbed up on a white rail fence, each of us craning our necks north toward the town's harbor, hoping to be the first to see the old cars arrive.

An impatient hour later, which seemed much longer in "boy time," our interest was definitely flagging. Where were those old cars? Our bottoms had gone numb perching on the bone-hard fence rail. Two of our number, their patience expired, left for the beach to search for empty tonic bottles left by beachgoers. The local store, Carberry's, paid two cents for each bottle turned in. Those were the days of five-cent candy bars, ten-cent soft drinks and, of course, penny candy. An hour's bottle search on the beach could be very rewarding.

With our two friends gone bottling, three of us were left on the fence awaiting the cars. Though anxious to see the spectacle described by our mailman, our growing physical discomfort and boyish fidgeting was wearing us down. So we began to explore the idea of abandoning our perch and going up Cable Road to Rand's Fields and the nearby spring, whose fresh water and watercress had fed and watered generations of Rye boys at play in the woods and fields.

Just then, as if sprung from the earth, a strange mechanical contraption came wheezing noisily into sight around the far bend, chugging unsteadily toward us down the hill from the harbor and the promontory known as Straws Point.

It must be one of Mr. Bean's old cars, we thought. But it looked more like the old-time, horse-drawn wagons and carriages we found abandoned in the town's woods, and used for cowboy and Indian games.

The apparition moving steadily toward us was black with gleaming brass headlights — or were they lanterns? — high on the front cowl. The wheels were narrow, even spindly, and all white, including the tread. The sound of the vehicle as it drew nearer was unlike any motor noise we'd ever heard, weak, like a MixMaster kitchen appliance whirring, as if it barely had the strength to move the car along.

There was a metal-framed glass windscreen, and a black canvas top suspended over wooden support bows. Everything about this ancient motorcar spoke of fragility. But on it came. As it drew near, its two middle-aged occupants came into better view. I call them middle-aged, though they were probably decades younger than I am now. But to boys just beginning grade school, they appeared as Mr. and Mrs. Methuselah.

And were they jovial! Broad smiles lit their faces when they saw us on the fence. We noticed that they were dressed in clothing to match the car's early century time frame. The man wore a black suit with turned-up stiff collar and round bowler hat. The woman was dressed in a great bustle of burgundy, with an outlandishly large hat, suggesting a large, colorful bird had mistakenly landed on her head.

As the couple and their old car drew near to pass us, they became more animated, smiling and waving. As we waved back, the man reached across the long tiller, which must have been the vehicle's steering control, and squeezed a large rubber bulb horn mounted on the outer edge of the windshield.

Ah-oo-gah! Ah-oo-gah! And with that raucous sound, the black vehicle and its occupants swept past us and continued south toward Massachusetts. It was followed over the next hour by dozens of old brass vehicles, grouped in twos and threes. Our waves drew smiles, and no few raspy horns in return, until the last car receded south in the distance, the chuffing sounds of those underpowered motors giving way to the accustomed silence of a small town summer.

Legs and bottoms more asleep than awake, we climbed down carefully from the rail fence, stretched our legs until they responded, and headed to the beach to do some bottle-hunting. We were hungry. Surely there were enough empties on the sand for us to earn a Baby Ruth, a Butterfinger, some root beer barrels, even a Coke or NuGrape.

Later, no one mentioned the car caravan for which we'd spent so much time waiting and watching. Apparently, my companions found the event interesting, but nothing more, and had already forgotten those unusual sights and sounds. But not me. From the moment I caught sight of the first antique car, until the last one chugged past, then faded from view as it passed the Sandpiper store, ran along the

Eel Pond beside the Atlantic, and disappeared around a corner, I was a changed little boy.

Suddenly, I took interest in every car I saw, comparing their appearances, their paint colors and interiors, the varying sounds of their motors. My father wore down under all my questions. I would often spend time in Carberry's store, examining the dozens of plastic Revell car kits, anticipating the day when a paper route became available, and its earnings allowed the means to buy and assemble some of those beautiful models.

I did not know it at the time, of course. But the Glidden Tour's passage through my little town, and straight into the innermost recesses of my heart, had given me the gift of a lifetime interest in all things automotive, an interest that would find decades of expression, participating in the many facets of the old car hobby, attending car shows, parades and other car-related events, visiting car museums and vintage car sales locations, buying and restoring a number of old cars and vintage trucks myself, and making friendships which continue to endure. Thank you, Postman Bean. The cathartic experience of an early 1950s Glidden Tour gave me a lifetime of pleasure just being around old cars. For that, I consider myself a lucky man.

* * *

It would, however, be incorrect to ascribe my love affair with cars only to the Glidden Tour. Growing up in a decade of increasingly fascinating automobiles and a car-crazy younger generation, there were ample influences around to feed my new frenzy.

Once or twice each year in the 1950s, local firehouses and fire-fighting volunteer companies polished their vehicles, then sent their shiny fire engines and burly firefighters to a weekend convention on a local field for a Firemen's Muster. In Rye, this usually took place on the broad, seaside lawn of the Drake House, an old wooden hotel on South Road opposite the Rye Beach Club.

Teams of firemen from nearby towns — Rye, Portsmouth, Exeter, Hampton, and North Hampton in New Hampshire, and sometimes from as far away as Haverhill, Massachusetts, and Kittery, Maine, would arrive at the muster with bright red pumpers and ladder trucks, quickly connect to nearby fire hydrants by running what appeared to be miles of hoses interlaced on the ground, then compete in fast-moving competitive firefighting drills in which speed, accuracy and practiced teamwork delivered a blue or red ribbon as reward.

Small boys, agog at the splendor of so much huge, red machinery, watched the goings-on in a state of amazement. A fortunate few were invited to climb high up onto the driver's seat, behind the horizontal steering wheel of the fire truck and, while wearing an oversized fireman's helmet, sit beside the dalmatian mascot in a near agony of the purest love.

Later in the day, the muster's competitions came to an end. Great quantities of hot dogs and hamburgers were eaten, beer and soft drinks ("tonic") swilled. The firefighting teams untangled and stowed their fire hoses, loaded all their equipment, and rode away with smiling faces and waves to appreciative young onlookers, some of the vehicles sporting brightly colored award ribbons pinned under a windshield wiper. To those of us already captivated by motor vehicles, the happy bedlam of a firemen's muster only intensified our desires.

Soon only the soaked lawn and excited crowd of wet little boys remained, replaying the antics of their firemen heroes, their minds still exulting over images of the muster field covered with huge red vehicles, men running and shouting while water gushed and splashed from a hundred hoses, enjoying their young and bright-eyed sense of such a large and exciting world.

* * *

From Rye's town center, which featured a town hall, the high-spired white church, a public library, the junior high school, and police and fire stations, Lang Road ran west a short bicycle ride to join Route 1's Lafayette Highway. On the corner was a junkyard — Ralph's. Around the roadside building were dozens of old or wrecked trucks, the apparent focus of the business. But further back, hidden by over-grown bushes, and by the stacked truck wrecks themselves, were several acres of old cars. A heaven and haven for little boys.

We would ride our bikes until we saw the old cars through the trees on our left. Then, dismounting, we hid the bikes well off the road among the trees and went exploring. Unlike the trucks, the cars were not piled on top of each other. They sat, disconsolate, in the high grass and low bushes. Appraising their lines, sitting behind steering wheels for imagined drives, one could almost sense the lives that had left them.

Often, the purpose of our visits was to remove chrome trim from wrecked cars to enhance the look of the crude soapbox derby racers we'd built. My racer was crude but formidable and ran well on its discarded lawn-mower wheels, with ropes for steering running from the front axle's ends into my hands. The racer sported a 2'x4' hand lever, which provided braking by friction on the road surface. Several coats of black paint were set off by chrome trim strips nailed on the body and frame. Auto taillights were attached to the rear. These childhood racers, used on untraveled back roads with just enough grade to allow coasting and simulated racing, had short lives. The quality control of ten-year-old racer builders left something to be desired. But they were a lot of fun.

Several luxury cars in Ralph's back lot caught my eye. One was a 1940 Cadillac sedan which looked as if it could be started and driven away. On the hood's forward edge was a beautifully fashioned shield, emblematic of the marque. I had to have it, not for my racer, but simply to possess something so beautiful. Using tools borrowed from my father's workshop, I opened the hood and backed off the nuts securing the badge. It came free. Into my pocket it went. I still have it. It sits beside my computer as I type these words.

Our trips to Ralph's became more challenging over time. The telephone company had been removing wooden, party-line, wall telephone units and installing modern telephones. It was, after all, the dawn of the "Space Age." As a result, several of us had accumulated dozens of the huge dry cell batteries from phone company workmen who, removing two batteries from every old telephone, had truck beds full of batteries to give away. These needed to be employed in useful ways. We decided to construct an electric shoe polisher for school and church shoes. But the batteries and polishing pad needed something to make it turn — a motor.

As it happened, the older wrecked vehicles at Ralph's were sometimes equipped with under-dash, accessory heaters. These metal boxes were on the floor, next to the car's firewall. They had access doors that opened, or could be left partly or fully closed. Hot water from the motor was directed to the heater, whose hot air kept the car's occupants warm in winter. To improve efficiency, many of these heaters were equipped with a fan driven by a quarter-horsepower electric motor. Our theory was that such a motor, small enough to fit in the palm of one's hand, was ideal to provide the power needed to bring our battery-powered shoe polisher to life.

The problem was access. Even for youthful bodies with small hands, it was difficult to crawl through the car's open front door, then take the heater housing apart, so that the fan motor could be removed. Several trips to Ralph's were made without success. Frustration, easily come by in young thieves, set in. But I had an idea. Rather than wedge oneself through the door and across the floor, I would lie upside down on the front seat of the car, legs hanging over the seat into the rear. My eyes would be in a position to see the heater up close, though upside down, and my hands would be free to perform the operation. All agreed this might work.

The next day, two of us pedaled Lang Road to Ralph's Truck Junkyard. We hid the bikes in the usual spot. I had borrowed additional tools from my father's workshop and carried them in a rolled up Pik-n-Pay shopping bag. It was a warm summer day. There were always bees buzzing around the cars. But they left us alone, as we made our way to one sedan we knew had a heater with better access than most.

This was a professional operation. I assumed my unusual posture on the front seat and, like a surgeon, began asking for various tools from my companion, who was standing beside the open driver's door. The work went smoothly. The heater doors and cowling were removed, then set on the floor. The fan and fan housing were more difficult. Though I had brought an assortment of tools, the next step required a tool we did not have. I struggled with make-do methods to obtain the prize.

My companion had been helpful and encouraged my progress. He passed the needed tools back and forth. I was so intent, trying to solve the mechanical riddle upside down in front of me, I failed to notice my friend's talking had ceased. I asked for a pair of small pliers. When there was no reply, I shifted my attention from what remained of the heater box and craned my neck to see what my friend was doing.

No friend. Where he had been were two huge, grown-up legs in dungarees anchored in black work-boots. In my odd position, I could not see the upper body or face, but two arms hung down with hands in heavy leather gloves. One of the gloved hands held a bolt cutter. Ralph!!! My heart felt like it had exploded. Those bolt cutters! I had to escape! With one desperate twisting motion, I drew my legs back over the front seat and dove through the open passenger door. I hit the ground running as fast as my legs would carry me, not looking back to see if I was being chased. Grabbing my bike I leapt aboard and tore down Lang Road intent only on putting distance between myself and the threat.

The bolt cutters were red — and they were huge.

I never retrieved my father's tools. I didn't have the courage to face the big man with the bolt cutters, and ask him to return the tools. After a suitable time had passed we did, however, return to the junkyard. Using the upside-down position in another car, this one as far away from the junkyard building as could be found, and with two cautious friends keeping a diligent watch, we were finally able to remove a fan motor for our use. It worked perfectly, buffing everyone's shoes to a gleaming shine, while our supply of dry cell batteries lasted.

But those big bolt cutters. Jeez Louise.

* * *

One of the many summer jobs available for teenagers in Rye was carrying golf bags for golfers at the venerable Abenaqui Golf Course, now the Abenaqui Country Club. One of the oldest courses in the country, Abenaqui opened in 1904. It was now the 1950s. For a twelve-year-old, the work was ideal, and paid well for that era. You met interesting people: doctors, lawyers, businessmen, and sometimes recognizable entertainment and sports figures. I remember caddying rounds with Johnny Mathis, Steve Lawrence and Eydie Gormé, Red Sox baseball player Jimmy Piersall, and several hockey professionals, including the Boston Bruins' Leo Boivin and the Montreal Canadiens' "Boom Boom" Geoffrion. The work was outside and involved lots of exercise.

It was often possible to carry one or even two "doubles" golfers' bags around the eighteen-hole course twice on a given day, a single round requiring about four hours. When not caddying on the course, there were other earning opportunities. One was to retrieve golf balls during member lessons given by the club professional, ranging around like a baseball outfielder to catch them on the fly in a canvas bag. In addition to being paid for "shagging" the flying golf balls, listening to the golf professional's pointers provided excellent tips to improve a caddy's own game. An added benefit of caddying at Abenaqui was the privilege of playing free on the course after 4 pm if, earlier in the day, you had caddied a round.

It was the late 1950s, and those of us who loved beautiful cars had only to walk out to the club parking lot to see dozens of our favorites, Fords and Chevrolets, of course, including the new Corvette and Thunderbird sports cars, but also Cadillacs, Lincolns and Chryslers, and a handful of low-slung foreign jobs, Jaguars, Austin-Healeys, Triumphs, and MGs.

Three of the club members drove the era's rarest car, the Lincoln Continental Mark II. Stately, sedate, beautifully low and wide, the hand-assembled $10,000 Mark II seemed to flow in slow motion over the road. I recall the golfers' deference when one of these cars drove by. Had the passing vehicle been a Cadillac Eldorado or Thunderbird convertible, the players would chime in with comments about the car, often ribald, particularly if the driver were a pert young woman. But when a Mark II passed, everyone's eyes followed until it drove out of sight.

At the end of the workday, caddies would often delay walking or bicycling home to search for lost golf balls along fairway roughs and in water hazards. Any golf ball having an unmarked outer cover brought a quarter at the pro shop. But an obviously new and unmarked ball from a major manufacturer, such as Titleist, paid fifty cents. This was at a time when carrying one bag for a four-hour round of eighteen holes paid two or three dollars, though good tipping often followed good caddying. Therefore, a caddy's search in the course's wet or "grongle" areas, where players were dissuaded from lost-ball searches by feasting mosquitos, might provide a lucrative return in the cooling sea breezes of a summer evening.

On one of those halcyon nights, sun slowly fading behind the western trees, three of us carefully combed several holes along Causeway Road, beating aside high grass and brush, and reaching beneath the sod edges of water hazards to locate our prizes. As we walked along, the sole possessors of the entire golf course, we stopped suddenly, awestruck at the discovery of a golden vision. Parked on the roadside grass alongside the fairway sat a 1957 Thunderbird, an image right out of a boy's imagination, its convertible top down and stored away. The color was a soft yellow. The interior was black and white. Overcoming our initial surprise, the three of us were drawn to the car as moths to flame. There we made a discovery almost beyond a boy's imagination. The keys had been left in the ignition. That discovery and its implications still bring an intake of breath sixty years later!

We stared at the car, and at each other, looking about nervously for the absent driver who was nowhere in sight. He was likely somewhere out on the course. The possibilities inherent in this situation struck three, car-crazy twelve-year-olds at the same time.

Someone said the magic words. "Let's take her for a spin." We moved closer to the car, then opened its doors and climbed in. Sitting in the driver's seat, I held my breath, reached forward and turned on the ignition key. The motor came immediately to life, throbbing with power. Fortunately, the car was equipped with an automatic transmission, so there was no clutch pedal to struggle with. Stretching my right leg, I could just reach the brake and gas pedal.

Recounting the adventure that followed, I'd enjoy describing our "peeling out" and leaving long strips of rubber on the road, roaring through turns with tires screaming, the chassis leaning, as we waved at startled adults, who looked up from lawn-mowing or getting their mail to see three underage boys ripping rapidly past in a beautiful roadster, horn honking, radio blaring, laughter floating in the air after their passage.

In comparison, the truth is boring. Unsure of ourselves, wondering every second when the absent owner might turn up, and with an unlicensed amateur behind the wheel, thoughts of prison bars in his head, we moved forward slowly onto the road. Then, barely touching the accelerator, we rolled slowly south on Causeway Road, so slowly that the car never shifted out of first gear. Turning around carefully, we retraced our path at the same crawl, reversed direction again, and placed the Thunderbird on what we hoped was the exact spot we'd found her. The car went silent as the key was turned off. Thus ended our joyride. As silently, we got out and gently closed the doors. Standing on the road eyeing the beautiful convertible we'd just driven, it came to each of us what a chance we'd taken, what an incredible experience we'd had, and how important it was that we not share the story with unbelieving and naturally jealous friends. And we didn't. Until now.

Looking back on the first illegal act of my life, I cannot suppress the smile that always leaks onto my face when calling up memories of youthful, risky events. "Fun, Fun, Fun," until our own well-founded, youthful fears, "took our TBird away."

* * *

On frigid winter weekends in Rye, after the ice had thickened, there was jalopy ice-racing on Burke's pond. The scene was right out of the John Travolta movie, *Grease*.

By mid-morning, as temperatures "soared" from frigid nighttime lows to an almost-survivable, just-below-freezing, a number of beaten-up, old vehicles drove up and parked in a pine grove off

Central Road, near the golf course, right beside the pond. The cars were backed into a rough circle under the pines, whereupon drivers and their helpers commenced making final adjustments to carburetors and equipment. Youngsters were not allowed near the chariots of these demigods. But we managed to skulk about. The cars were near-wrecks and looked ready, even overdue, for the crusher. Bent and crumpled fenders, running boards flattened by collision or removed, rusty and unpainted or amateurishly hand-sprayed in garish colors, tires bald, cord showing, interiors shredded or removed altogether, the vehicles existed for one purpose only. Racing on the Burke's Pond ice.

The drivers and their friends wore a sort of uniform, setting themselves apart from the traditional residents of our small town. Motorcycle boots, faded dungarees, black leather motorcycle jackets, replete with chromed buttons and assorted chains. No gloves, scarves or hats, despite the frigid air, the better to expose the swept-back and heavily greased "DA" haircuts they wore. These fell forward over the forehead, James Dean-style, when working on their motors, and had to be combed frequently to keep the bad boy image in its improper place.

Among those who came to observe the jalopy ice races was my personal hero, Eddie. Older, wiser, infinitely cooler, he drove a chopped and channeled black 1949 Mercury coupe which was, in a phrase, "the cat's mustache." Far too cool to race on the ice, his uniform impeccably perfect for a young hood, he drove slowly with a studied nonchalance, glancing sideways as if bored by life. Picture Marlon Brando in the film, *The Wild Bunch*. Slicked-back dark hair with a prominent wave in front and the requisite "DA" sculpting in back. Worn jeans, a tired motorcycle jacket but, uppermost, an ineffable practiced aloofness that lent itself to brash idolizing by impressionable youngsters like myself. "Bye, Bye, Birdie!" Eddie! Eddie! Eddie! Even today, I can instantly summon an image of him driving slowly by in that mean black Merc.

The din caused by every driver's constant throttling after each adjustment, the shouted challenges and friendly obscenities, lasted for perhaps an hour, after which, as if on some secret signal, the wretched vehicles drove out of the pines and onto the ice, one after another.

The fun began. Burke's Pond was not large. Fed by an eastbound stream, and feeding in turn the Eel Pond near the coast through the rocky conduit of a long-fallow millrace, it formed an oval perhaps eight hundred feet long by four hundred feet wide, sufficient, indeed ideal, for the informal antic racing to come.

Each race began informally and lasted perhaps a half hour, when it came to a raucous end, equally informally. Collisions were not only inevitable, with a group of young testosterone-stuffed madmen driving hotrods pell-mell on a glassy, frictionless surface, but seemed intended as part of the overall design. The crunching sounds of car striking car was a constant. Given the wasted state of the vehicles, and the fact that the cars in the race were already slipping and sliding as they caromed around the icy oval, it was surprising that no one was injured. Participating cars would drive back under the shelter of the pine grove as the race ended, looking about the same as when they began the race. Which, of course, was not saying much.

All in all, the effect of watching this pre-NASCAR activity was of a busy, bustling, noisy bedlam full of sound and fury. Fun in the frigid winter outdoors. The races were not unlike the dodgem electric cars we rode and crashed around in during weekend visits to a nearby amusement park in Massachusetts. But the visuals were stunning. Twenty or more roaring, exhaust-less motors motivating an equal number of past-prime running wrecks at full throttle around the frozen fringes of a small, snow-surrounded pond, horns honking, drivers laughing and swearing at each other, while crowds of locals stamped their feet for warmth as they watched the carnage from the snowy shore.

Occasionally a car would spin off the track out of control or be bumped from the pack. One might bounce off the shoreline, only to rebound, downshift, and reenter the auto jousts. No jalopy ever broke through the foot-thick ice. The steadfast townspeople, though not exactly approving, sought and found a noisy, energetic weekend's entertainment without charge while standing, and stamping, on the shoreline of Burke's Pond.

* * *

These and many other car events served to build within me a deep and abiding love of the automobile, indeed a love of all things mechanical. Seeing colorful 1950s Chryslers, Desotos, and Dodges with their long tail fins, sporty Hudson Hollywoods with their rear-mounted continental spare tires, and stubby Nash Rambler wood-sided station wagons in bright, and sometimes awkwardly unmatched paint schemes, while pedaling my Hercules bicycle around the neighborhood delivering the *Portsmouth Herald* newspaper in rain, shine, snow or ice, six days a week, further embedded an unquenchable desire to have the automobile always remain part of my life.

That interest was enhanced with the help of a neighbor, John Carberry, a truck driver and welder with a large family, who possessed an innate grasp of all things mechanical, and who was willing to share with his newsboy the essentials of tuning motors, adjusting and rebuilding carburetors, doing valve and brake jobs, and removing and replacing radiators, exhaust systems, instrument clusters, body panels, and the like. In deference to my parents' concerns, I would race around my newspaper route in the post-school afternoon. Seeing the man's truck parked in his driveway, I planned my route to deliver my last paper at his front door. That done, I'd duck behind the house to find him at his garage workbench, or bent over a motor, intent on solving some automobile challenge. Those dozens of half-hour visits, with an adult willing to explain and demonstrate auto repairs and adjustments to an interested youngster, formed the knowledge base for what became a lifetime of taking old cars and trucks apart, and putting them back together.

But nothing drove the lance of automotive attraction deeper than my father's earnest promise, born of his concern that my indifferent scholastic interest would result in an equally indifferent collegiate and adult life, to furnish me with an old Ford or Chevy coupe to commute in if I passed the entrance exam and was accepted to a nearby prep school. Content with the modest challenges of high school, unwilling to study harder than the half-hearted student I had long been, the prospect of owning my own souped-up jalopy quickly altered my thinking, supercharged my study habits and test-taking skills, and won me the prize. Or so I thought.

I left Portsmouth High School, after two easygoing but undistinguished years, for two far less easygoing years at Phillips Exeter Academy, an all-male, two-century-old institution of very serious learning. Students were required to attend classes six days a week. As was my custom, I made a modest beginning in this demanding scholastic environment, while focused completely on the prospective arrival of my car.

Then the axe fell. My father withdrew his offer, reasoning, correctly and quite reasonably from my present perspective as a father and grandfather, but tragically and dishonestly from that of a sixteen-year-old freshly licensed to drive, that I would definitely fail in that demanding school because of the nights and weekends I would spend doting on the car. I know now that he was correct in his thesis and in his decision. That in no way lessened the blow at the time.

A broken-hearted sixteen-year-old, I was, of course, unaware that my eventual college, the U.S. Naval Academy at Annapolis, Maryland, would have its own draconian rules. These banned car ownership until late spring of senior year, shortly before graduation and commissioning, from whence graduates went to sea — and, in my case and many of my classmates, to service in Vietnam. I would be a car-starved, twenty-two-year-old before I saw my name on a car title and sat behind the steering wheel of a car I owned.

And that's our next story. Let's take a ride together in a 1960s muscle car.

2

The Pontiac GTO:
Redline Reverie

*The basic position of Zen is that it has
nothing to say, nothing to teach.*

Sometimes, driving home in the uneven surges of Washington,
D.C.'s heavy afternoon traffic, surrounded by a drab herd of economy models, my thoughts wander back to an earlier time. My eyes
lingering over the most beautiful air-scooped hood ever designed,
one hand on a faux wood sport steering wheel, the other cradling the
ball of a Hurst 4-speed shifter, the powerful hum of a tri-powered
389 in my ears, I remember the day we first met, this car and I —
almost nineteen years ago. My God, nineteen years! I was twenty-
one. Can it have been that long? As if in answer, the slim teal-green
car smartly answers the downshift and slight touch of the wheel,
and darts swiftly onto the exit ramp and off the George Washington
Memorial Parkway in Alexandria, Virginia. As we travel the winding
country roads deeper into suburbia, alone and free once more, time
rolls backward to that first fateful meeting.

* * *

It was a cold December night in 1965. It began to drizzle as I left
the Naval Academy main gate and trudged up Maryland Avenue
in Annapolis. Pulling my midshipman's cap down, and my bridge
coat collar up, my walk became brisker — a man on a mission.

17

True enough. Only two weeks earlier, I had determinedly ended over two decades as an unwilling pedestrian by spending virtually every cent of my savings on a young man's dream — a 1966 Pontiac GTO convertible: $3245.45. It had everything, of course, but, most importantly, it possessed what every aspiring Navy carrier pilot valued most — speed.

I walked faster as the drizzle turned to rain. Saturday, the next day, was the promised delivery, late in the afternoon. But, as my growing impatience swept me along, I felt determined to follow my hunch that she was already there, just waiting for me. Ten minutes later, practically running, I reached Marbert Motors on West Street. Sweeping past the display models at the front of the lot, I reached the fence that surrounded the storage area at the rear of the dealership. Wiping the dripping rain from my cap brim, I peered intently into the dark.

What followed was one of those electrically memorable moments that happen but very few times in a person's life. There she was. Almost alone on the lot, facing me with what seemed a taut impatience, her white vinyl top still encased in its protective plastic, spinner wire wheel hubcaps shining, tiger-eye parking lenses gleaming in piquant promise to the intense feelings a young man can experience for something as supposedly inanimate as a car. I got the message. Thinking back on that magic moment, I knew even then that this car and I were destined to travel many thousands of miles together, grow older gracefully as good friends, and share the telltale dings, wrinkles, and other honorable badges of a life well lived.

* * *

Two weeks later I aimed the GTO northward for my home in New Hampshire. So much power. Each time I'd set the pedal at 65, the legal speed limit, the car would creep higher as if daring me to follow. Finally, on the New Jersey Turnpike, a dour-faced state trooper pulled me over, gave me a firm warning, admired the GTO, and brought me back down to earth. But not for long. Back among my friends in New England, four challenging years away at a service academy were now to be rewarded by a car that could take on anything on the road. Or so I thought.

On Christmas Eve I sat waiting at the red light outside Pease Air Force Base in Portsmouth. Suddenly a '55 Oldsmobile, black and flashy, pulled alongside. The driver revved his engine to a roar, and flashed a toothy grin, then the famous V-sign offering a challenge. I smiled back, and nodded affirmatively past my date, who knew just enough to be turning pale.

As the light turned green, I was ready. Inexperienced in drag racing — as in *totally* inexperienced — I assumed I needed lots of accelerator and zero clutch simultaneously. Initially it seemed I'd made the right choice. The GTO literally exploded through the light, tires screaming. The Olds faded back out of view. Then things changed rapidly. The car began a slow but uncontrollable swerve, nearing the snowy shoulder. I fought the wheel, still holding the gas pedal full down, but the turn continued, bringing the GTO closer and closer to the road's edge. Exasperated, and probably more scared than I would care to admit, I let off the accelerator, braked hard, and brought the car to a halt off the shoulder, partially imbedded in a snowbank. The Olds hurtled past, all smiles and loud honks on the horn. Crestfallen, I swallowed my defeat like a man, swearing revenge on the Oldsmobile and its occupants. You'd have thought a budding engineer would have known a bit more about torque!

Later that week, I evened the record. For years, the young and restless along the seacoast had proven their driving mettle by racing for time through a twisting series of curves on heavily wooded Love Lane. More than one vehicle had wound up in a stream bed below the narrow bridge, which bracketed the final two sharp turns. One driver had died, his hot rod upside down in the water.

Our discussion began at dinner, then continued at the movies. My friend and both our dates felt the GTO could handle the local "dead man's curve" with ease at 60 mph, the well-known local record. Braver, or simply more foolish, I maintained the car could do 65 all the way.

Eleven o'clock found the four of us sitting a quarter mile up

the road from the famed bridge and its twisting curves, silently sum-
moning our courage. Twice we had driven the course to reassure
ourselves, once at 40, then again at 45. At those speeds, the positraction, quick steering, and power brakes made it look easy. My plan
for the final run was set. Coming down the straightaway at about
70, the GTO would have to take the first downward, left-breaking
curve as close — I mean, *close* — as possible to the massive granite
blocks that framed each end of the bridge. But then things would get
tricky. Halfway through that first curve, the car would need to have
its traction broken. Then it could be drifted to the road's centerline
as it crossed the bridge where, after a brief acceleration and upshift,
she would again be broken free for the level, 90-degree hairpin to
the right which followed.

The talking ended, the eerie effect of the silence heightened
in the dim glow of Rally gauges on the instrument panel. Looking
around, I noticed how large everyone's eyes were. No one seemed to
be breathing. My friend offered to watch the speedometer from the
rear seat and certify the run, while my date would look for headlights
ahead. We knew we needed all of the narrow country road between
the curves.

The GTO slid smoothly forward, then accelerated quickly to
70 mph. I stopped watching the gauges, and stared over the hood,
as the car raced toward its fate. My face tightened as I gripped the
wheel and shifted through the gears.

It happened fast and was done. Entering the first curve felt
like going over the highest peak of a roller-coaster, the GTO almost
touching the granite pillar just inches outside my window. Sliding
precisely, the car picked the exact centerline as it crossed the bridge,
then broke free to slide through the hairpin leaving rubber streaks
on the road. Victory!

I slowed and pulled to the side of the road, my hands clammy
on the wheel, as my lungs welcomed air again. My friend in the
rear looked at the dashboard instruments admiringly. "Jeez," he said,
"71— all the way!" I felt a heady surge of high achievement, until I
focused on my date. She looked terribly pale ... and very ill.

Hours of cleaning and scrubbing took away all the telltale evidence. But that marvelous record-breaking GTO never regained its special "new car smell."

* * *

Oh, how the memories carry you along, once you unlock that treasured mental storehouse.

New Year's Day, 1966. Sixty-three degrees outside, an all-time New England record. And you guessed it, eight hours of top-down driving to celebrate, followed by three weeks in the hospital with double pneumonia.

Picking up my fiancé at Dulles Airport, west of Washington, D.C., and returning to Annapolis on the beltway surrounding the city at speeds guaranteed to impress, or distress, depending upon one's penchant for thrills: 80 ... 90 ... 100 ... 110 ... 120 ... Then, as the speed keeps building, the speedo needle bends downward, until it strikes its physical limit — but *not* the accelerator pedal limit. Still plenty of that left. Are all those other cars stuck in first gear?

Graduation Day at the Naval Academy. Hundreds of midshipmen caps thrown in the air. An "officer and gentleman" by an Act of Congress. Parents, relatives, and friends beaming, then a royal exit, top down, in a marina turquoise jewel with an ash-blonde ponytail by my side. My Lord, it's a car fit for God's gift to the Navy — a brand new ensign.

A Cape Cod *Surfin' Safari* on graduation leave. Eight-foot Hawaiian surfboard stretched from dashboard to mid-trunk. Had to stop for gas every hour or so. What, your wallet's in the trunk? Just hold that board up, so I can get to my cash. What was that awful noise? Oh, no — the windshield!

Off to flight school in Pensacola, Florida, everything I own in the trunk or on the backseat. South of Washington, D.C., it's 120 all the way on the smooth superhighway. Only eight miles to a gallon with those thirsty tri-power carbs sucking away, but you make great time. Sun's up, so top's down. Blew out the radio speaker. Natch.

Weekends on the Florida Panhandle's clear, white sand. Hotdogs, footballs, and folk guitars. But Vietnam and death lurk in the background. The first numbing news arrives of Marine friends killed in action. Then, shaking off the news, though we knew we'd soon be headed to the risk-filled skies of Southeast Asia, more sun, sand, and surf, and the thrill of driving three GTO convertibles just inches apart at 90 mph down narrow back roads to our barracks. We'd grin wildly with the wind in our faces and shout to each other, "It's like flying our aircraft in close formation!" Right on, Junior Birdmen!

Nineteen years ago. Some, most of us, came home from that war after a year or two. Some — those slowly fading names and faces, that special song, the Sunday touch football or soccer game of so long ago — did not. For bold cars and brave young men, the fast lane takes its toll.

* * *

Eventually almost everyone sold their GTOs. Wore 'em out. Tore the guts away in a long, jarring succession of memorable thrills. Life is now mostly business and profession, and everything's so expensive. The world demands something practical for transportation. Small, unstylish, and economical and, preferably, fifty miles per gallon.

But, hot damn, when old tales are told by peppery-haired daredevils at late night airbase "Happy Hours" around the world, they always talk about the same three things — their airplanes, their girls, and their favorite cars. And the GTO is always remembered. Always. The Goat. The Beast. The '60s premier muscle car. They sing the peerless pop hit *Little GTO*, warbling badly in their Budweiser-strengthened voices, remembering Ronny and the Daytonas — and the quickening memories of youth, sand and sky, and clear starlit nights, racing with tops down and radios blaring, brighten to brilliance yet again.

A few years ago, at a college football game and class reunion, I parked the GTO, clean and waxed, on the grass beside the class tent. Oh, the stares and sighs, the fond caressing of those well-remembered curves. You think men don't really *love* the great cars they've owned? "Can I sit in it?" "Would you start it up, so we can hear that great

V8 motor one more time?" "Oh, yeah, I remember one wild night with my Goat when ..." And, as always, a weakness in the strong, more than one tear appearing at the corner of an eye.

* * *

I turn left onto the street where I live, a tranquil scene of serene homes, lawns, and families. Like the thoroughbred she is, the GTO responds to my backing into second gear with smooth power, the motor's rumbling throatiness subtly reminding that, while this gentrified boulevard driving is fine, whatever else you might have in mind — *whatever* — is fine as well.

I nose the car slowly into the driveway, coming to a stop beside my family's Volvo station wagon. Volvo? Wagon? Ah, domestic bliss. Off goes the radio. I set the parking brake. Oil pressure, water temperature, and engine idle check normal. It's been a long tiring workday. I feel spent and reach for the ignition key to shut down.

But then I pause, as a thought crosses my mind. With a slow grin spreading from the corners of my mouth, I tap down on the accelerator. Vroom! A second time. Vroom! And once again, in response to that memorable sound, the exciting tingle runs up and down my spine, as it has so many, many times before.

The key turns the magnificent sound, that unmistakable throaty, throbbing power of the GTO's big V8, to silence. As I sit there in the afterglow, listening to the motor's heat ticking, my mind's eye again sees the colorful glow of the jukebox across all the years, the dancing saddle shoes and chinos, poodle skirts and white sox, the laughing happy voices, and the characteristic beat of 1960s music, with those still achingly familiar words —

"Three deuces and a four-speed — and a 389."

GTO REDUX

"Redline Reverie" was written several decades ago for the Royal Pontiac GTO Club. The short story covers the period 1965 to 1984, and appeared in several magazines, including *High Performance Pontiac*. The recollections are factual, with one exception. I amalgamated two

1966 Pontiac GTO convertibles, pre- and post-Vietnam, to simplify the story line. Other GTOs followed over the next four decades. This is their story.

* * *

Marina turquoise, a bright dark teal, was a captivating color on Pontiac's first model year GTO in 1966. While the GTO option was available on the 1964 and 1965 Tempest, 1966 was the year in which the car was first classified as a model — long, wide, sleek, and breathing thirstily through its tri-power carburetors.

It was — it is — a beautiful automobile and harkens to a time when Detroit first became aware of the burgeoning youth market and its "need for speed." Though there would later be many so-called "muscle cars," John DeLorean, a flashy young Pontiac division executive, captured the pole position with the GTO, and never looked back. With marketing genius Jim Wangers avidly embellishing the concept, the GTO became the symbol of a new and dynamic breed of powerful, big-engined intermediate cars that brought eye-opening thrills back to the driving experience.

Five of these cars have graced my life. All five were 1966 convertibles. All clad in marina turquoise. Returning from overseas in the early 1980s, I located a long-stored example in the basement of a rural Baltimore suburb. After minor mechanical repairs and upgrades, and fresh paint, the GTO became my commuter car around Washington, D.C. for several years.

One intemperate winter's day, the morning's heavy snowfall caused the federal government to shut down. Suddenly, thousands of federal employees were struggling to wade to their cars and drive home. Leaving the Pentagon, I could see solid taillights in every direction — total gridlock. Instead of driving south away from the city, I drove into the city, against the grain, crossing the 14th Street bridge over the Potomac River just minutes after an Air Florida jet had missed its landing at nearby National Airport in the limited visibility, grazed the bridge, and crashed into the river. This brought the chaos of emergency responders, and a frenzied life-and-death situation to a city already under a foot of snow, with thousands of stalled or wrecked cars on the roads.

I learned a lot about the GTO that day. Unable to go faster than a crawl, picking our way around deep snow drifts, and past inoperable vehicles slowly disappearing beneath a thickening white blanket, the car's ample power, manual transmission and, particularly, its positraction rear end, allowed us to avoid becoming another roadside snow sculpture.

In first or second gear, at speeds of no more than five miles an hour, the car never stalled or bogged down, though the snow was sometimes deeper than the car's underbody. We crossed the southern edge of the city eastbound, made our way into Maryland turning south, then drove back across the Potomac into Virginia well south of Washington, then home on the George Washington Parkway. Pulling into the driveway, and letting the air out of my lungs in relief, I noted it was 6:15 pm. I'd left the Pentagon parking lot just after noon. Six hours to drive twelve miles. But we'd made it. All credit to the GTO.

* * *

In time, I decided to sell the car. I placed an advertisement and was rewarded with some interest, but no buyer strongly interested in the car. Later, I received a call from a man in Chillicothe, Ohio. A bachelor in his forties, who owned a trucking business, and Oldsmobile 442 and Camaro Z28 muscle cars, he'd bought a green GTO convertible as his first car in December 1965. This was quite a coincidence, which I kept highlighting in our conversations. I'd bought my first GTO in the same month. The man bit at the baited hook and agreed to drive east with his brother to see the GTO.

The two men left Ohio after work on a Friday, drove all night, and arrived in our driveway just as our family finished breakfast Saturday morning. Both men had the washed-out, thousand-yard stare of a long night's drive. We sat them down to breakfast and coffee, lots of coffee, and began discussing the GTO. The prospective owner had walked past the car coming through the garage into the house and obviously liked what he saw. He asked if we could take a ride together. I rose from my chair.

Initially, I drove. I wanted him to hear and feel the GTO. After a mile or two, he looked over and told me that everything about the car seemed exactly like the memories of his GTO. I pulled over, and we exchanged seats. He drove well, and was respectful of a car that was not yet his. But it was going to be. The constant smile on his face during his half-hour drive was the tell.

We returned home. Before exiting the GTO, he told me he was going to buy the car. I was surprised, because I'd asked top dollar for a good-looking and good-driving, but hardly collector-quality, example. But when someone bites hook, line, and sinker, thoughts of negotiating a better price often get lost in the shuffle. I'd been there. We entered the kitchen and rejoined my wife and his brother. As everyone had more coffee, he opened his briefcase and handed over a cashier's check. I responded with a signed title, bill of sale, a folder with maintenance and repair bills, and other paperwork documenting the car's history. He put these away. It was time for the brothers to begin their long drive back to Ohio.

But the buyer looked at me and said he wanted to share how he'd come to find and buy my car. He loved his Olds and the Chevrolet, he said, but for years he'd had recurring thoughts of finding a car to replicate his first automobile. Though the idea tugged at him, he'd been too busy in his work to take action. Then, just a few months ago, he'd read a story about a GTO in an old magazine given him by a friend. It changed everything. He knew he had to have another 1966 GTO convertible, and that it had to be green. But green was not a popular color for the GTO. He'd looked in vain, until he'd seen my advertisement.

He looked directly at me as he reached into his briefcase and, as if handling something sacred, which I guess for him it was, lifted out the magazine. He held it up. It was an issue of *High Performance Pontiac*, some years old. I looked again. There was something familiar about the magazine's cover. He opened the pages, found what he was looking for and, holding the pages open, turned the magazine around to show me. My throat constricted. I couldn't breathe. Somehow, after a pause, I found the words, "Can I see it?" After a moment, and somewhat reluctantly, he handed me the magazine with my story, "Redline Reverie," open at the centerfold.

How could this have happened? Though this man had driven four hundred miles, and bought my car because of an ad I placed in a car magazine, he was actually sitting in front of me with the GTO's keys in his hand because he'd been influenced by an article I'd written years in the past, and he was completely unaware of that fact. I looked at the familiar article, the artwork, and asked if he had a pen.

"Certainly," he replied and retrieved one from his briefcase. But, alarmed as I bent to write something in his prized magazine, he rose from his chair, arms outstretched and waving. "No! No!," he said loudly, "Not in that magazine. Please. It's old. I'll never find another."

I didn't move, allowing him to relax and recover himself, then said, "In a minute or so, you're going to be very happy with what I'm going to write." Seeing that he had settled down, I bent to the task. "To John," I wrote, "who inherits the very car featured in this story. Enjoy this great GTO — your once and future car." I signed my name beneath my printed name in the article, then handed the magazine back to its owner.

It took a moment, but soon I saw his eyes well with tears. It had finally struck him. A minute later, his brother, who'd been leaning over his shoulder, had tears running down his cheeks. Mine were already wet. Three men around a breakfast table, all crying like babies. But what else could we do? It was such an unexpected surprise. The infinitely small statistical possibility had somehow happened, and here we all were — overwhelmed.

Soon the GTO backed out of the driveway and drove off down the road, followed by the truck. It hurt to watch the twin rows of louvered taillights disappear. But I knew the GTO had a new owner absolutely dedicated to its care. The proof? For a decade or more, I received a Christmas card each year from the owner. It was all about the GTO. Pictures were included. He would report that, after careful thought, he'd replaced the chrome GTO badges on the rear fenders with those painted black inside, removing those painted white that I'd had on the car. He hoped I didn't object. How could I? But I was pleased to see how that beautiful Pontiac was doted upon.

* * *

Years went by. Other car projects came and, after a time, went. I thought often of the GTO and, now and again, looked over the examples available. The good ones had become much more expensive. A few had reached six figures. But I never saw a green GTO for sale. I decided it was just as well. Looking in the mirror, I seemed somewhat old to be driving a muscle car. I resigned myself to the fact that my GTO chapter was history.

I had all but stopped looking when, much to my surprise, a perfect example in marina turquoise came to my attention. It had not been advertised in the usual publications. In fact, I was looking for a very different automobile, when there it was on my computer screen — unbidden. The price was reasonable. A superb driver-level car. But what impressed me most was its equipment list. While all Pontiacs in the 1960s came laden with lots of extras, usually concentrated on performance-enhancing equipment, this car was unusual by even that standard.

Its 389 V8 was equipped with the desirable tri-power carburetors, which raised horsepower from 335 to 360. It had a positraction rear end, with power steering and brakes. But there Pontiac muscle normalcy ended. For the car had an automatic transmission, and factory air conditioning, reportedly working. It was, in fact, the perfect GTO for a mature owner, who sought performance, but comfort and ease of use as well.

After a trip to inspect and drive the car, it was purchased and brought home. What a find. Everything worked as new. It was remarkably easy to drive but definitely capable of whatever its driver might demand. And in summers, when convertibles are the proverbial "cat's mustache" vehicle for happy cruising, the antidote for a hot and humid day was to raise the top and turn on the AC. Suddenly, volunteers were readily available for rides in any weather.

The return of another green GTO convertible — the fourth — came at a stage in my life when such things could truly be enjoyed. Retired with time to tinker, clean and polish, or to take a drive down a favorite "memory lane," the car was used regularly, mostly in the local area, but occasionally to attend distant old car events. I was not surprised to find the GTO still of keen interest to the hobby community. But I was impressed that, approaching fifty years of age, a certain adulation of the model was now evident. I'd never made a practice of leaving the hood gaped open at car shows, believing it did not show the GTO's lines to advantage. Now, if I was anywhere near the vehicle, I was asked repeatedly to raise the hood and expose the V8 motor with its tri-power "trips." John DeLorean and Jim Wangers had built an enduring brand. Everyone loved the GTO.

Each year, we took the car to an event at Walter Reed Army Medical Center, just north of Washington, D.C., which as a veteran I found particularly enjoyable. In fact, touchingly enjoyable. Afghanistan and Iraq, as have all of America's wars, had taken their toll on our country's young men. Many of those most seriously wounded were being treated at Walter Reed's Wounded Warrior Center. The car show, put on for their benefit over a summer weekend, was unlike any other. While trophies were awarded, the spirit of the event was to encourage the wounded soldiers to see, touch, sit, and ride around in our cars.

Something suddenly catches in one's throat when a nineteen-year-old with missing legs tells you he's never seen a GTO in his life, asks if he can sit in it, but expresses concern that, in bringing his wheelchair close enough to transfer to the car seat, he might damage the vehicle. As sad as the spectacle was through a normal frame of reference, it was such a privilege to meet those young men engaged in a struggle to overcome their physical infirmities, and recover as much normalcy in their lives as was possible — to see how they took lost limbs in stride, while maintaining their morale, and confirming anew the high quality of today's young soldiers. All day long we assisted these heroes in and out of the GTO, took them for rides around the hospital grounds, and brought a brief, fun-filled respite to their months and years of recovery.

Having a GTO back in our family brought a recurring idea to mind. When I was engaged to be married, driving around in GTO #1 in the mid-1960s, a youngster half our ages adopted my future wife and me, and always expected to accompany us on our local outings. Even on dates! His name was Paul Dentler. He was from Massachusetts, but his family spent summers in my hometown on the New Hampshire coast. The three of us formed a very close friendship which has endured. One day in 1966, a friend took a picture of my wife and me in the GTO, top down, with Paul sitting in the back seat. At ten, Paul's head could hardly be seen above the car's rear fender, a little, dark-haired cherub with a friendly smile.

In 1986, Paul came to Washington, D.C. on business, and had time to visit us in northern Virginia. It was great to catch up with the young business professional. Someone recalled the memorable 1966 photo taken of the three of us and, noting that it was now twenty years later, suggested we reprise the scene. Fortunately, GTO #3 was parked in the garage. It was driven onto the front lawn. The three of us took our former positions in the car, and one of our daughters snapped several photos. These revealed my wife and me to be older, as expected, and I had greying hair. But in the back seat the pipsqueak was gone. In his place was an adult sitting up straight and tall. We had quite a moment comparing the 1966 and 1986 photos. Time flies, as they say, and it showed.

We had always stayed in touch with Paul, who had married and had two children, ultimately moving to California for a career opportunity. Our families got together when possible, always reliving our common memories. In 2006 Paul visited us again in Virginia, only to learn there was yet another green convertible in the garage, GTO #4. A "three-peat" was suddenly on everyone's mind. As before, the car was driven onto the front lawn, and the familiar photo taken. We didn't look that different after another twenty years, except that all three of us now had greying or grey hair. And one of us, who prefers to remain unidentified, was looking — how does one put this diplomatically? — more "substantial."

Two years later, a New Hampshire summer get-together took place that included everyone in both families, including our six grandchildren. After a rollicking day of food, fun, games, laughter, and many recollections, two identical plaques were presented, one for each family. Against a marina turquoise background, the three photos of our threesome were placed vertically, with the year inscribed beneath each picture. 1966. 1986. 2006. Replica "GTO" and "6.5 Liter" emblems were fastened above and below the pictures. The caption read:

> *"Once young kids; now old goats,*
> *Friends for Forty Years"*

* * *

Three weeks later, I received a strange call. A lady in New Jersey wanted to purchase the GTO, which hadn't been advertised, and wasn't for sale. She was an older woman, she said, and her husband was soon to have his eightieth birthday. The only thing in the world he wanted, and did not have, was a teal-green GTO convertible like the one he'd bought new in 1966. She added that his health was not good. For this reason, she felt it was important that she buy the GTO for his birthday. She knew my car, she said, somewhat ruefully, and had gone to see and drive it years ago. I'd apparently purchased the car while she was still considering making the purchase. She had obtained my contact information from the seller.

I told the lady that, while the car wasn't for sale and I was enjoying its use, I'd think over our conversation and her request. She added two comments for me to weigh. She said she was willing to pay whatever I asked for the GTO, as long as it was within the bounds of reason and, should the car ever become available, she would be willing to sell it back to me. She thanked me for listening, and we concluded the call.

I was of two minds. Selling the car for a good, and possibly very good, price was certainly tempting, and someone making such an open-ended offer would seem to have both the inclination and means to take proper care of the vehicle. I couldn't see a man of eighty wearing out the tires and drivetrain as I'd tried to do with my first GTO decades earlier. On the other hand, would agreeing to the sale bring about the end of my long love affair with such a special car? I knew that GTO values were climbing, which was a factor. But the small population of convertibles in marina turquoise meant, just as the caller had known in contacting me, that few examples remained. Of those, only a handful would have been kept or restored to a high level.

Ultimately, I decided to sell the GTO. I liked everything about its prospective new owners from the standpoint of the car's prosperity. And I was paid my asking price promptly, a price I'd set at a level almost, but not quite, embarrassing. Before payment was made, I did spend a long afternoon and evening with a friend of the buyers, a serious car collector and car show judge, who gave the GTO the most comprehensive inspection I'd ever witnessed. Fortunately, the car passed with flying colors and, within days, had been collected and delivered to New Jersey. Later, I received a touching thank-you note with a photo of the beaming birthday gentleman sitting behind the steering wheel of his dream car.

Looking at the photo, I concluded that I'd done a good thing for both parties involved and life went back to normal, though, for some time, I'd open the garage door, surprised not to see what had long been there. Then, in a major change in our lives, my wife and I decided to sell our home of thirty-five years in Virginia and return to our home town in New Hampshire. Soon my wife found a lot for sale, which we bought, determined to build a new home together, after owning or renting existing homes for five decades. We considered the purchase a fiftieth wedding anniversary gift to ourselves. The process took almost two years, and absorbed all of our time, attention, energy, and resources. Eventually, we settled in, and began to enjoy a layout specifically designed to meet our current and future needs. Throughout the project, there'd been little time to think about old cars. Possible future projects, long the focus of my daydreams, had been replaced by permit requests, construction decisions and, of course, invoices.

Three years went by, the new home and its occupants growing into each other gracefully. I'd all but decided that the lengthy house-building interregnum had indirectly heralded my quiet retirement from the old car hobby. Getting older, much of my old car-questing fervor seemed to have left me. I no longer tracked various marques or models of interest online. I'd stopped watching the January classic car auctions in Scottsdale, Arizona, on the television. Reading my *Hemmings Motor News* each month had once required a full evening's study, and sometimes more. Instead, my *Hemmings* "bible" had become an hour of speedy skimming.

Then she called.

I knew the voice immediately, authoritative but kind, and the obvious New Jersey accent. She thanked me again for the pleasure the GTO had brought her husband and, through him, to her as well. He had passed away a few months ago, she said. She was slowly rearranging her life in consequence, and planning to move to a new, smaller home along the coast. I told her how sorry I was to hear her sad news, but how pleased I'd been to receive the photograph some years back of her husband in the GTO with his smiling face showing his pleasure.

She was quiet for a minute, reflecting perhaps, then said she'd been thinking for some time about the car. Every time she went out through the garage on errands, she saw it parked to the side under its cover and remembered its arrival at the eightieth birthday party and the delight it brought that day. She recalled her promise to me, then asked if I was still interested, and would I like to welcome the GTO home for a second time.

What a question.

I did welcome the car home again. Our fifth GTO but also our fourth. It arrived in New Hampshire in exactly the condition it had left our home in Virginia six years earlier. A beautiful teal-green convertible that drove as well as it looked. And, though I would always miss the idea of a four-speed manual shifter in the center console, the practicality of the two-speed automatic, as the sands of time brought my eighth decade closer, was not lost on me. Nor was the factory air-conditioning for those hot summer days when, top up or top down, a convertible driver is often found wanting for companionship unless, of course, there's that switch to be thrown, bringing a level of refreshing comfort to the interior.

An old friend and local car collector provided the final element for the car's return, introducing me to an experienced local mechanic capable of maintaining the GTO at its current level. A championship drag racer for more than fifty years, a fact recognized by his being honored with membership in three Racing Halls of Fame, Bob Broadbent, proprietor of Seacoast Auto Repair in Hampton, New Hampshire, is and will remain the only person, besides myself, putting hands and wrenches on the GTO.

The sudden re-immersion in a much-beloved hobby I'd almost talked myself out of has, somewhat surprisingly, led to few other changes. My interest in car events remains pallid. The time I spend involved in old car topics continues to decline. But there is that one exception. The GTO sits in the garage radiating green. She is very compelling. I think I'm in love.

So I've been thinking. No one can dependably predict the future. As a result, it's good practice not to assume one's future plans will all work out in life's latter stages. But we have kept in close touch with our good friend Paul, once a ten-year-old pipsqueak, now a sixty-five-year-old contemplating retirement. And 2026 lies only six years off in the future. What about the car? Hah! The GTO is probably healthier than the two of us. So perhaps there can be yet another photograph taken on some front lawn in 2026, the three of us again sitting in a marina turquoise GTO convertible. A four-peat?

Of course, we'll then have to have the two plaques redone. But what the hell?

3

Packard:
"Ask the man who owns one"

*While Zen does not imply a specific course
of action, since it has no purpose and
no motivation, the Zen devotee turns
unhesitatingly to anything that presents itself
to be done.*

While in grade school, I found a book in our local library about
the two Packard brothers who built the Packard automobile, one of
America's premier luxury automobiles, during the first half of the
twentieth century. It was the kind of American success story that a
youngster could get between his teeth.

James Ward Packard was a successful mechanical engineer and
sought to convince Alexander Winton, principal of the Winton
Motor Carriage Company, one of the first American companies
to manufacture and sell automobiles, that he could build a better
motorcar. Apparently, the conversation between the two determined
and outspoken men almost came to blows.

Subsequently, Packard, his brother William, and Winton stock-
holder, George Lewis Weiss, built a factory in Warren, Ohio, and
produced the first Packard automobile there in late 1899. Between
1899 and 1903, the factory produced about 400 automobiles. Their
vehicle featured a steering wheel, when most cars at that time utilized
a steering rudder. A single-cylinder motor was used. From the first,
Packards were sold as a car for the wealthy, with prices starting at

almost $3000. At that time, a basic Ford or Oldsmobile could be bought for about $400.

In 1903, success allowed the firm, now incorporated as the Packard Motor Car Company, to build a modern manufacturing plant in Detroit, Michigan. The plant produced luxury motorcars for domestic and foreign buyers. By the early 1920s, Packard was exporting more cars each year than any other company in the high-end class.

The Great Depression changed everything. Many automobile manufacturers were forced to merge or went out of business. Packard's modern, single-line production method, and efficient cost controls, bought time. But by late 1934, the company, and the luxury car business, were both in deep trouble. Packard's response was to develop a low-priced, lower-quality car, a Packard only in the shape of its radiator grille. The strategy was successful. The new, mass-produced 110 and 120 model Packards sold well. Sales tripled in 1935 and doubled again in 1936.

But in saving the company, the future of Packard was imperiled. Wealthy buyers were accustomed to purchasing distinctive, well-respected, and often customized luxury cars. They looked down grimly upon the throngs of mass-produced models on the roads sporting the distinctive Packard grille. Chagrined, they began to buy cars from other high end manufacturers, including those in Europe. Foreign luxury automobiles provided a noticeable cachet on American roads, driven by the discerning who could afford them.

Packard never recovered. Lagging their competitors in styling and mechanical upgrades after the war, the company fell further behind. They were no longer able to compete with Cadillac and Lincoln for luxury sales leadership. In time, Packard was forced to merge with Studebaker, another troubled carmaker, to become Studebaker-Packard. The last Packards were produced in 1958.

For me, the Packard memories lingered. Reading about the two brothers and the rise of their brand as a schoolboy left a strong impression, though it was rare to see a Packard on the road in the 1950s, when I was becoming interested in automobiles. Much later, in my mid-twenties, I was finally in a position to take action. But the first old car I found and decided to buy was not a Packard. It was a 1934 Dodge Brothers four-door sedan with rear suicide doors. Seeing the car parked beside the road in western Rhode Island, I was taken with its smooth lines, which looked especially attractive to me in black.

There was a "For Sale" sign on the car's windshield, but without a price. I offered $200 for the car, all the cash I had. This was refused. Only after adding my $5 weekly lunch money was I able to get a nod of assent from the owner. The car ran well, and I enjoyed tinkering and learning with it. I drove it on country roads, and sometimes to work. But soon I faced a dilemma. The Navy was sending me to Japan, where I would fly rescue missions. What to do with the Dodge Brothers sedan, which I'd planned to keep? A friend offered to store it in the unused half of his double garage. I prepped the car for storage, backed it into the garage, disconnected the battery, and left for the overseas assignment.

Months went by. One day a letter arrived from someone in Rhode Island, a name I did not recognize. It was an offer to purchase the Dodge for about three times what I'd paid. A puzzlement — but not for long. I accepted. Now, as a high finance car collector in good standing, I began to read *Hemmings Motor News*, the monthly classified advertisement bible of the old car hobby. The search for a vintage Packard began in earnest.

Still in Japan, I soon found what appeared to be a gem, and an apparent bargain as well. Located in Burlington, Vermont, and thus near friends in New Hampshire, who could store the car while I remained overseas, the project seemed a good fit. Sight unseen, I purchased the 1937 Packard 120 four-door sedan, and paid to have it delivered into storage.

A year later, I returned home to visit my parents. After some catching up, I excused myself to go view my purchase nearby. A doubtful look in my friend's eye was a harbinger I missed in my zeal to see my first Packard. From the opening of the garage door, it took only minutes to utterly dishearten me. Sitting awkwardly on its bald, sagging tires, the Packard was an early and graphic lesson on the need to buy old cars with discernment and due care.

Mired in self pity, I reviewed the car's *Hemmings* advertisement. I soon saw where the fault lay. The ad was truthful. The Packard was complete. It ran. What the ad did not say was that the poor old car was completely worn out, just like its tires. It needed everything. Exterior paint, chrome, glass, interior side panels, wool seat covers, and carpet. Probably a motor and transmission rebuild, as well. And the exhaust system needed replacement. The seller had not misrepresented the car. I had misrepresented the car to myself. I'd seen in the advertisement what I'd wanted to see, a car similar in condition to my 1934 Dodge, which had aged gracefully and not been used up. I faced the fact that my active but overreaching imagination must never play a role in the purchase of a vintage car again.

But what to do? My investment in the vehicle, including transport, was only $400. My salary and modest savings could never handle the cost to bring this sad car back to life, even if it did sport the flashy Packard radiator grille with chrome louvers. And so, applying P.T. Barnum's theory of the "greater fool," I put an ad in the local paper to sell the car. The Packard name produced the desired interest. Within a week the car was gone, having found a new home. I had priced the Packard at $500, and accepted $400. This was the sum I'd mailed a year ago from Japan to Vermont. I was whole.

Relieved of that burden, my wife and I set out for a rustic mountain village in northern New Hampshire, where the sole entertainment was to sit on a bench in the town's central park, watching the shift changes at the nearby lumber mill. After two years of excitement overseas, it was the perfect remedy, a tactical time-out, before reporting for training to be a test pilot on the shores of Chesapeake Bay. We rested. We read. We walked. We languished, and watched the autumn leaves turn brilliant colors and fall to the ground. Rested, we returned to our coastal hometown for a few days, before our drive to the new assignment in Maryland.

They say "fate is the hunter." This would seem to suggest that we are the hunted. A day or two later, while wandering around local back roads, we drove through Exeter, site of the state's revolutionary capital, where I'd once attended school. Following Front Street west along Route 111, we were surprised to spot three vintage cars parked in front of a closed car dealership. We debated going on, but the lure proved too powerful. Inside we met the proprietor, who walked us through his inventory, an inventory which included a Packard sedan.

Oh, my. There she sat, radiating 1930s high style and a stately composure. Black with sweeping front fenders, a rear-mounted, metal-covered spare tire, and sporting the famous flying lady ornament as its radiator cap, the 1934 11th Series, Model 1100, four-door sedan had been owned by the same local family from new. The heritage showed. The only minor flaw on the car's polished exterior was a minor paint irregularity on the driver's front fender, where a misplaced bag of winter road salt had shriveled the finish.

There were no disappointments inside the Packard. A rich gray wool broadcloth covered the seats and side panels. The dashboard, instrument panel, and controls looked as if the car was still in a showroom which, of course, it was, though almost four decades after its production. It was love at first sight. The price, however, was somewhat daunting. We decided to return home to discuss the situation. It turned out to be a short conversation.

We drove back to our hometown in our new Packard the following afternoon, rolling quietly through the colorful autumn leaves. What a pleasure to drive such a car along winding country roads. A century earlier, they'd been cow paths; centuries before that, the footpaths of America's native peoples. How imposing the old car looked in the driveway. Finally, a genuine Packard in the family!

We relaxed for our final vacation days, driving the sedan around town, pleased by her behavior and good manners. The question of whether it was wise to drive the 500 miles to Maryland was resolved by the consistent, confidence-building roadworthiness of the car. When the day came, it seemed natural to load both the Packard and our Volvo wagon with our belongings, and set out southbound early in the morning. The Packard ran well. The Volvo looked diminutive, following the stately old sedan, as we motored through Massachusetts.

Passing through downtown Providence, Rhode Island, on I-95 an hour later brought a sudden change to our plans. I'd noticed a slight decrease in engine oil pressure, then watched as it continued lower. Then the coolant temperature began to rise, along with my eyebrows.

It was time to leave the highway and find help. We knew an auto mechanic in nearby East Greenwich. His skills had earlier kept our first old car, the 1934 Dodge, on the road. We drove to his garage and pulled up to his business, breathing hard in relief. The mechanic liked the car. It was a larger and higher quality car than our former Dodge, but otherwise similar. The two cars shared the same production year. Within an hour, he'd prepared a repair estimate.

The engine problem proved simple. The head gasket, dried out from long-term storage, and used only locally since our purchase, had simply dissolved at sustained highway speeds. Replacement was straightforward. Both radiator hoses were also deteriorated and had started to leak. The mechanic recommended an inspection of all safety systems and suggested we replace all five tires, which were dry-rotted. We agreed, made a deposit on the work, and continued to Maryland in our Volvo.

So began a golden two years in which I drove daily to work in a classic 1934 Packard. I'd fly a variety of fixed- or rotary-wing aircraft, then amble home to family, content to glide along the country road, freewheeling the final half mile downhill into my driveway. One day, stopped at a red light just outside the naval air station, an older couple, waiting on the curb to cross the street, noted my flight suit and asked me why a test pilot would drive such an old car.

I beckoned the couple over to the passenger door. They moved closer and looked inside, curiosity overcoming their homespun reluctance.

"Can you see the lever just above the steering column?," I asked.

"Yes," they replied. "It's called 'Ride Control'. It lets me select four positions for altering the firmness or softness of the ride."

"Over here is a similar lever marked 'Brakes'. With it, I can use the basic brake system, or supplement the braking power with hydraulic assist."

"Just beneath the brake lever is a small pull chain. It's called a Bijur Lubricator and was invented by a Frenchman named Bijur in the 1890s. By pulling on the chain, eight noisy locations on the car's chassis receive a drop or two of heavy oil, which dampens or eliminates the occasional squeak."

"The forty-year-old AM radio you see there in the dashboard still works without a single tube change. Inside the running board on the passenger side runs its antenna. It's over four hundred feet long. During the days, that antenna ensures a wide selection of local radio stations. When I complete a night flight and drive home afterward, the nighttime atmospherics let me listen to broadcasts from London, Paris, Vienna, even Moscow."

"Finally," I said, looking up and noticing that the red light was about to change, "the motor in this car has nine main bearings. It was built to last a century with regular use. The transmission, though not synchronized, is just as durable. To demonstrate, I will shift to high gear, and move forward as the light turns green. You'll hear no motor or transmission sound at all. I'd consider buying a modern automobile for commuting. But I doubt I can find one with any of these unusual features, let alone all of them. I'm very happy with this fine old Packard."

The couple smiled and moved to the curb. I smiled back at them. The Packard smiled too as it smoothly and silently pulled away, passed through the light, and proceeded on its way.

Over our memorable years of driving the Packard, I received occasional visits from a local minister who lived further down the same country lane we lived on. The reverend had developed a slight obsession with the car. He would sometimes drop by in the evening to discuss the car and, after a time, asked if it might be for sale. My answer always avoided the question by repeating the obvious. I enjoyed driving the car every day, tinkering with it on weekends, washing and waxing it every few weeks, and participating in vintage car events in the local area. Why would I ever consider selling something which brought me so much pleasure?

The minister, however, continued his hopeful visits. Then, altering his approach, he asked what amount I would sell the car for, should I ever decide to sell it. I thought about his question for a while, considering what had been put into the car, then responded the next time he stopped by with a figure roughly twice that amount, confident that such a sum would be unaffordable for the minister of a small rural congregation. I'd found a way to blunt his interest by turning the tables on his question. I did not see the man for a week and congratulated myself for cleverly countering his interest. The price I'd given the minister had obviously cooled his ardor. l expected he would now admire the Packard only in passing.

But I was wrong. As I was still congratulating myself on my successful diplomacy, the minister dropped by one evening with a shoe box in his hands. Handing the box to me, he waited while I opened it. It was full of hundred dollar bills. Was this gentle man a bank robber? Flustered, I asked how a minister could possess such a sum from church earnings. He laughed and said he wouldn't be able to purchase a Model T from that source. However, his grandfather had wisely purchased land in Oklahoma before the war, land that was now leased to oil and gas companies. Those leases provided royalties to his generation of the family. Each month, a check arrived to supplement his church salary. The contents of the shoe box were the result of his grandfather's vision and largesse.

I agreed to sell on the spot, writing out a bill of sale, and signing over the title, after confirming that all the green stacks in the shoe box added up to the correct amount. It was emotional to watch the Packard's new owner climb into the car, start the motor, back slowly out of our driveway and, with a jaunty wave and broad smile, drive the old sedan down the road to his home. It was years before I again heard from the minister. He had moved to a new church near Atlanta. His note said he still owned and loved the Packard. How could he not?

So there we were, my wife and I, standing on our front lawn, as our Packard sedan was driven away. She had always been supportive of my involvement with old cars. Supportive, but not overly interested, a reasonable position in a marriage, and one for which I was grateful. I knew men in the car hobby who pursued their vintage auto dreams despite the disinterest or opposition of their spouses, a situation which probably dashed their enjoyment in the hobby.

So it was a complete surprise to hear her say, as the sight and sound of our former Packard receded, that the car was very distinctive, had served us well, and that she would miss its presence in our lives. Stunned at her words, I stared in silence. Then she continued, "But if you want to know about my dream Packard, one that I doubt we could ever afford or own, it would be a classic convertible or roadster, built a few years earlier than our sedan, the "Great Gatsby" kind with twin side-mounted tires on the front fenders, and a large leather-covered travel trunk on a rear rack, large headlights alongside a chromed radiator grille, driving lights mounted on the front bumper, an ornamental radiator cap, and a tonneau windshield for the rear seat, with the canvas top set at a rakish angle, a classic late-1920s senior Packard."

Whew! She had captured the vision so clearly I saw it in technicolor. But it was a vision so extreme and unaffordable, considering our circumstances, that I felt diminished at first in the face of such an unreachable but fascinating objective. But as we turned toward the front door, an idea had begun to form. I sensed the possibility of automotive adventure stirring in the air. Who was it that said, "If you can imagine it, it can be made to happen?"

Later that night, my wife turned out her reading light and turned over to sleep. Free to let the adventuring spirits free to fly, I reached into my night table drawer for two booklets and three Marks-A-Lot coloring pens I'd put there after dinner. The publications contained membership lists for the two major Packard clubs: the Packard Club and Packards International. The roster information included the name and address of each Packard owner, and the year and model of the cars he or she owned.

I began with a green pen, outlining every convertible senior Packard that fit my wife's clear-eyed description of our ideal possession and, coincidentally, of my own. There were hundreds of members in each club. Many owned multiple vehicles. So the process was slow. By midnight it was finished. I counted the green boxes. I had outlined 177 cars, any one of which we would be thrilled to own.

Sleepy, but too enrapt to consider sleep, I reached for the blue pen, intent on further reducing the total to one hundred. It was challenging to choose among such desirable models. But an hour later, it was done. Finally, I used the red pen to cut the distinguished list of classic automobiles in half. I had decided to mail a handwritten letter to each of the fifty car owners, hoping to convince a stranger to consider parting with their Packard. "Within our reach," wrote Browning, "but beyond our grasp. But what's a heaven for?" As dawn broke, I turned off my light and slipped into a brief but satisfied sleep.

It took a week to craft the letter. The Packard owners who were to receive it were people of means and citizens of the world. They would see through any ruse, and would quickly toss any stranger's missive sounding presumptuous or lacking the ring of truth.

In preparing the letter, I reminded myself to lower expectations. Not one of the fifty cars I was asking to purchase was within our financial reach. Some would have been in the same family for generations, and were not only highly valued, but treasured as well. My thought was that one or more of the owners might have passed, with their Packard having become part of an estate settlement. I reasoned that an estate might be turned over to attorneys, hired to sell its assets, who might not know the exact value of a vintage Packard automobile, and might then be inclined to sell for a reasonable price to close the estate. These thoughts occurred as I drafted and re-drafted the letter to be mailed on our wings of hope.

It was finally ready. Much altered and shortened from earlier attempts, it told the simple truth. I was a young Navy pilot recently returned from Vietnam. I had previously owned two Packards, and was hoping to purchase another, preferably a convertible. Should the recipient be interested in selling, I would be grateful to be considered as a purchaser.

That was it. A classic long shot. It took several evenings to address and copy the fifty letters in a neat longhand, address envelopes, then put them in the mail. Having done this, I suddenly felt depressed. No one would trouble themselves to reply to a well-written but presumptuous letter sent by an unrealistic military fellow who happened to have a dream about Packard convertibles. This was a concept laughable on its face. No one would answer those foolish letters. What had I been thinking?

A week went by, then another. I gathered I'd wasted time and energy. The fifty outbound letters had likely found their way to fifty wastebaskets. I'd known at the outset that the plan was an unlikely concept, dependent upon people I didn't know being sufficiently stimulated to respond. I'd left no room for error by soliciting only the most prized and sought-after senior convertibles from the golden era of America's classic automobiles. I shouldn't feel I'd failed, only that I'd attempted something far too daring to succeed.

Then the first reply arrived. Though positive and encouraging, it did not contain an offer of sale. The next day, another. This time an elegant Packard was available for purchase, but at a price equal to several years of my salary. And so it went. For several weeks I received letters, altogether about twenty. All were positive. Many suggested I continue pursuing my dream. A number of cars were offered, but none were remotely within our financial reach. One of them, a 1934 custom Packard convertible located in Texas, still haunts me. Finished in sage and dark green, it was priced at $65,000, the documented cost of restoration. This sum was about three times the price of the house we'd recently purchased, our first. As I penned short thank-you notes to the replies, I realized what an overreach I'd made, attempting to intrude into the social and financial stratosphere of senior classic automobiles. Soon the replies to my earnest, but vainglorious, letter stopped arriving.

Two weeks later a day came when everything changed. It was a hot and humid Saturday morning in southern Maryland. The lawn needed to be cut, a lesson in the joys of sweat equity, but also a task which, when completed, would allow the rest of Saturday, and all of Sunday, to relax and enjoy family activities. Finishing the chore, I stored the lawn mower in the garage, wiped my face and arms with a towel, and entered the house to get a glass of sun tea. Realizing it was almost noon, I told my wife I'd go out to check the mailbox for the day's mail. Sliding open the family room door, and more in jest than not — or was it? — I called to her that I'd be bringing in the letter with her classic Packard convertible.

Did I sense something? Who knows? But as I reached the bottom of the driveway and approached our mailbox, it seemed to be vibrating slightly. An unusual, expectant trembling. Was it the ruffling wind? Probably. But, real or imagined, that apparition of movement caused me to pause, transfixed, wondering what was going on. I reached forward and opened the mailbox door, lifting out the stack of advertisements, bills, and such. As I walked back to the rear of our home, I riffled through the stack in my hand. Near the bottom was a small envelope addressed to me in a scratchy longhand. Hmm… The return address was to a Nicholas V. Brower, 308 Avenue F, Redondo Beach, California. I went into the house, walked over to my wife, and presented the envelope. "Here," I said without irony, "is your Packard." She took the letter with a smile which suggested she was humoring me. As I guess she was.

We both felt forced to sit down after reading the first few lines together. We were being offered an opportunity to purchase a 1929 Packard, a 6th Series Custom Sport Phaeton.

Together, we read the two-page handwritten letter over and over. Mr Brower thanked me for my letter, and agreed that the unique qualities of the Packard automobile were well worth our pursuit. His personal collecting objective, he wrote, had been early brass vehicles, primitive automobiles that he could tinker with. A 1904 Knox was his favorite. A geological engineer, his company had sent him for a year in Portugal to help develop the Algarve region in the south of the country for tourism.

While on a visit to Lisbon to attend business meetings, he'd read in the newspaper of an estate sale auctioning off the assets of former Portuguese royalty, the late Count and Countess of Cacem, whose palatial estate was located near the seaside cities of Cascais and Estoril. Included in the auction were two notable European motorcars of early vintage, but also a 1929 Packard convertible. The Packard caught his attention. Out of curiosity, Brower attended the auction, only to find a cabal of wealthy Portuguese car collectors assembled to ensure the two rare European cars remained in the country. As the group had little interest in the American automobile, he was able to purchase the Packard.

Following the auction settlement, the Packard was moved out of the estate carriage house under its own power with fresh gasoline and a new battery, then put on a transport, and taken to the nearby Serradas-Rio de Mouro workshop of Arsenio Valentim, one of Portugal's foremost automotive restorers, where it would be disassembled and restored over several years.

Brower's letter closed with a series of warnings. Things move slowly in Portugal, he wrote, but he found the people to be unfailingly honest. Valentim, the Packard's restorer had completed a number of superb restorations in the decades since the war. All became European award winners. Brower believed there was significant potential in the restoration of the Packard. But Valentim and his wife were getting on in years and spoke no English. Although the Packard was complete and running before its disassembly, and had only 12,000 kilometers (about 7500 miles) showing on its instrument panel, there was simply no telling how long a restoration would take, nor its cost.

If I was willing to take on such a project, given the risks and uncertainties he'd discussed, he would sell me the car for his investment, "as is and where is." The price of $3120 dollars included the winning $3000 auction bid, a $20 battery, and the $100 transport fee to the restorer.

We bought Mr. Brower's car. It required taking equity from our life insurance policies to assemble the funds. But we did it and without hesitation. We'd seen classic car values rising steadily, and convinced ourselves that the Packard might well be our only opportunity to enter the hallowed circle of classic owners. We also had what the Disneyland song called "high hopes." We believed the Packard, once restored, would prove a solid investment. We also assumed we had the patience and means to see the project to a successful conclusion.

Looking back, it was a very tall order, not to mention an utter leap of faith. But we were young, driven to accomplish and achieve, and had a certain brash confidence that we would endure and bring the thing off.

And, God bless us, we did. It took nineteen long years to complete the restoration. Yet even the elderly restorer survived the experience. Thankfully, he maintained his peerless standards as he aged. Along the way, of course, there were the requisite trials and tribulations.

On my first visit to Portugal, a year after purchasing the Packard, I hired a translator and took a taxi to Serradas-Rio de Mouro, having previously asked Brower to write the restorer, explain he had sold the car, and introduce me as the new owner, who would visit him to discuss the restoration. The village was small and gave the impression it hadn't changed in centuries. The workshop, with a family apartment upstairs, was small and its exterior unpainted. Could this be the same shop that had dazzled Europe with its perfected restorations of European classics?

It was.

We met the Arsenio Valentim and his wife, both guardedly friendly and possessing a quiet dignity, qualities I encountered widely among the Portuguese I met, regardless of social or economic level. The couple looked old to me, then in my mid-twenties. Today, a half century later, he would appear to me a somewhat younger man. He asked if I would like to see the Packard, then turned without waiting for my reply, and opened the door into the shop. The lights were turned on. There it was. Our 1929 Packard. But where exactly? Well, everywhere. The motor was on an ancient workstand against the far wall. The transmission and rear end were nearby, perched on a bench.

The car's large body sat in another area, its canvas top and bows still installed. The remnants of the leather seats had been removed, and set on another worktable. Against one wall, which included the entrance into Valentim's office, were the six 20-inch tires, mounted on disc wheels. These included the two side-mounted spares for the front fenders. While the condition of the disassembled Packard was sobering, to say the least, it was obvious that the complete car was present in the garage's work area. I was determined to feel encouraged.

As his wife left to return to the apartment, the restorer invited me into his office to discuss the project. By this time, night had fallen. I had been awake since early the previous day and was feeling the fatigue. The translator and I followed the restorer into his office, As we sat down in chairs around a desk, I expected we would outline the major restoration steps together, and establish a framework for costs and time frames. I expressed this idea, then watched the man frown. Then he surprised me by asking how old I was. After I responded, he told the translator to inform me that he was unwilling to restore the Packard for me. Stunned and suddenly wide awake, I asked why. He replied that I was too young to understand what a Packard was.

I disagreed, but he would not relent. I explained that I had owned two other Packards, including a 1930s senior sedan. He was unmoved. Given the slowness of our communications, and the need to speak back and forth through the translator, it was now past 11 pm. I was again becoming seriously sleepy. Still, the man was not convinced, and remained adamant that I was not old enough to understand the importance of a Packard. He would not, he claimed, spend years of his life on a worthy car for, as he hinted, an unworthy owner.

I sensed that, were I to surrender, it would be the end of my dream. I had realized during the exchanges that this formal old man could not be reached through logic or emotion. So I was surprised when he asked if I was willing to take a car ride with him. The middle-aged translator worked for an hourly fee, so she was willing, though also visibly tired. In my position, and without a hand to play, I agreed to go along, while wondering where we might go this late in the evening, when most Portuguese were in bed asleep. We went outside. The restorer pointed to a tiny Fiat parked across the street. We all got in and soon had left the village headed west toward the sea.

Minutes later, we entered a vast gated estate, with beautiful trees and shrubs outlined by subtle lighting. At the end of a wide entrance road, we came to a grand house. Only a light or two remained on. We were asked to remain in the car, while Valentim spoke to one of the housekeepers, then proceeded around the side of the palatial home in the semi-darkness. We sat. He returned, asking us to follow him to the garage. He told us that this was the home of the head of Firestone Rubber in Portugal, a wealthy executive for whom he had restored a valuable Bentley. I began to understand what we were about on this nocturnal tour.

Entering the garage and turning on the overhead lights, the restorer's purpose became clear. There sat a stunning 1920s Bentley, its dark green exterior, shiny bumpers, and chrome trim gleaming. Feeling disloyal, I realized that my heart beat faster at this shining vision than it had at first glimpsing the disassembled Packard. We were shown the finished details of the vehicle. Then, without getting behind the steering wheel, instead sitting on the garage floor, the old man used his hands to depress the clutch pedal and accelerator, shift the car out of gear, crack open the choke, and, satisfied, bring the Bentley's motor to life by turning on the ignition and pressing the starter button. This produced the kind of smooth sound one would expect from a classic luxury vehicle in such perfect condition.

I was not asked to comment so, though drooping eyelids, I paid rapt attention and tried, through facial gestures and body language, to convey an appreciation for the man's superior skill, the restoration's quality details, and the extravagantly beautiful motorcar which had resulted. As my awe was indeed genuine, I must have been convincing for, after a time, the motor was silenced, the garage door closed, and we returned to the Fiat.

We were driven the short distance to my hotel in Lisbon. Valentim used the time en route to explain, through the interpreter, that he had changed his mind, and decided to restore the car for me. He would not predict the project completion. I should expect the project to take several years. The work would best move forward if, when he submitted handwritten bills, I would see that he was paid promptly, and in Portuguese escudos. What was the neophyte owner of a Packard classic to do but agree? I thanked the old man for his time *and* for his favorable decision, saw the bone-tired translator to her car on the street, paid and thanked her, then stumbled to my room, falling dead asleep on the bed, fully clothed, until late afternoon the next day.

From this unusual beginning in 1971, it was to be nineteen years before the Packard restoration was complete. It was a slogging experience, but one that remained positive throughout. The restorer reported his progress in some detail about twice a year, in a letter which included a bill, both in Portuguese. I had them translated, and found a way to pay him in his currency. From time to time, replacement parts were needed, which I found and shipped over to the Valentim's workshop. It was an altogether archaic system but it worked.

Two notable events occurred during those years. Either could have taken the project completely off the rails.

I brought the first on myself. Seeking a more efficient way of dealing with the restorer across distance, languages, and currencies, I hired a well-recommended attorney in Lisbon to act on my behalf, passing on translated letters and bills, handling the relatively small amounts of money, and quietly watching and reporting on the progress of the restoration. An improved system, this worked until Portugal underwent its "Carnation Revolution" in late 1974, which brought the economy to a halt. Soldiers put carnations in their rifle barrels to signify peaceful intent, even as military tanks rolled through the streets.

My connection with the attorney was broken for several months. Then I received a fervent if self-serving apology in answer to several of my inquiring letters. He admitted that, with the country's economy in shambles and martial law firmly in place, he'd had to use my funds to buy food and pay his rent. No mention was made of restitution. I tried unsuccessfully to feel sympathy, then wrote the Packard restorer directly to explain what had happened and reestablish our primitive but reliable communications system. The project was then able to sustain what passes for progress in Portugal.

The second event was more pervasive, and far more threatening. Persistent rumors reached us of a dark but politically important chapter in the Packard's history. In the mid-1920s a young but highly creative swindler named Alves Reis had created a counterfeiting operation on such a grand scale that he and his co-conspirators effectively took over the financially bereft Portuguese colony of Angola in Africa. When the crimes were brought to light, and the conspirators caught in December 1925, they were well along in pursuit of their ultimate objective, the takeover of Portugal's central bank and control of the country itself.

Reis's high crimes were beyond Portugal's, and the world's, imaginations. The stunned and embarrassed government demanded Reis be made an example at his trial. He was found guilty and sentenced to twenty years without possibility of parole or pardon, the first two incommunicado. All of which he served. But to balance the heinous crime Reis committed, there was the undeniable fact that, even as Europe descended into depression, Portugal had experienced a golden economic era, as tens of millions of counterfeit escudos flooded the business and consumer sectors. The Portuguese people and its business community were grateful to Reis for their improved lives. Some spoke of electing him Minister of Finance, even Prime Minister. Noting this favored reaction from the populace, the government placed Reis in the Palacio Cacem through the 1930s, a gilded cage of a prison, and a macabre reward for the indirect and unintended gifts his clever chicanery had brought to the people of Portugal.

Although he could not leave the iron-gated confines of the vast estate, he lived well within this luxury. He was allowed to receive visitors at the palace gate, but only through its locked bars. To proceed from the palace the considerable distance to meet his visitors at the gate, Reis was allowed to drive a certain 1929 Packard sport phaeton, which had been delivered to the estate's late owners, the Count and Countess of Cacem, in December 1928, and was owned by the last surviving heir, a son. Many thought the Packard belonged to Reis. It did not.

As the years rolled by, the restoration proceeded steadily, if glacially. Our family was living in Naples, Italy, in the late 1970s. For several years, I was able to visit Lisbon more easily, and spend time with the Valentim and with the Packard. Things were going well and, with the restorer aware of my increased visits, more rapidly as well. By now, the story of Alves Reis and the Packard had become common knowledge, as was the rumor that the government was actively seeking the car to confiscate as a national treasure, and to display at the National Coach Museum near the Tagus River in Lisbon.

Hearing these stories created stress and a certain pressure to move the car out of Portugal. But, with the restoration proceeding apace, and the work of unquestionably high quality, such a decision seemed ill-advised. Cost remained an important factor. As someone of modest means committed to a long-term project with a pay-as-you-go restorer, I was able to manage the Packard's restoration, without taking out loans, only because labor and material costs in Portugal were a small fraction of a similar effort in the United States, yet about equal in quality. After anguishing over the risk, I decided to stay the course.

Years went by, then a troubling trend appeared in the late 1980s. As the restoration neared its conclusion, progress began to slow. After eighteen years, I though I'd seen everything. Sensing something was amiss, I flew to Lisbon, intent on taking whatever time was needed to discover the problem and find resolution. Unsurprisingly, the problem turned out to be the restorer.

Valentim had come to closely identify himself with the Packard, an understandable reaction to its oft-discussed connection to the infamous swindler, but also in full accord with the respect he'd long enjoyed among Europe's wealthy vintage car collectors. At his advanced age, completion of the Packard was unlikely to be followed by other commissions. Thus, the project was slowed to delay the inevitable. It was an entirely human reaction by this humble, elderly man, who had labored many years to restore the Packard. But something had to be done.

I met with two of Portugal's best interior fabrication experts, a father and son team, who I'd hired earlier to furnish the Packard's leather interior, fit a canvas top to the oak top bows, and construct side curtains and canvas covers for the twin side-mounts and the Packard trunk. They had learned of my predicament and were willing to intercede. They suggested that they might best convince the restorer that the car, now running and drivable, leave him, and begin its finishing phase in their shop. As I watched the old man listening to the fabricators' quiet words in his own language, tears in his eyes, and his wife by his side, I felt sad for him. I certainly understood his plight. But I was frankly relieved when, without speaking, he nodded in quiet assent.

The next day the Packard was moved from the workshop for the first time since Nicholas Brower's transport had delivered his Cacem estate auction prize there in the late 1960s. It was now 1988. I knew that the fabricators, who were to finish the Packard, had spent fifteen years pursuing their trade in Canada, had sterling reputations and excellent references from their time in North America, spoke fluent English, and would accept payments in dollars. Through the long darkness, finally, a glimmer of light. A lingering threat remained that the government might locate the car at the penultimate moment, and appropriate it for national purpose. At such a late stage, it was a risk that we decided to accept.

The Packard was finished four months later. My wife, Nancy, and our two daughters, Noelle and Christine, joined me on what we hoped was a celebratory visit to Lisbon to close out the project, and see our car hoisted onto a ship for delivery to Baltimore. The restored car was stunning from any angle. Finished in bright blue on its fenders, hood, lower panels and trim, with oyster-white motor cowls, doors and rear, and the dark-red leather interior, its lustrous appearance made it difficult not to imagine we'd actually arrived at the finish line.

In truth, we hadn't. With our "sword of Damocles" concerns about government usurpation, we walked the Lisbon waterfront seeking a shipping company competent to deliver our prize to its homeland. I had decided to be candid with those I met, concerning possible government interest in the car. Predictably, the first three shippers we met listened sympathetically, but politely declined the assignment. On the edge of panic, I thought of renting a rollback, and driving the Packard across the border to a less-conflicted shipping location in France or Spain.

The young professional at our fourth stop on the waterfront disabused us of this unrealistic notion. Alert, and with a level eye-to-eye gaze, he listened calmly to our story, then simply told us that he would be pleased to ship the car for us. My heart rate slowed perceptively. With everyone now understanding the factors and risks, I asked what the plan was, and the price for his services. Consulting several plastic-covered documents and a thick folio filled with paperwork, he quoted a figure almost double our expectation. Unnerved, I asked if this amount was solely for shipping. Looking directly into my eyes, he replied simply, "No." He was apparently letting us know that, to manage this delicate matter for us, other payments must be made. We went through the business process, signed documents, and made payment.

The plan was simple. "When," the young man asked, "can you deliver the Packard to a warehouse near the airport?" With a few calls, we agreed on early the following afternoon. He remained mute regarding other arrangements, but his business acumen and quiet self-confidence were persuasive. We left the shipping office sensing we might have crossed a high bridge over troubled water. An evening of wonderful frivolity and good food followed at our favorite seaside restaurante, which our daughters had laughingly dubbed "Fat Frank's Frango" after its burly owner and chef. We left full of mouth-watering chicken and fried potatoes, looking more confidently toward the events of the following day.

After the Packard was safely loaded in the late morning, we followed the transporter across Lisbon in our rental car to the airport area. Wandering down alleys between dingy warehouses, we half expected to see a government swat team, dressed in black, drop out of nowhere and claim their masterful swindler's favorite motorcar. But nothing of the kind occurred, and, after further searching through the vast storage labyrinth, we found the proper address and correct warehouse. Standing at the door in casual clothes, wearing an enigmatic "Mona Lisa" smile, was our young man from the shipping office. Seeing him relaxed, we relaxed as well.

It was all done professionally. The Packard was treated like an elderly dowager empress. Removed from the transporter, she was hand-pushed onto the base of a shipping container by a team of stevedores, then completely swaddled in several layers of protective insulation, after her undercarriage had been strapped tightly to several of the container floor's eyebolts. The four sides were carefully raised and attached to the floor. The container's roof was lowered by a small crane and bolted down tightly. Only the clamshell doors at one end remained open, we presumed for the customs inspection, after which the container would be officially sealed. With a youthful flourish, our young shipper walked to the container, and closed and latched its doors. Then, reaching into his pants pocket, he withdrew the customs seals and clamped them securely to the locked door handles. We now understood what the higher shipping fees had paid for.

We shook hands, and were told we would receive a phone call just as soon as our "package" was considered safely beyond the reach of the Portuguese authorities. Impressed, I asked when the ship that would carry the Packard might be at sea.

He smiled back: "6 pm, on the tide."

I looked at my watch. It read 3 pm. That night we were awakened from a sound sleep at 1 am. It was the shipping agent.

"You will see your car in Baltimore in ten days."

Suddenly wide awake, I asked, "Where is she now?"

"In Algeciras, Spain," he answered, "being craned from our ship to a Spanish ship which will carry her to your country."

He explained further that, in order to confuse any party seeking to intercept the car, he had arranged a cross-deck transfer of the container in the Spanish harbor to make interdiction impossible. Thanking our young James Bond a final time, we returned to our beds, though the welcome news made sleeping less important than lying there awake, feeling we could finally allow realization of our hard-fought success out of its box of concern.

Our family flew back home to Washington, D.C. two days later. There we waited for notification from our coordinating firm in Baltimore to advise the Packard's arrival. We planned to be on hand, rented flatbed truck and driver at the ready, to see the container open and the first appearance of our red, white, and blue classic Packard, colors I'd selected more than two decades before, expecting to drive the car in parades celebrating our nation's bicentennial in 1976. It was now July, 1989.

Before proceeding, I thank you, earnest reader, for your persistence following this complicated, but I hope interesting, story through its many twists and turns. At this point you may also be doing the same math I've done. You might think, having accounted for only nineteen years of this story to this point, that you still have a very long way to go, covering yet another twenty years.

Please set aside your concerns. While the Packard project brought serious challenges of distance and language, amid the rumored risk of government seizure, the unique trials and tribulations found in the search, acquisition, and restoration of *any* vintage automobile form the central interest of any car story and, for many of us, of the project itself. What follows is the ownership period, interesting enough for those directly involved but, lacking serious or threatening problems, much less interesting for the reader. Such a story is typically brought to its conclusion by briefly revealing the car's fate. And so it shall be here.

We were notified that the car had arrived at the Port of Baltimore. Our family drove to the shipping port, where we met the transport and driver hired to bring the Packard to our home in Alexandria, Virginia. What followed was the exact reverse of what we'd witnessed in the Lisbon warehouse. The container was carefully disassembled, the packing around the car removed, and the chains and bolts holding the vehicle to the container base loosened and disconnected. The Packard was carefully hand-pushed from the disassembled container. The gentleness employed by the six brawny stevedores was touching, as was their awe upon being told how much their efforts were appreciated helping to return an American car to its homeland after sixty-one years in Europe.

The trip to our home in northern Virginia was uneventful. The transporter helped get the Packard into the garage, was thanked and paid, then left. There we were with this colorful classic convertible parked in our garage alongside a Volvo station wagon, a study in contrasts. I confess to feeling a certain emptiness at seeing this two-decade, European project merged into our family life and home. There were to be no more distant crises. No more angst over news of Portugal in magazines and newspapers. No more explaining to doubting friends that the mythic object of a distant and seemingly endless project would one day appear in Virginia.

For here she was, sitting formidably with her distinctive flying lady radiator ornament, chromed radiator shell and louvers, staring out at the world. As the evening's dark descended, the rest of the family turned in, emotionally drained by the day's events. Though devoid of energy, I found I could not sleep. Sitting in my study, staring vacantly into the darkness outside, I got up time and again, went to the garage, opened the door, and turned on the light. Each time the Packard was still there; I hadn't dreamed the day's events. Finally, nodding off at my desk, I was able to accept that the project I'd begun at twenty-six was now concluded at forty-five. I slept late the next morning.

With gasoline and oil servicing, and the recharged six-volt battery reconnected, the Packard was running and driving around the local area by the next afternoon, still wearing its 1928 license plates from Lisbon. Each drive was more ambitious, taking us on forays farther from home. Stopping at a service station to add fuel to the gallon I'd initially put in the tank, I got my initial experience with the show-stopping capacity of our large and colorful car. "Beautiful." "What is it?" Or "What year?" I heard these and other interested comments again and again.

Let me relieve the suspense. In the two decades of ownership that followed, the seventy-five-year-old Packard *always* started and ran without problem or complaint. Ironclad. A trouper. The handcraft builders at the Packard factory, and Arsenio Valentim, the Portuguese restorer, had done their work to the highest standard. The car could drive in traffic at 65 mph without difficulty, if you didn't consider the wide-eyed fellow drivers who, upon seeing this anachronistic vision in the next lane, rolling along at highway speeds, had a concerning tendency to drive much too close, trying to get within hailing distance to shout a question or compliment.

The Packard often attended old car shows, where it won praise and its share of awards. It also drove occasionally in parades. But it was most often used in local or neighborhood events. This exposure brought requests for participation in weddings, and we were always pleased to participate. There's something very special, seeing a young bride and groom emerge from a church married just minutes earlier, then helping them climb into a classic Packard convertible, and overhear their first married words to each other, after "I do," while chauffeuring them to their reception.

Then it was our family's turn. Our eldest daughter, Noelle, was to be married in Charlottesville, Virginia, about a two-hour drive from our Alexandria home. She and her intended asked to have the Packard ferry them to events throughout their wedding day, which it did without incident. Because it was such a special occasion, I had taken the opportunity to have the hood, fenders, and rear end repainted in the dark Washington blue I'd specified more than twenty years earlier. In Portugal, the color blue is most appreciated in a lighter shade which, though appealing, was not the color I'd wanted for those 1976 bicentennial parades. The dark blue in contrast with the oyster-white sides, and the red trim and interior, perfectly featured the Packard's classic lines.

The old car never became a central element in our family life, but remained a distinctive possession for two additional decades. Driven regularly, its reliability was assumed. But over the years it was driven less and less. Other car projects and career commitments relegated the Packard to a lesser role.

There had been regular inquiries from collectors wanting to purchase the car but we had no interest in selling. Finally, someone out west, who seemed as interested in the Packard's initial royal ownership as in the car itself, made an impressive offer at a time when the Packard seemed to be sitting more than driving. The family discussed the offer, one of us observing that we seemed to be considering the sale of a family member. And, in a sense, we were. Thirty-eight years is a long time and strong bonds form.

Ultimately, we decided to let the Packard go to a new owner, who had impressed us with his plan to have another professional restoration undertaken, something we believed the car did not need, but which would improve its long-term fate. So, as we watched, our Packard was loaded into an enclosed transporter and departed for delivery to its new owner — "somewhere west of Laramie."

The departure left a large hole, not only in our garage, but in our hearts as well, a hole which took time to fill. But other projects inevitably took the Packard's place. A mahogany 1965 Chris-Craft Constellation 46-foot, flush-deck motor yacht, needing complete restoration, which remained with us for twenty-four years. And an original 1966 Lamborghini 400GT V12 coupe, which needed nothing at all, which would be in our family for almost twenty years.

The story of our 1929 Packard Sport Phaeton did not end as we watched the trailer drive away. Several years later, the car's next owner got in contact, asking for the history of the vehicle. Something had gone awry for the man who'd bought the car from us. The restoration, though begun, was not completed. The businessman who called had purchased the car and completed the restoration. It subsequently won many impressive *concours d'elegance* victories and achieved the sought-after status of a full Senior Classic. The Packard now resides in Florida and lives exactly the pampered, sheltered life such royalty deserves. In a mere decade, she will celebrate her centennial.

Some years ago, my wife attended a business conference in Lisbon, representing Motorola, her employer. At a dinner event, she sat at a table with several Portuguese businessmen, who regaled her with the many interesting things to see and do around their beloved city. They were quite surprised to learn she was already familiar with the city and its surroundings, had visited Portugal a number of times, and loved everything about the country: its people, food, culture, and music. Pressed about her familiarity, she mentioned that she and her husband had, decades past, purchased a 1920s Packard convertible in Portugal, restored it in the vicinity of Lisbon, then taken it back to the United States. She went on to tell the men that the car was rumored to have been used regularly by the infamous counterfeiter and swindler, Alves Reis, during the years he was incarcerated for high crimes in the gilded palace-prison of Cacem outside Lisbon.

The men's jaws dropped at hearing her story, as did my wife's when one of them added a sequel to her tale of our family's involvement with the Packard. At the present moment, the man related, a play about Alves Reis and his infamous plan to take over the country's central bank was showing in central Lisbon. He had gone to see the play, as it was the talk of the city. It had taken many decades for such a sensational topic to be allowed public exposure, so total had been the government's official embarrassment in the 1920s. In the play's concluding scene, a full-sized replica of a 1929 Packard convertible was rolled onto the stage. It was the conveyance used by the actor playing Reis to meet his guests at the locked gate of the Cacem palace.

History had repeated itself through art.

Looking left, then right, another of the businessmen leaned forward and guardedly whispered to my wife, "In several reviews of the play I've read, it was mentioned that the government is still quietly looking to locate and obtain the Packard."

Ask the man who owned one. He'd probably say, "Good luck with that ..."

4

Cadillac: The Turret Top V-12

Zen begins at a point where there is nothing further to seek.

I'd never owned a Cadillac. My family never owned a Cadillac. I never thought to own a Cadillac. Our having owned a 1929 Packard phaeton for almost four decades seemed to have completely filled our family's need for a classic luxury car.

Such penchants did not prevent me from feeling an electric ripple along my hairline and down my spine when, lazily reading a Sunday paper in Monterey, California, in early 1975, I spotted a 1936 Cadillac sedan for sale in the car classifieds.

Working at the time on two project cars, a 1956 Lincoln Continental Mark II and a 1954 Chevrolet Corvette, while studying my way through graduate school, one could have argued that enough was enough. Unless, of course, it wasn't.

As in other suspended moments of my life, the weight of two ongoing car projects proved a lesser influence than the exciting prospect of a possible automotive challenge. The search. The confrontation with possibility. The research. The anticipation. The journey.

I called the phone number in the ad. It rang and rang and rang. Finally, just as I was about to end the call, a man answered. He was pleasant, a high school teacher nearing retirement in nearby Carmel Valley. He had bought the car in San Francisco to enjoy in his old age. His new condominium in Monterey was costing more than he'd anticipated. More funds were needed. The Cadillac needed to find a new home.

Neither warmed nor cooled by the owner's description of the old sedan, I agreed to meet him several days later at a commercial address in Carmel Valley, where he rented storage space in a former gas station. The day came. I drove the Volvo wagon south, then east, following his directions. Arriving and introducing myself, I noted the rundown appearance of the building, which helped restrain my animal spirits from building up a head of steam.

We approached the two clamshell doors which, after a padlock was removed, resisted our efforts to be opened. Together we pulled and pried for a time until, finally, the right door surrendered to our effort, and we were able to drag it ajar, scraping along the concrete. We slipped past into the gloom.

Three feet away sat an imposing 1930s Cadillac sedan, one of the tall "turret top" models. What got my attention in the middle of the chrome grill, however, was a small chromed bezel. It read "V12." I attempted to suppress my excitement at this discovery, which had gone unmentioned in both the ad and the phone conversation, Before me was a full classic.

After more struggle, both garage doors were opened wide. The Cadillac could be seen in better light. The exterior color was dark green, which appeared black, unless in sunlight, and was accented by bright chrome trim. The interior seats and panels were a rich tan wool broadcloth. A gray wool headliner completed the impressive interior. Inside and out, the car appeared complete, original, and in excellent overall condition. The instrument cluster showed a mere fifty-four thousand miles. A radio was installed in the dash. A walk around revealed wide whitewall tires and full wheel hubcaps, hard rubber running boards, and a huge trunk with spare tire and tire-changing tools, a space large enough to hold a Volkswagen Beetle.

We lifted both engine cowls, and stared at the V12 engine with its chromed brightwork and head bolts, dual down-draft carburetors, a rare and unusual Duo-Coil twin coil system, and a dorsal chrome tube to insulate the twelve spark plug wires from the motor's heat.

The owner started the car. She caught immediately, without fuss, smoke, or smell, and ran smoothly. The Cadillac was driven outside onto the station's pavement. The green paint and chrome brightwork gleamed in the late afternoon sun.

We went for a short drive along Carmel Valley's winding roads, the owner driving outbound, so that I experienced the car's riding qualities, its sounds, and road character. Then I took the wheel, returning to the storage site. I enjoyed the power of the V12 motor, and the long-armed, floor gearshift. The owner described the Cadillac's original "San Francisco" rear end, geared especially for the steep hills of that city. I later heard the humorous claim that cars equipped with those special rear ends could climb vertically up the trunks of California's huge redwoods. The Cadillac drove, shifted, and stopped easily, and almost noiselessly. Its performance served to confirm the owner's comment that, before his ownership, the Cadillac had belonged for almost forty years to a prominent San Francisco family, who'd bought it new.

The Cadillac was shut down and stored, the obstinate doors forced shut, and the padlock reinstalled. Negotiations followed on a sun-drenched wooden bench nearby, and were amiably concluded with the car purchased for less than I would have expected to pay for a similar model in lesser condition, and with a more common V8 motor, not the much rarer V12. The following day, we met and settled. I drove the Cadillac home. I owned my first Cadillac.

The months of study stretched on. In the spring Monarch butterflies flooded the Monterey Peninsula, bringing their vibrant orange and black colors to every bush and flower. John Steinbeck's Cannery Row had become commercialized, but still smelled pungent from the decades of marine product processed there. Actor Clint Eastwood was elected mayor of Carmel and opened his restaurant, "The Hog's Breath" in Carmel. Life was good in Lotusland.

I commuted to school in the Cadillac, enjoying every minute behind the wheel of such a grand motorcar. Though she received lots of attention, my real pleasure in her ownership was experiencing her behavior on the road. A real lady. The only mechanical problem I encountered was floats sticking in the down-draft carburetors. These occasionally prevented starting. A tap of a knuckle on the carburetor bowl usually freed the floats, and allowed the car to proceed.

My confidence in the turret top grew to a point that I suggested we take the car on a drive to San Jose, and attend a weekend old car gathering. Loading our baby daughter, and her three-year-old sister, diapers, baby formula containers, and spare clothng items, we headed north along the coast. We stopped in Castroville, the "Artichoke Capital of the World" for lunch, and tried the famous fried artichokes. Walking to the Cadillac after our meal, we gazed through the showroom windows of a Mercedes dealership, and spotted a car which utterly captured us.

It was a 1975 107 series 450SLC coupe, silver with bright red leather interior, a limited production five-seat model based upon the 450SL roadster, but stretched a foot in length. Designed with trademark louvered opera windows accenting its artful C pillar, the SLC's price exceeded my annual salary at the time. We broke away and drove on. After all, "we knew the way to San Jose!" Departing Castroville, we promised ourselves that one day, probably far in the future, we would own an SLC. The promise proved prophetic. We owned several SLC coupes over the ensuing decades, one of them, a 1973 example, for thirty years.

California cars exist in a uniquely beneficent, auto-centric culture, a perfected climate, and in a state of being intensely appreciated most conducive to their longevity. The car show was a wonder. Hundreds of old and new collectible cars and exotics were ranged across a green field under a bright blue sky. We enjoyed viewing the vehicles, as we pushed the strollers through row after row of beautiful show cars. Hours later, as the children wore down, we returned to our Cadillac and found it surrounded by car buffs. Some seemed unnerved to see small children and diaper bags disappearing into the spacious rear seat for the ride home. Smiles, handshakes all around, and we were on the road heading south.

Or were we? Passing Santa Cruz, and climbing up a long grade at sixty miles per hour, I noticed steam rising from the radiator ornament's base, though the car continued running smoothly. A check of the instruments indicated that our relaxed drive homeward was about to change. The water temperature was rising steadily, while engine oil pressure slowly dropped. With anxious thoughts of what it must cost to rebuild a forty-year-old twelve-cylinder motor, I shifted to neutral, shut off the motor, and glided to the shoulder, where I found a wide, level grassy area to examine what had happened under the hood.

It did not take long to determine the cause of our interrupted journey. Peering at the motor after lifting the cowl, I saw a round hole, high on the left side of the engine block, still dripping green coolant. A "freeze plug" had popped free, probably from the higher internal pressures generated by climbing a long grade at speed.

So there we were. Stuck. No communications. Miles from any-where, while nearby trees threw ever-lengthening shadows over us, and the sun began its long descent into the Pacific. As if to heighten our helplessness, my wife announced that her diaper inventory was down to three. Three diapers and two little girls suggested we might soon be facing a second crisis. We looked at each other as if to say, "What comes next?"

What came next was an answer to unspoken prayers. A blue school bus, its sides and rear covered in huge, brightly-painted flow-ers, pulled in beside us. Two heavily-bearded men in bib overalls emerged. Hippies? Who knew? They walked over to the Cadillac, trying to see inside. We responded by rolling up the windows and locking the doors.

One of the men spoke. "Hey, man. This is an awesome old car. Really tubular." In answer, I rolled the driver's window down three inches.

"Need help?" queried the other man.

"I do." I replied.

"What's wrong?" he asked.

They didn't look like members of the Manson family, and their smiles seemed genuine. By this time they'd been joined by four long-haired women in loose flowery dresses, and a bevy of long-haired little children, all now walking toward the Cadillac. I got out, shook each man's hand, acknowledged the gathering audience, and lifted the cowl, so they could see the missing freeze plug that had left us inert beside the highway. We agreed that a new freeze plug, a hammer, and a quantity of coolant or water would be needed to get us back on the road. If such things could be found late on a Saturday afternoon in northern California.

What I needed was a phone to call my friend and fellow naval aviator, Mike "Oakie" Stansel, a man with encyclopedic knowledge of automobiles and clever enough to tackle any vehicular challenge. But he was in Monterey, forty miles away. We were parked beside the highway south of Santa Cruz.

Reading my mind, one of the men told me that, though they were traveling south, they were willing to take me north into Santa Cruz to find a phone or the necessary repair materials, then bring me back to my family and our silent sedan. I accepted their offer gladly, and joined the hippie commune in the flower-covered blue bus, standing amidst goats, pigs and dogs, plus bedrolls, worn suitcases, piles of clothing hung on hooks, and cartons of food — a genuine menagerie.

A work table at the rear of the bus was covered in leather materials, from which the group fashioned belts, vests, and what-all to sell for their cash needs, mostly food and fuel. Under the work table was a fenced-off space with a row of cardboard boxes, each containing a laying hen. If you've lived and worked on a farm, you probably have a memory of the distinctive barnyard smells found there — and on that bus.

But the hippie group could not have been more friendly or helpful and, true to their word, the bus soon pulled up to a pharmacy in Santa Cruz that was open, where I was able to call my friend, explain the circumstances, and relax in the knowledge that a rescue mission was on its way. The busload of hippies dropped me off at the Cadillac, and left with waves and smiles, knowing that help would soon arrive. As it soon did. Within the hour, a flashy jade green 1969 Mustang fastback, its 390 V8 rumbling noisily, slid alongside and stopped.

Mike had brought various sizes of freeze plugs, a hammer, and containers of water. We inserted several plugs in the motor block's opening. None fit. Too big or too small. Thankfully, the last he'd brought did fit. A few hammer taps to depress the plug's concavity and seal the block, then refilling the radiator, completed the repair. The V12 started up and ran smoothly. We checked that engine oil pressure and coolant temperatures were now in normal ranges, and noted no steam venting from the radiator cap, before following the Mustang's taillights back to Monterey and home.

Everyone felt relief as we pulled into our driveway, my wife mentioning that she'd just used the final diaper. Somehow, using my various senses, I'd already known that.

Before moving on in this tale, please allow me a brief diversion. Ever wonder why vintage motor blocks needed freeze plugs? Fact: those so-called plugs had nothing to do with cold weather, nor were they intended to pop free to prevent the block being cracked in winter's extreme cold, though that was often the tale told by dealerships in the day. Truth is often stranger than fiction. Freeze plugs were a purposeful design for production, but a weakness to the motor's integrity. The holes filled by the plugs, usually four, were there to accommodate transverse iron bars, allowing the heavy engine blocks to be moved to various assembly areas easily during the production process. "Freeze plugs" indeed!

The Cadillac continued as a daily driver back and forth to my classes. Some evenings, I confess, she served as an alternative to studying. Mike and I would find something that needed slight adjustment. Or we'd simply consume the evening hours together, reflecting on the many examples of quality and innovation found in a machine produced four decades in the past.

Inevitably, our time in graduate school came to an end. With a pending move south to San Diego, and some family health issues threatening to challenge our pocket book, it seemed prudent to seek a new owner for the Cadillac. I put an advertisement in the *San Francisco Chronicle* where, ironically, I'd first found the car advertised. The ad indicated the car's history and condition, and highlighted its redwood-climbing San Francisco rear end. She was sold to the first person who called, then drove down from her original home town to see the car.

Another great old car had left me. I knew I'd never see her again.

But I was wrong.

Years later, having lived for a decade in Alexandria, Virginia, where I worked in the Pentagon, my wife and I decided it was time to retire from the Navy, and seek other professional challenges. I had joined the military at the age of eighteen, and was now past forty. Our two daughters were doing well in local schools. There were excellent colleges throughout Virginia. We reasoned that ending our frequent moves around the world would provide stability for our family at a critical stage, and allow our girls to complete high school, and possibly college, while living at the same address — which was how it turned out. Personally, I looked forward to trying my hand in business, and finding a fresh challenge.

Big changes in a family's life bring certain risks, known and unknown, and definitely increase anxiety. We had a suburban home, which came with a mortgage. The Washington, D.C. metropolitan region is a relatively expensive place to live. College tuitions loomed. These considerations exerted pressure to take the safe and stable path, and remain in uniform. Instead we followed our sense of discovery, and went through with the retirement. "Two roads diverged in a wood…"

On the other hand, it seemed prudent to hedge our bets to the degree possible, and find ways to cushion our exit from the military and hoped-for entry into the business world. Having planned ahead and set savings aside to meet family needs until a new job was found relieved some of the pressure. We decided to purchase a new car with a multi-year warranty, expecting to eliminate repair costs through the career transition and beyond.

I went in search of a new sedan, intending to purchase an Olds-mobile, a car I knew well, having helped my in-laws purchase one the previous year. Good looking, well-reviewed and sporting an efficient

3.8 liter, six-cylinder motor, I began my search for a new Olds at two local dealerships. But the car's sterling qualities and reputation had preceded it. Buyers flocked to Oldsmobile that year. In the timeframe I was looking, there were backlogs of orders at most dealerships. It became obvious that expecting a discount deal for a new Oldsmobile was impractical. Dealerships I visited were charging pricing premiums to impatient buyers. Unable and unwilling to compete for a new car, I moved on.

Though I did not see our family in a Cadillac, I wanted to find out if another General Motors division might be under less buyer pressure and hungrier for sales. I made an appointment at a northern Virginia dealer. Happily, there were basic Sedan de Ville models all over their lot. I found salesmen willing, even eager, to negotiate prices, and soon concluded a favorable agreement for a new 1986 Sedan de Ville in medium metallic blue with a blue leather interior. Ironically, the car's price was less than the premium-priced Oldsmobile I'd tried to buy earlier.

Our family loved the new Cadillac. But, aside from the pride of owning our first new luxury vehicle, we sensed this purchase was to be one of the stable underpinnings for our new and as yet undefined life detached from our military past. On the day we were to visit the dealership, complete settlement, and drive off in our new car, we were all a bit giddy. We'd been told we would meet with the general manager, who would present Cadillac's widely-advertised Gold Key Service, with its gold-plated ignition keys and other perks of luxury car ownership.

We arrived at the dealership, went inside to meet with the green eyeshade folks, then had a tour of the dealership, which emphasized the service department and its capabilities. We were joined by the general manager, who brought us to his spacious office and thanked us for our business. Finally, the moment had arrived. We followed the GM through the dealership's offices and out into a long tunnel, which traversed the dealership,, and allowed new car deliveries to take place in inclement weather. The scene had been well set.

The tunnel, though three or four car widths wide, was not well lit. This gave our new Cadillac an almost ethereal appearance, as it basked in the soft glow of the indirect lighting coming from nearby office windows. Our daughters gasped. My wife and I probably gasped as well. It was the perfect setting to take possession of a new car. The general manager couldn't have been nicer, pointing out the various characteristics of our new vehicle, demonstrating how various systems worked, and finally presenting the set of gold keys to my wife in a courtly gesture.

At that moment, my radar antenna directed my eyes forward of our new car, searching in the gloom ahead for something that my unconscious had sensed but my eyes had not yet seen. We were not alone. Almost at the exit door, at the far end of the tunnel, and well ahead of our car, another vehicle was parked in the near darkness. Only a dim outline was visible. But I could tell it was not a modern automobile. Much taller and more broad. Formidable. It was an old car. 1930s or 1940s, I guessed, based upon what little I could see.

I waited impatiently while the general manager had my wife sit in the Sedan de Ville driver's seat, He explained the dashboard functions to her. Finally he finished and I caught his eye. I asked what sort of car was parked ahead of us.

"An old Cadillac," he replied.

"What year?" I asked.

"1936," he answered, "Those old sedans were known as turret tops."

"A V8?" I asked.

"No. It's a V12, which is much rarer," he said, causing the hair on the back of my neck to rise unbidden.

By now, my car collector's radar was locked on and tracking. Furiously. It might have already shifted into hyperdrive. Be still, my beating heart.

I spoke slowly, pronouncing my words as if talking to a child. "I once owned a similar car while living in northern California a decade ago. I bought it in Carmel from a retiring school teacher. He'd bought it from the original owner in San Francisco. He was told that it was delivered with a special San Francisco rear end for navigating the city's inclined streets. When I moved to southern California in 1975, I sold it to a collector in San Francisco."

His eyes widened. "I bought this car in San Francisco about a year ago."

Such a coincidence, I thought. Then, "But ours was a dark green. Your's appears to be black."

"Only because of the poor light," said the general manager, "Its actually dark green."

Hmmm ...

We were both silent, thinking the same thought. Could it be? We looked again at the car, then at each other, both of us knowing that we had to have an answer to this improbable but still possible occurrence. We turned together, and walked toward the old car. The general manager stopped for a moment to turn on additional overhead lights. We walked up to the 1936 Cadillac as she sat quietly, keeping her secrets for another moment or two. The color was definitely green.

I told the man that there were two oddities on my California car that might help us identify if this car was, by the strangest of chance, the same. Most cars of 1930s vintage had a pair of fog or driving lights mounted on the front bumper, in addition to the normal headlights on the fenders or alongside the hood cowl. Only one yellow fog light had been installed on my car.

The second oddity was that one day, driving down Highway 1 along the beautiful Big Sur coastline, I'd heard a rear hubcap come loose, and spin noisily off the road into a pine grove. A thorough search failed to reveal the escaped and well-hidden culprit, which was actually the outer trim ring, not the intact center chrome cap. I had to continue on without it. In time, I was able to find a replacement, but one of marked lesser quality than the rest of the car, and its clean and unmarked original hubcaps and trim rings.

We approached the car together. Bending down, we looked carefully at the right rear chrome beauty ring on its wide white-wall tire, then did the same to the front tire to make comparison. The former was obviously of less quality than the latter. We made similar comparisons with the hubcaps and beauty rings on the left side of the car,. They confirmed our finding.

I sensed in both of us a reluctance to break the spell, and walk to the front of the car. It had been such a fascinating, if accidental, interlude. We looked at each other for a moment, then strode out in front of the old Cadillac.

Only a single yellow fog light was mounted on the bumper.

Bingo!

We'd once owned this very car. What effort the fates had to have made to position our former 1936 Cadillac V12 turret top sedan in the dealership tunnel with our just-purchased 1986 Sedan de Ville. Two cars. Both Cadillacs. Produced fifty years apart. One we'd once owned 3000 miles away, and more than a decade in the past. One we'd bought within the hour.

What were the chances?

Broad smiles. Laughter. And a certain dryness in my throat as, with the owner's permission, I opened the driver's door and slid behind the wheel, looked at the chrome-bezeled dashboard instruments, then, through the split windshield and over the long lovely hood, to the beautiful radiator ornament. It was quite a moment. Something to savor.

"Does the radio still play?" I asked.

"Of course," he answered.

Of course...

Minutes later, having thanked the general manager with whom we'd just shared the most unlikely of odd discoveries, the tunnel door was lifted for our departure. We drove slowly past the stately old Cadillac, our family proud and happy with our new car, enjoying its many safety features and comfort systems, all developed over the five decades separating our new car from the beautiful old classic we were passing.

As we pulled out on the highway, homeward bound, I found myself feeling quite emotional about the grand old girl we'd just left behind us.

Again.

5

Studebaker:
Horse-drawn Carriages to
Motor Cars

*The taste of Zen (ch'an) and the taste of tea
(ch'a) are the same.*

Always be careful what you pray for, particularly in the old car
hobby. Those of us who dream of finding old automobiles lost in
time, and who chronically survey passing roadsides for candidate
vehicles, should keep that adage in mind as we quest for old cars.

One of my bizarre habits over the years was to leave a note
expressing interest in a desirable vehicle parked in some public place.
The envelope, scrap of paper or napkin was left under the windshield
wiper on the driver's side, in the hope that the car's owner might
notice before getting in the car, or while just starting out, before
speed shredded the message or tore it away.

What was in the note? The usual. A knowledgeable compliment
about the vehicle. An attempt to establish car-collecting bona fides.
A request that, should the car ever become available, I would be
interested in discussing purchase. And finally my contact information which, in those simpler days before cell phones and the internet,
consisted of my name, address, and home phone number.

How many of these notes have I left? Dozens, surely. Hundreds, perhaps. I don't really know. Even to me, this appears to be
an over-optimistic addiction run wild. I guess it was. I knew it was

unrealistic to expect a reply which, in all but one of those vain-glorious communiques, proved the rule. But the one captivating exception was powerful enough to keep me leaving windshield notes for years afterward.

Still do, in fact. Though only now and then.

Strangely enough, the single success involved a marque I had always admired, but had little interest in owning. It was a 1947 Studebaker Commander convertible, a rare collectible, though not highly valued in the 1970s, an era not that long after the company tried to survive by merging with Packard, another troubled manufacturer. Both later failed and passed into history.

Studebaker cars had always been an acquired taste. Even the best of their design efforts left many car aficionados wondering what really went on during those late nights in the company's design studio. Studebakers always seemed either way ahead, or well behind, the other automobile manufacturers in their design concepts. They appeared to be daring potential customers to consider their latest wingless aircraft on wheels. For those who know something of the marque, the bullet-nosed Starlight coupes of the early 1950s come readily to mind.

It wasn't the car's design, but its uniquely original condition, that attracted me to stop in the San Diego grocery store parking lot sometime in the late 1970s. Staring through the Studebaker's side window on a rare sunless day, I noted that the mileage, seen with difficulty in the dim interior, appeared to be in the forty-thousand-mile range. Though the car's exterior had an off-putting metallic green paint, the body itself, and its brown Naugahyde interior and tan canvas top, appeared to be original. The left rear fender and an adjacent section of the trunk had a slight but noticeable paint fade, suggesting the Studebaker might have been parked in the same carport location for many years, allowing the California sun to slowly bake away some of the paint color on those areas not under cover.

I went back to my car, obtained a pen and scrap of paper, and wrote what I hoped was a compelling note. I left it under the wiper on the window and drove home. After a few days, I came to the usual conclusion. The owner was either not interested in selling or the note had blown away before it was noticed.

More than two years passed. Then one evening, while the family occupied itself with homework, conversation and television, not necessarily in that order, the phone rang in the kitchen. I walked over and answered. An obviously elderly gentleman was on the line, his voice thin, and somewhat hoarse. He asked if I was the person who had left a note on the windshield of his Studebaker. That last word registered like the hammer hitting the anvil at the end of Jack Webb's *Dragnet* episodes on television.

The caller was talking about the old convertible at the grocery store, the one showing such gentle use almost thirty years into its life. Was my long record as a loser in the windshield note business finally going to produce a winner, in what had previously been such an unproductive lottery through the years? The prize, I reminded myself, was an actual collector car, a convertible at that.

It was. It did. Mr. Howard Vanderbilt, eighty-eight years young, was calling to offer me the car. He had saved my note for two years, leaving it in the car's glovebox. His cataracts had finally gotten to a point where he felt unsafe behind the wheel. His wife and eye doctor both seconded the opinion. Vanderbilt knew that Studebaker was considered something of an "odd duck" as a make. But he'd bought it new after the war, taken good care of it, kept it mostly inside when not in use, and had decided it ought to go to someone who'd been sufficiently attracted to leave a note on the windshield expressing interest. Who was I to argue with such helpful logic?

I asked if I could drop by after work the next day to see the car. He agreed, and furnished an address on one of Coronado's broad streets, not far from its famous white sand beach, the Pacific Ocean, and the venerable Del Coronado Hotel. I arrived at the agreed time and rang the front door bell. Tall and spare, Mr. Vanderbilt opened the door and greeted me, then led me to the driveway, where we struggled together to tug open the heavy two-car garage door. No carport? The Vanderbilts, I decided, must have lived elsewhere for much of the Studebaker's life, given the faded paint. This supposition was later confirmed.

Parked alongside another vehicle hidden beneath a cover, the Studebaker looked exactly as I remembered. Its owner explained its distinctive aspects as I walked slowly around the car, then sat inside. I spent time evaluating the motor bay, trunk and lastly, but slowly and carefully, the undercarriage. Everything was in good order, with no evidence of rust or collision repair. Similar conclusions were drawn from the condition of the sheet metal, end to end. All panels were remarkably straight. The paint, including the faded area, was undeniably original.

A break in Mr. Vanderbilt's explanations gave me opportunity to reveal my own minor Studebaker connection. Early in the last century, the Studebaker family, founders of the only horse-drawn carriage company to successfully transition to the manufacture of automobiles, built a beautiful seaside mansion in my New Hampshire home town. They lived there through the 1930s Great Depression years. Other wealthy families had followed, successive owners of "the Studebaker mansion." As a result, the imposing wood structure remained occupied and well-kept in an era that had seen many of the coastal region's largest wooden residences and hotels either burned or torn down. The property had recently changed hands. Newly landscaped and freshly painted, it looked imposing, though of a style lost in time.

Sooner rather than later, even before a courtesy test drive, Mr. Vanderbilt told me the price he was seeking for the Studebaker. Having done my homework, I knew that his figure was reasonable, so we shook hands in agreement, and the sale was concluded, contingent only upon a satisfactory driving test, which took place soon thereafter and was successful. The car's inline six-cylinder motor was so smooth and quiet that, at stop lights, it was difficult not to reach down and press the starter button, since there was no tachometer, and the silence suggested the car had stalled, though it had not.

I paid for the Studebaker the following day, exchanged paperwork, waited as Mr. Vanderbilt said his goodbyes, and prepared to drive the car to my home nearby. But before taking my departure, curiosity demanded I ask what mystery car he'd stored under a cloth cover alongside the Studebaker. He told me it was a Chevrolet he'd owned for many years.

"What year?" I asked.

"1963," he replied.

"May I take a look at it?"

"Yes, you may," he answered. We worked together to lift the cover from the car.

It was a tan Chevrolet Impala sedan with a white accent panel on its rear fender. Behind the wheel well on the front fender was a "409" badge, indicating that the sedan had Chevrolet's biggest mill under the hood, though equipped with an automatic transmission. It was also one of Chevrolet's fiftieth Anniversary models. I leaned in through the open driver's side front window to see the mileage. Could it be true? The odometer read a mere twenty-nine-thousand miles. I could feel my heart rate rising, thumping away at this news.

"Would this car also be for sale?" I asked, reasoning that the cataracts would probably prevent Vanderbilt's driving at all in the future.

With a smile at the corner of his eyes, he laughed, then replied, "Not at this time, young man, but I note your interest. I'll be in touch should that decision ever be taken."

I asked if he still had my windshield note with my contract information. He nodded in affirmation. The old Studebaker and I drove south down San Diego's Silver Strand in the direction of Imperial Beach and home.

I hardly spent a dime on the car over the next year and used it regularly to and from work and on weekend outings. It was a convertible, after all, and southern California's perennially sunny skies called. Though I did not intend to keep the car long term, it was nice to have it around, and so straightforward to operate, that I simply enjoyed owning and driving it.

Besides, I had a plan for the car. Another Navy pilot in the area drove a 1953 Studebaker Hawk coupe as his daily driver. He dropped by one day, having seen me around town. He told me that his father had once owned a 1947 Commander, finished in light yellow. He told me he'd be interested in purchase when and if I decided to sell. I thanked him but did not get back in touch. I'd learned that if someone really wants one of your old cars, they will return on their own. And if they do return, they are far less price sensitive than had I initiated contact.

Eventually the Hawk owner did return and, after a short conversation, agreed to buy the car for the price I thought it should bring. Two days later, the 1947 Studebaker Commander convertible had moved on to its new home. I began a fresh search for another car project. I was involved in doing that several weeks later when, as if on cue, I received a phone call. It was Mr. Vanderbilt, now 90, on the line.

"Young man, are you still interested in my Chevrolet?" he inquired without preamble. It took me a moment to unscramble my thoughts at having received such an unexpected question before I could answer.

"Yes, sir, I am. May I ask why you've decided to sell?"

"I've had an accident," he replied in a subdued voice. "I thought I could still drive safely with my cataracts if I kept the speed down. But I missed a stop sign, and a lady in a big station wagon ran right into my passenger door. It was all my fault, of course."

"Were you injured, Mr. Vanderbilt?" I asked.

"Just my pride, son," he answered, "I'm fairly certain that the damage is limited to the door. It's been badly pushed in."

Vanderbilt was correct, and fortunately so. Inspecting the Chevrolet the next afternoon, I thought it miraculous that the front and rear fenders, and the rocker panel beneath the damaged door were unmarked. Not even paint scrapes or mars could be seen. The damaged door, on the other hand, was beyond repair, its structure having taken the brunt of the collision. But its interior panel and hardware, matched to the rest of the car's interior and undamaged, could be used with a replacement door. In consequence of the damage, and perhaps his complicity in its creation, Mr. Vanderbilt had significantly reduced his price. We were able to quickly agree on the sale.

By the time I visited the Vanderbilt home to pay for the car, I'd gone to a local junk yard and bought a used 1963 Chevrolet passenger door, loading it into our Volvo wagon. Later, as I drove home in the damaged Impala, the throaty resonance of its 409 V8 a symphony to my ears, I wondered whether this acquisition would prove a "keeper." It certainly seemed so.

Twenty-nine thousand miles and all original — except, of course, the passenger door.

"She's real fine, my 409."

Then, in one of those quirky episodes which seem to pervade the old car hobby — or at least *my* old car hobby — I received a letter from a good friend, a fellow pilot I'd flown with in Southeast Asia. He wrote that he was about to complete his flying assignment at Adak, a barren island off the coast of Alaska, and would soon return to San Diego with his family.

Did I, by merest chance, have a lead for him on a good used car? Did I ever.

The 1963 Chevrolet Impala found a new home with my friend and his family. I always wondered what he thought when he opened the trunk, and found the replacement passenger door hiding there.

6

Lamborghini:
Farm Tractors to Supercars

*A good haiku is a pebble thrown into the
pool of a listener's mind.*

Doesn't every aspiring car collector secretly wish to own a Ferrari?
I did. And, as a result, spent years of mental wanderlust salivating at
pictures in magazine articles, followed marque offerings in *Hemmings
Motor News* and, very occasionally, encountered the actual blindingly
bright physical presence of one of those mythic red chariots.

I knew it was never to be more than a dream, after further investigation revealed the exorbitant costs required to maintain and repair
those ethereal machines. Given that the cost of a single scheduled
maintenance visit, as reported, exceeded my budget for purchasing
such a car, it became less difficult to let the dream go. This information was about late models. Vintage Ferraris, which captured my
interest, required greater sums for even mundane mechanical service.
With that daunting news, I surrendered to the inevitable.

The years flew by. I received a three-year assignment to Naples,
Italy, a city settled before the Greeks and Romans, standing seaside
opposite the legendary Isle of Capri, and beneath the shadow of
Mount Vesuvius. This seemed a perfect base from which to mount a
search for Italian automobiles countrywide. I did, with vigor.

After a year in which success proved elusive, I'd learned a good
deal about the Italians and their exotic machines and fallen head-
over-heels for the country, its people and culture and, particularly,

81

its food. Unlike the thoroughgoing care with which American car collectors cosseted their exotics, Italian owners seemed intent on driving them regularly — and hard. But they seemed only minimally interested in maintenance. In traveling to inspect possible purchases, from Sicily in the south, to Milan in the north, it was apparent that, while each car could be driven to its limits, the evidence of neglected maintenance and deferred servicing was everywhere. Drivetrain and frame rattles. Oil leaks. Inoperative systems.

The cars always looked clean and undamaged, possibly due to the moderate California-like climate. They started and drove competently. Despite the obvious flaws, prices were typically at or above the U.S. market, though the need for significant drivetrain investment was a commonplace and, in most cases, beyond my means. Realizing that a purchase of any of these candidates would involve paying twice, once for the vehicle, then again to overcome the mechanical neglect, I ended my search. Morose over the turn of events, my weekends were soon occupied with tours of museums and ruins, instead of long drives on the Autostrada to inspect a distant prospect.

Then, as happens when we come to the end of one pursuit, only to have fate present us with another, I chanced to see a car driving in the vicinity of my workplace with an appearance so powerful that it took my breath away. Long-nosed, a deep black, and with perfected contours that could only have been fashioned in Italy, its throbbing exhaust note had me reversing my red Fiat Cinquecento, and following that svelte monster down the street. When it pulled over and parked, I was surprised to see an American naval officer emerge.

I parked the Fiat and introduced myself. The officer was friendly, and willing to respond to my questions. The car was a 1967 Lamborghini 400GT coupe. The motor a V12. He had bought the car locally from a retired businessman, the original owner, and used it around Naples as basic transportation. The manufacturer was the same Lamborghini who'd built his business success manufacturing farm tractors and, later, heating and air-conditioning systems. The story was that the man's previously close friendship with Enzo Ferrari ended over an argument between the two men over what

Lamborghini saw as insufficient quality standards in new Ferraris. Lamborghini had owned several. Outraged, Ferrari is said to have shouted at his erstwhile friend that if he was convinced Ferraris were being built poorly, he ought to go and build something better.

Lamborghini did just that.

Having met another American living in Italy who'd successfully found and bought an exotic, I renewed my search in my months remaining in the country. As before, every car I inspected and drove revealed the lack of care and maintenance I'd seen earlier. Since repair and restoration costs could exceed asking prices, I passed on these prospects.

The objective of the search had changed. While I remained interested in *any* Italian V12 exotic, my desire for a Ferrari had faded, while rarity and uniqueness, and an unlikely story of a tractor manufacturer trying to outdo the Ferrari legend, refocused my search on Lamborghini. However, while there were many older Ferraris for sale in Italy in the 1970s, there were a mere handful of vintage Lamborghinis, due to limited production in the marque's early years. From 1963 through 1967, only 120 350GTs and 247 400GTs were produced, a total of 367 cars. In addition, only 108 of the Lamborghini Miura P400 were sold by the end of 1967. Predictably, I returned home without that long-sought Italian car.

It was good to be home. We missed life in Italy, living within such a dynamic culture and enjoying its unique richness, while regularly traveling to other European countries, as part of my work. The USA had no ready answer for Italian cuisine, its wonderful pastas, espresso and cappuccino, and the deliciously thin Neapolitan pizzas drenched in olive oil. As I settled into a new assignment at the Pentagon, we eventually found ourselves re-Americanized. Our years in Naples became fond memories, but memories nonetheless.

Having sought without success to find and purchase an Italian supercar while living in the country of their origin for several years, I knew my chances of finding an affordable example in the United States were remote — a "hen's tooth." Nevertheless, I kept my eyes open and my nose to the ground. Sometimes success involves nothing more than patience and perspicacity.

But years went by and nothing rose to view. I became discouraged. I made a decision limiting my prospects for success. There were numbers of modern Lamborghinis available in the major exotic markets of California, Florida, and New York City. Angular and aerodynamic, these sharply configured designs were not to my taste. Late models also had higher values.

I found myself captivated by the original 350GT and 400GT models, sleek, low slung, refined and with unerringly simple but stunning styling. These cars had been built in very limited numbers, and in GT or GT 2+2 configurations. The two-seated GT model became my focus. The gorgeous Miura had also became available. Though eventually to become Lamborghini's most valued and collectible mode, its mid-engine design failed to excite my aesthetic sense.

Given this *reductio ad absurdum*, and though I kept searching, I was far from sanguine that I would succeed in my narrowed quest. More time passed. Lots of time. Then one day at a local car show, while engaged in a time-passing conversation with a fellow collector, a chance remark caused a bright light to illuminate at the end of a long dark tunnel. Mentioning my years of fruitless searching for an early Lamborghini and the missed opportunity I'd experienced while living several years in Italy, the man perked up. He told me that he'd heard of exactly such a car owned by an elderly doctor, and stored in a tobacco barn, somewhere near Richmond, Virginia.

I was on full alert. Richmond, the seat of Virginia's Commonwealth, was only ninety miles away. Italy was 4000 miles away. Did the owner have a name? Was the location even approximately known? Who knew of this car and had it actually been seen? The man had no answers. No problem, as today's young often say mindlessly. My gratitude knew no bounds. This fellow collector had given me hope, the greatest stimulant to action available to the human race.

It took several months of letter-writing, phone-calling and pre-Internet basic research before the breakthrough came. Ultimately I was able to get a name, then an address, and finally a phone number. Thus began my six-year odyssey with one of the nicest men I've ever had the pleasure of meeting and, eventually, doing business. An older doctor, but still practicing medicine, he spent much pro bono time serving the poor in a small clinic in Haiti, his gift to humanity, captured and symbolized by the many colorful oil and watercolor paintings of Haitian life on the walls of his cozy study.

I was hesitant to make the first call, knowing how suddenly dreams can be vaporized by a dose of harsh reality. Finally, late one weekend, I called, introduced myself, and told the doctor of my interest in his Lamborghini. He replied helpfully that he would like for us to meet, and invited me the following weekend to visit his tobacco farm on Richmond's outskirts. Encouraged, I read his remarks optimistically, and assumed he must have an interest in a sale. This feeling was strengthened when, nearing the end of our conversation, he told me in his soft Southern voice that, while he had a great appreciation for his car's unique design, he had always been reluctant to drive it because of, as he put it, its "race car performance." A 1966 400GT V12, and one of seventeen rare "interim" models, according to the factory, the doctor told me had bought the car new about twenty years previous, and had driven it less than 11,000 miles. My heart probably skipped a beat or two at this news.

The weekend visit to the doctor's farm seemed a conspicuous success. The doctor and his wife were the picture of friendly, Southern hospitality, offered homemade sweet ice tea, and, then, in the course of conversation, offered to show me the still-hidden Lamborghini. We went outside, then over to a small, one-bay garage at some distance from the house. These structures, and several outbuildings nearby for farm equipment storage, were literally an island in a great undulating sea of waving tobacco leaves.

Fortunately, the car was sitting on a concrete floor, overriding my concern that it might have been kept on an earthen floor, with all the unfortunate possibilities of such storage manifest in its undercarriage, rocker and quarter panels. The 400GT sat in the semi-darkness, very dusty but otherwise beautifully poised. The light-blue metallic finish, minimalist rear bumper and chrome, appeared darker in the half-light. The long, low design, and overlarge rear window glass, created an impression of great beauty and, remembering the V12 motor residing under the long hood, great speed. It was a gorgeous "rocket ship."

After a good deal of my breathless gaping and staring, the doctor broke the silence, offering to move the car outside into the bright afternoon sunlight. It started immediately, if somewhat roughly, but settled into a throaty rumble through its twin tailpipes. There was a significant difference, I noted, between the sharp, ear-splitting "blat" of a Ferrari V12, and the more sonorous, richer sound of the Lamborghini. Soon it was parked on the unpaved driveway. Staring at the car — how could one not? —anyone would readily admit to being in the presence of one of the most beautiful automobiles to ever grace the earth. The Lamborghini sat in stately solitude, the waving tobacco its backdrop, and was completely captivating.

The doctor explained what he had learned, owning and driving the car over the years. Driven conservatively, as he had explained on the phone, the 400GT had never experienced a failure, nor needed a repair. He gave credit for this record to Lamborghini himself, whom he'd once briefly met. Because of his demanding standards, and tractor-building expertise, Lamborghini's concept was to build a product with great strength and quality, but as simply as possible. It was for these qualities the doctor had decided upon a Lamborghini instead of a Ferrari.

As he opened the hood and trunk for my inspection, the doctor explained how he operated and cared for the car. Reviewing its few prejudices and preferences, and pointing through the gauges and switches on the leather-paneled dashboard and instrument panel, he made a surprising comment.

"Why don't you and your wife take a ride in the car?" he suggested.

I had difficulty believing my ears. Had he really made such a trusting offer? If we disappeared with his valuable vehicle, he'd have only an old Volvo to show for his trust. Overcoming my surprise, I quickly accepted his offer.

I found my wife enjoying a relaxed conversation with the doctor's wife, and extended the doctor's invitation. Her eyes registered how surprised she was at such a kindness, a look probably similar to my own upon hearing the doctor's words. We went out to the car, got in, started the motor, placed the car in gear, and drove down the long pebbled driveway to the paved road.

Soon we were experiencing the driving characteristics of a true supercar. The Lamborghini was so easy to drive, the car almost anticipating the driver's commands. Behind the wheel, one's sense of confident control was complete. Any awareness of speed was dulled by the car's inveterate smoothness over the road. At one point, alone on a winding country road with good forward visibility and no vehicles or dwellings in sight, I asked my wife to guess our speed, without glancing at the instruments. She looked at me, then off to the side, and finally to the road ahead.

"We'll, I don't really know," she responded. "Seventy."

I smiled and pointed at the instruments. She leaned over, then sat back quickly in amazement.

"It says 120." she exclaimed, nervously. "Is that correct?"

It was. Yet the car hadn't reached high gear.

We returned to the doctor's residence, parked the 400GT at his front door, and turned off the ignition key to the stirring echoes of the magnificent V12's rumbling. We sat there for a minute in the afterglow of a ride beyond description, drinking in the car's features, the well-organized dashboard and instrument panel, the look, smell and feel of the ultra-soft Italian leather seats and side panels. The excellent fit and function of everything. The carefully understated pure beauty of the entire motorcar.

As we exited the Lamborghini and went to thank the doctor and his wife for their hospitality, and for the thrilling driving opportunity, I felt a certain confidence, born of the day's events, that my purchase of the car had become a definite possibility. The owner had readily agreed to meet and frankly shared his love of the car as well as his fear of driving it. Then he'd issued the unexpected invitation to drive the car without his being present. These facts suggested that

I would soon find an opportunity to make an offer, which would be accepted. The doctor's inviting me into his study for a man-to-man conversation before our departure only strengthened that notion.

Minutes later, the bubble had burst. The doctor, as it turned out, knew a great deal about Lamborghinis and their current values. His asking price, though quite reasonable in the 1980s market, was approximately twice what I could offer and afford. My counter was closer to his original purchase price for the car in late 1966, a fact of which we were both aware. Unable to reach agreement, our conversation deflected to other topics, the doctor's medical career, his experiences in Haiti, my naval career and work as a rescue pilot in Vietnam. It seemed we had become friends. As I rose to find my wife and depart for northern Virginia, the doctor and I agreed to continue our conversation about the car. It had been a pleasant day in the company of two courtly people we were pleased to have met. Chastened by my inability to complete a purchase, I thanked the couple again for their hospitality, and resolved to remain in touch with my new friend.

We did remain in touch — for the next six years. Intermittently, one of us would call the other to catch up, then discuss the car. Over all that time, the doctor said several things I found encouraging. He received regular expressions of interest in his car from all over the world: England, Japan, France, Argentina, and, of course, Italy. He did not react positively to those offers because, as he shared with me, he believed the callers were looking to buy, and then resell, the car for profit. "But you," he once said in perhaps our fourth year of these discussions, "show me a genuine appreciation for what a Lamborghini is, and what it stands for." Naturally, I was elated at his words. But then he continued, laughing, "However, it seems you are either too poor or too cheap to meet my price and conclude a sale."

So it was that, on a cold, snowy December evening, I found myself on my twentieth anniversary deep in the bowels of the Pentagon, working alone on a priority project that required a finished product before the next workday. I was at my desk in a vast office warren, my desk light the only illumination except for overhead lights in a distant hallway. Not a sound could be heard except that of my pen scratching — just as it is at this moment.

Suddenly the phone on my desk rang. I immediately stopped writing in surprise. I answered quickly, thinking of a possible emergency at home. It was the doctor in Richmond, apologizing for calling me so late at night. He had called my home and then, discovering I was not there, asked my wife for my work number, which she provided. Feelings welled up in me. I thought about the six years of congenial but frustrating conversations. My discontent at having a job which required my being away from home on an anniversary evening entered in as well. Life seemed to be pressing down on me. Without thinking, I interrupted the doctor's Christmas greeting, and said to him, pointedly, that I found six years a very long time for two men to discuss the purchase of a car. Any car. After a short pause, he quietly agreed.

Deciding to remain on the initiative, I followed with, "Let me propose an idea which, should we both agree, would settle the issue one way or the other. Tonight. And finally." The gauntlet had been thrown. The doctor said nothing, apparently waiting for more, or perhaps shocked at my being so forward. "Let us put our phones down for five minutes." I said. "I'll use the time to determine what funds our family can spare, and add that sum to our previous offer. The result would definitely be a best and final offer for your Lamborghini. In return, Doctor, I ask you to please practice a word I've not heard from you in over six years. That word is 'yes'. You decide, of course, whether to use it. But I'd like to know you have that word somewhere in mind when we both are back on the phone."

The doctor agreed and the phones were set down. Reaching for a writing pad, I hastily scratched down the offer made six years previous, and not altered since. Next to that number, I began listing possible additions, a little from savings not labeled for college educations, some funds on the side from writing projects and, finally, the dregs, my own lunch money. Totaling the sum, it looked meager. Paltry. Not noticeably greater than the offer made years earlier. Moreover, I had now placed us in an endgame from which there was no return.

Five minutes had passed. I picked up the phone and spoke. The doctor, already on the line, immediately, almost but not quite impatiently, asked for my offer. I paused for a moment, looking for some persuasive comment to preview my answer. He pushed aside my pause, perhaps sensing evasion, and asked again. I swallowed hard, found my voice, and gave our offer.

Was it me? Had another ten minutes passed in pregnant silence? Probably not. It was my altered perception of time, as I tried to suppress my impatience. The doctor cleared his throat, then said something. What was it? I had no idea. I asked if he would mind repeating what he'd said.

"No." he said, and my heart dropped hearing the dreaded word. "No." he repeated, "I would not mind." Then, echoing down through the years spent chasing a seemingly unattainable object, I clearly heard him say "Yes."

What anticlimax. And yet there I was, the new owner of a 1966 Lamborghini 400GT. I thanked the doctor. We agreed that I would visit his farm two days later, exchange payment and paperwork, after which I would drive the car north to our home. We said our good nights. I turned off my reading light, locked my desk and headed for home, the project I'd been working on now forgotten. As late as it was, I had an anniversary, and a prized new possession, to celebrate. My heart was no longer in the writing, having flown south to a small garage surrounded by acres of tobacco, within which I imagined myself sitting behind the polished hardwood steering wheel of the greatest automobile I would ever be privileged to own.

Two days later, the yellow Volvo wagon rolled south down I-95 to the doctor's home, this time with all family along. In my pocket was a certified check made to the doctor, who greeted us pleasantly, as we pulled up alongside the stunning, blue-green Italian car, the one about to join our family. The proper exchanges, documents, handshakes and well-wishing completed, our two cars drove north. The Lamborghini drove as I remembered, smoothly and powerfully, instantly responsive to the slightest touch of hand or foot. Only when the car was parked, silent in our garage, did I allow myself to feel a wave of exultation. The sheer magnitude of a long-sought achievement finally realized.

Much rarer than a Ferrari, particularly in the United States, a Lamborghini is welcomed at any vintage car event. Over the years, we attended our share. Its presence was prized for its obvious originality, the seductive exhaust tone, and, hopefully, the humble joys of ownership evident in its driver, as he shared the rare car with other interested collectors, answered questions, and recited the marque's history. It was all great fun, and deeply satisfying, made better by a vehicle built as perfectly as humans could ever manage.

In our eighteen years together, three incidents stand out in my memory as indicative of the Lamborghini's unique perfection. Each illustrates how very different such a rare car is treated in the world. None proved daunting to car or driver, though each, in its own way, was most instructive. All, decades later, remain vivid in my mind.

One Sunday, our eldest daughter asked for a ride to the nearby stable where she often rode. Always looking for an excuse, I backed the 400GT out of the garage and picked up my fare. We drove the short distance to the stable, as I listened to her excited plans for a weekend ride on her favorite horse. We stopped before the stable entrance. I was bidding her good-bye as she exited, asking her to take care riding when, with a concerned look, she stared at the front of the car, and asked if smoke was supposed to be coming from under the hood. Alarmed, I jerked my head back to look through the long angular windshield. Smoke *was* billowing from around the hood. We were on fire!

Even as I shut down the Lamborghini, pulled its hood release, and jumped from the car, I was calling to my daughter to run for a fire extinguisher in the nearby barn. Lifting the hood, I quickly saw that only a small area was actually aflame on the left side of the motor. Concerned for the fire's spreading further, and the possibility of explosion, I removed my favorite tweed sport coat, and used it to smother the flames, bringing the crisis to an end. Troubleshooting revealed a minute fuel line leak, and a cracked Bakelite spark plug receptor, which exposed the spark to the leaked fuel and caused the fire. Driving home I was aware of how close this call had been, and how lucky, at least on that day, was the star under which I was born.

The second incident involved a wealthy Dutchman who regularly attended old car events in the Washington, D.C. area. He arrived in a Rolls-Royce or Bentley, typically a convertible, and had a tedious habit of running down or mocking every collector's car he deigned to inspect. One day at a summer meet, with dozens of beautiful cars on the field, he came by my car. After walking around it several times, he stopped to favor me with his thoughts. He said he liked the car's obvious originality, and knew it to be rare. However, in his years as a collector of fine automobiles, he knew that Lamborghini's motors were not in the same class as those built by Ferrari and race-proven. They were, he added, prone to breaking down, often needed low-mileage rebuilding, and so on.

"Why," he exclaimed, "I bet this old model, when warmed up and at speed, would begin to lose oil pressure. It might even suffer internal damage." I looked at this haughty prig with eyes I hoped appeared steely, and asked what he was willing to bet. "$100," he responded. "Get in the car," I responded, sounding more like Clint Eastwood's "Dirty Harry Callahan" than was probably needed. He nodded, and bent to enter the vehicle.

The car meet was in Laurel, Maryland, a few miles east of the Washington metropolitan center. Route 50 extends from the federal capital to Annapolis, Maryland's capital, a distance of about forty miles. Speed limits on that highway range from 55 to 65 mph. At 160 mph, and literally flying on this road, though with only light traffic, I glanced at my companion, the formerly haughty, now heavily sweating man in the passenger seat beside me, with a two-handed death grip on the dashboard grab bar, and shouted over the wind noise, "Look over here. We're warmed up now. Check the engine oil pressure at well over 80 psi, the same as when we left the car show. There's still a little pedal left, if you'd like to check again at a higher speed."

"No! *No!!*," was his exasperated response. "You win. Please — *Please* — slow this monster down."

As we pulled into my space back at the car show, he handed over a $100 bill, smiling weakly. I took it, and thanked him for being a good sport, though he really wasn't. He'd simply picked the wrong test pilot to whom he issued a challenge. Not only was I feeling "the need for speed," like Tom Cruise's Maverick in *Top Gun*. But that need was ably matched by the stunning performance capability of an old but still fierce Italian supercar. I later heard that the Dutchman lost some of his abusive habits at later meets. When we bumped into each other from time to time, he never spoke to me, but always smiled. Bashfully. Or was it ruefully?

On another occasion, an old Navy friend was in town for business and came to dinner. This friend, who was also a car collector, had once done me a significant service during the two decades I spent restoring a classic Packard convertible in Portugal. I needed six twenty-inch tires delivered to the restorer there to replace the dry-rotted set on the car. In command of a Navy frigate scheduled to visit Lisbon on a port call, my friend agreed to take delivery of the tires in Florida and see that they were delivered to the restorer in Portugal. What I learned, only after the fact, was that, in order to do this within Navy regulations, he was obliged to store the stack of huge tires in his own small stateroom, leaving negligible space for himself, while crossing the Atlantic. *That* is the definition of a good friend.

Late in the evening, we finished dinner and the usual dessert of endless, rollicking "sea stories." My friend asked if I'd take him for a ride in the Lamborghini, which he'd seen for the first time. Pleased to oblige such requests, we left so hurriedly I failed to take my wallet. We drove to the traffic circle at George Washington's Mount Vernon estate, intending to air out the car on the northbound parkway. Its smooth hills and gentle twists and turns ran alongside the Potomac River. Built in 1932 by the Civilian Conservation Corps ("CCC"), the road was well kept, and usually devoid of traffic late at night. In any event, headlights seen to front or rear should warn us of other vehicles.

Circling the traffic circle, we followed another car. Our headlights revealed a grey, late-model Ford sedan, and the driver's cropped blond hair. I wondered if, by chance, the vehicle might be an unmarked police car. It was unlikely this late at night. In almost three decades of daily commuting along the parkway, I'd seen only a few members of the Park Police patrolling that road, and more had been on horses than in cars. Of the latter, all were marked vehicles. As the other car continued around the circle, apparently intending to head south, I set aside my concerns, downshifted and sped north, letting my friend see and experience what a Lamborghini could do once the car got rolling.

Soon we were flying, as I demonstrated the power and responsiveness of the car, which tended to feel sluggish until it found its higher gears, passed into triple digit speeds, and became more aerodynamic and responsive. At that point, the motor reaching 5000-6000 rpm, the V12 sounds became sweet bedlam and steering response quickened noticeably. These conditions brought the 400GT alive, and showed its instinctive desire to run and run hard. I let it do so. The road ahead looked like an airport runway. Ahead and above, the stars shone brightly in a dark sky. It was a journey into space, a pure moment of unleashed driving pleasure. Then, quite suddenly, the darkness was shattered by a piercing blue circulating light behind us.

For a brief moment, I thought to outrun the police car and find a hiding place deep in some residential warren, as I had once done with one of my daughters one dark night on this same roadway when, accelerating the Lamborghini into Han Solo's "hyperspace," we unexpectedly flew past a plainly marked Park Police cruiser alongside the road without lights. The decal was all I really saw, as I hit the afterburners. "Don't you ever let me catch you doing what I've just done, young lady." Considering the communications capabilities that would quickly bring others to the scene, I decided not to attempt escape with my friend a captive to circumstance. Instead, we pulled off the parkway onto an intersecting road, and awaited our fate.

It took little time for the unmarked Park Police vehicle to arrive and pull in close behind us. Nothing happened for several minutes. No one got out of the police car. Strange. Then two more Park

Police cars, both marked and with blue lights flashing, arrived. All three officers left their cars. Meeting at the last car to arrive, the one farthest from us, they commenced a discussion, which lasted about fifteen minutes. Watching and waiting, I had my first intimation that, owing to my excessive speed, I was to be forced to my knees on the street and summarily executed. At the very least, I had likely ended my driving career in the Commonwealth of Virginia, and perhaps elsewhere. The longer my friend and I waited in the dark, as the meeting continued, the more convinced I became that the night was not to end on a high note. But, to our amazement, it did.

The meeting that I'd watched in the rearview mirror came to an end. Two of the police officers got into their two marked cars, reversed their direction, and departed. The officer from the unmarked car came to my driver's door. I lowered the window. Strange, I thought, the officer had a smile on his face, as he looked down into the car. He paused a moment as if silently rehearsing his lines, then said, "Well, good evening. I try to begin these pull-over conversations with an attempt at humor. I've been told it lowers the stress everyone feels in these situations." I made certain he knew he had my full attention. Then he continued, "But in a case where the speed of the apprehended vehicle is more than one hundred miles over the posted 45 mph speed limit, I must say that words fail me."

I almost laughed at the cleverness and sincerity in the officer's short speech but, with the imagined image of my execution still in mind, managed to nod soberly that I understood, and silently awaited the unknown but inevitable. The officer asked for my license and registration. I produced the registration, but told him that my wallet and license had been left at home, which was nearby if he wanted me to obtain it. After all, I thought to myself, I'd probably never need them again. But he seemed nonplussed. "That's not necessary. Wait here while I check this on the computer. With that, he returned to his cruiser with the car's registration, while my friend and I sat quietly conversing about things like lawyers and, well, lawyers.

The park policeman returned. He asked me to leave my vehicle and accompany him to his vehicle. Obeying, I noticed a clipboard on the hood with what appeared to be dozens of yellow ticket forms. I remained silent as he turned off the whirling blue light atop his car, handed my registration back to me, and retrieved the clipboard. The moment of truth had arrived.

Coughing twice, he began, "You may have been concerned, seeing the three police cars lined up behind you." Indeed I had. "The drivers of those other cars were my two supervisors. I wanted to ask both of them what the limits of my authority were in this unusual traffic situation and in my prosecuting this case." Authority? Prosecuting? *Case?* My heart rate tripled, as I again contemplated the execution image. This is how we treat extreme speeders, miscreant! On your knees!!!

Then, breaking in upon my incipient panic attack, he went on. "These are some thoughts that I would like to share with you in what we both know is a unique situation. I have loved reading or watching television programs about classic Italian exotic automobiles though, until tonight's adventure, I'd never set eyes on one. I suspect these cars exist in a dimension all their own. I imagine that, when driving such a car, the presence of a 45 mph speed sign on a quiet, untraveled road late at night cannot compete with the compelling sense of power and speed such a car delivers to its driver. There may be a living animal spirit within the machine itself. These personal impressions, and my concerns about them, were the reason I needed to meet with my supervisors before speaking with you and settling the matter with you."

I didn't know what to say, so I said nothing. My policeman had morphed into an exotic car aficionado, not to mention something of a philosopher. Such thoughtful words. I was not only amazed, I was touched by the officer's insights, knowing firsthand the truths he'd just spoken. Still pending, however, was the matter of the radar's 156 mph reading. Surely that evidence required something be done I was certain not to enjoy. Having practiced my silence throughout, I remained attentive, but also in that mode.

He continued, looking directly at me. "These thoughts weighed on me, so I sought advice on what the correct response of the Park

Police should be. But there was another factor that weighed even more heavily. I've been patrolling this parkway for over eight years. In that time, I've stopped hundreds of errant motorists for a wide range of traffic infractions, most minor, a few serious. In those encounters I've heard every excuse invented by man that the broken rule was caused by an endless list of reasons other than the driver."

"Never did a single driver ever accept responsibility. Ever. That is, until tonight."

"When I asked for an explanation, you immediately took responsibility, and offered no excuse for the facts, which were, in any case, not in dispute. I have decided, with the backing of my supervisors, that I am not going to give a ticket to the first person among hundreds to accept responsibility for breaking the rules we live by on the road. Have a good evening, sir, and take good care of that beautiful automobile."

Without further conversation — I was speechless, and he had had his say — the park police officer turned and got into his car. I watched as he took off his hat, started the cruiser, turned slowly back to the parkway, and was soon gone. I walked back to the Lamborghini, got in, reassured my friend that all had gone better than expected, without going into detail. Who would possibly believe such a story? I started up the Lamborghini and drove home. Slowly.

These unusual examples bear little resemblance to our everyday use of the 400GT over the two decades that followed. Mostly, she sat in our garage or occasionally in our driveway, was driven on weekends in good weather to various car events, the occasional parade, but typically in what, the old doctor termed "a gentle manner," over country roads. Many relatives and friends took their turns behind the hardwood steering wheel and enjoyed their brief rides in a rare Italian exotic.

Other than regular changes of oil and filters, and an occasional tuning of the six Webers, perhaps three times in twenty years of driving, the Lamborghini proved a tribute to its namesake and manufacturer, and continued the doctor's reported two decades of performing without dint of repair, until it reached four decades without needing a repair or suffering a breakdown. And, as you know, this Lamborghini had, on occasion, been driven to speeds seriously challenging any motorcar. But not, apparently, this one.

I did, at one point, remove both gas tanks from their location in the trunk, wedged tightly under each rear fender. I took them to a specialist to remove sludge, perform a cleaning, and seal them internally. This seemed the easier path, rather than waiting for the detritus in the tanks to claim the six Weber carburetors. Reinstallation of the gas tanks took twenty minutes, as gas lines and sender unit wires were reconnected, and the tanks secured in the rear fenders.

As with most of the unique automobiles I'd collected over the decades, there was never a plan to sell the Lamborghini. We assumed it would be with us for the duration. Over the years, the car received steady interest, and had a few offers. Not unlike the former owner's reaction to such blandishments, we felt that those interested were primarily looking to buy the car and re-sell it. As is often the case for those who acquire a rare or unique motorcar, it wants to be another member of the family, always in our garage. But matters have their own way of happening, and usually for the best.

One evening, shortly before bedtime, I received a call from an area code in the Los Angeles area. An editor for a prestigious car magazine, the *Robb Report*, asked if I still owned a 1966 Lamborghini 400GT V12, vehicle #0517. I replied that I did, for many years, and noted that the car was not for sale. Ignoring my comment, the caller then inquired if I had purchased the car from an elderly doctor in Richmond, Virginia. "Yes, I did," I replied.

The caller tasked me to be patient and give him time to explain himself. When he was a small boy in the late 1960s, his father had owned a Porsche 912. Going to the dealership with his father, he'd seen early Lamborghini models on sale there. The strong impression those cars made never left him. Now, as an unmarried, forty-something professional with a secure position, an important objective in his life was to find, buy, restore, and ultimately create the finest 350/400GT Lamborghini in the world. I found myself wanting to laugh out loud at such nonsense. But the man's serious tone made plain that he believed every word he'd spoken.

He went on to tell me that he had spent years searching for the car around which his dream could be developed. His research led him to conclude that #0517 was probably the best, original, low-mileage Lamborghini in the world. My car, he concluded, would furnish him the optimal starting point to achieve his objective.

Then he surprised me. He had already signed a contract with a Ferrari restoration shop in California to perform the restoration once, of course, he provided the subject automobile. He was willing to forward a copy, which I could review and confirm that he had a definite plan. A few days later, the contract arrived in the mail. True to his description, it was for the amount he'd stated, and for the purpose he'd described. I noted in the details that the instrument panel's gauges were to be removed, disassembled, restored, then calibrated before being reinstallation.

Discussions about the car took place over several months, including references to price. Our family determined that the decision should be more for the car's sake than for our own. The 400GT remained a pristine car, and completely original. Approaching its fifth decade, yet showing only about 19,000 miles, there were small evidences of age, here and there, that a discerning eye would see. As a result of countless washings and polishings, red primer was showing through the blue paint along the fenders' raised edges, and on the hood and trunk. The motor remained clean and functional, but its appearance was no longer crisp to the eye. The Webers, in particular, were stained, and would benefit from removal and cleaning.

What was really being offered? The Lamborghini was to be completely re-manufactured to become as-new. This realization finally tipped the scales. With our daughters both in high school, and years of college bills ahead, I knew that I wouldn't be providing the car an opportunity for new life for many years, if ever. An elemental truth was that I actually preferred the car in its original state, warts and all. Because, in this way, it remained just what it was, a car, and not instead a shiny, revered object, somehow less material and real. So the decision to sell was taken. The day came when, as the family watched from our garage, the 400GT was loaded into an enclosed trailer to begin its coast-to-coast journey, then to enter a restoration process resulting in its rebirth.

Over several years, the car's new owner kept in regular touch. The restoration took longer than expected and cost more than agreed in the contract. Don't they always? Some three years after we'd seen the Lamborghini rolled into its trailer and headed west, we received an invitation to visit the owner at his home on the Pacific coast, north of Los Angeles, to see his vision come alive. As it happened, my wife and I had business meetings in California. We included the invitation in our travel plans.

The address was off the Pacific Coast Highway at the end of Malibu Canyon. We arrived at the suggested time to find our host pulling into the driveway beside us. We greeted each other warmly, then went in to his home, a large but not overly imposing structure, closely sited among other similar homes in the contemporary California style. Once inside, we realized an addition had been constructed at the rear of the two-car garage. We followed our host in that direction, noting the sign over the addition's entrance. *Tutti Italiano*, it said. All things Italian.

Walking into the new space, we found ourselves in another country. Rome? Milan? Naples? Without any doubt, it was an Italian location. The large bay was walled with tall mirrors, even the wide entrance door at the opposite end. The mirrors' reflections gave an impression of endless space. Thick carpeting covered the floor. In one corner was a sitting area with chairs and couches in supple tan Italian leather. A full bar, and formidable copper and brass espresso machine, stood nearby, completing the cultured imagery.

Am I forgetting something? Yes, I am. A vintage Ducati motorcycle stood in a far corner. And there, in the precise center of the space, sat the newly restored Lamborghini 400GT, an object of recently perfected splendor, an effect repeated many times in the faceted wall mirrors surrounding the car. It was a stunning presentation, thoughtfully imagined to provoke the maximum focus on its central object. But it was lost on me. I had eyes only for the glowing apparition before me, its familiar lines resplendently shiny and new.

The Lamborghini was perfect, or as perfect as human hands can fashion. A virtually new 1966 400GT in the flesh. Unable to relax on the couch, seeing an old and dear friend only at a distance, I spent more than an hour crawling around, over, and under the exterior and interior of the car, then through its motor bay and trunk. Everything — *Everything* — was perfectly done. Paint. Chrome. The fabulous V12 motor with its polished Webers. The Borrani wire knockoff wheels. Everything.

Concluding my inspection and reacquaintance with my former supercar, I was deeply touched by this opportunity to see a man's dream come literally true, and to recognize and accept that earlier I'd made a difficult but correct decision. The end, in this case, had justified the means. The Lamborghini had gone from chrysalis to butterfly. It had found a far better fate than our family could ever have provided. Sitting back on the soft leather couch, sipping a perfect espresso, and congratulating the car's owner with sincerity on his successful fashioning of this beautiful exotic car from the stuff of his own dreams, we could not have known that this Lamborghini would capture every prestige award at the foremost West Coast concours d'elegance, including those at Hillsborough, and the annual, late-summer frenzy on the Monterey Peninsula.

It was a humbling yet enervating experience to see this fine old Italian machine, built by a perfection-oriented manufacturer of farm tractors, an automobile we'd once owned after years of anguished anticipation. The Lamborghini had experienced a genuine rebirth. In that transformation, it became the best of its type in the world. We thanked its owner for extending the invitation to visit. The tears did not come until we had pulled away from his home. The deep sense of satisfaction that the best outcome for the car had, quite visibly, taken place, would prove our lasting solace.

Ciao, bella …

7

Italian Cars: Fiat, Alfa Romeo & Maserati

In Zen, all grasping is futile, because there is nothing to be grasped.

I'd spent years searching for an affordable vintage Ferrari, and later an early Lamborghini, blithely unaware that "affordable" and "vintage" were a contradiction in terms for such ethereal machines. That effort was renewed when I lived in southern Italy. Later, I found and bought a 1960s Lamborghini 400GT V12 coupe less than a hundred miles from my Virginia home. I'd never been interested in other old Italian cars. But that was to change.

While living in Italy, I'd gone native and bought a red 1970 Fiat Cinquecento (500 cc) to use commuting around the ancient city of Naples and for weekend family excursions into the narrow streets of that city, where a full-sized automobile rarely escaped with fenders intact. The little Fiat was a reliable microcar, with its two-cylinder, air-cooled engine, four-speed manual transmission, and thirteen-inch tires, ideal for navigating the Grand Prix simulation of Italian city driving.

Looking as if it fit into an American car's trunk, the Fiat could comfortably carry two adults up front, two children and a small dog in the rear. It was equipped with a sliding fabric roof, providing a ragtop experience in sunny southern Italy. It got 60 mpg on regular gas. Our memories of this appealing little vehicle remain among the favorite of our time overseas.

Returning to the States, then almost magically finding the vintage Lamborghini, allayed whatever interest I might have had in vintage Italian motorcars. But that's not how it works. A car collector's constant scanning of newspapers, magazines, and every road he drives on, often provides opportunities lying at the outer fringe of one's imagination. So it was for me.

While living in Newport, Rhode Island, in 1980, I read *The Providence Journal* on Sundays. The news and sports sections took a half hour. Another half hour, sometimes longer, was spent tracing the used car advertisements, particularly the classic car section. I'd done this for months without finding a single ad worthy of a call or visit. But then — as the football odds-makers say, "on any given Sunday" — I found a listing in the classic section for a 1941 Alfa Romeo convertible. There was no other information except the price, a few thousand dollars.

According to sources, there was no Alfa Romeo production in 1941. Early in WWII, British Lancaster bombers bombed Italian armaments factories to cripple the country's contribution to Axis war efforts. Vehicle, aircraft, and motor factories were completely destroyed. If there was a 1941 Alfa Romeo in existence, it would be extremely rare, or perhaps a fake. I planned to call for information, then visit to have a look at what automotive historians claimed did not exist.

The call exceeded my expectations. It was compelling. The owner's father, an Army major, had somehow managed to import the car to the United States at the end of the war. It was stored in the father's single car detached garage. When he died, the property and the Alfa passed to the son. The son was starting a livery business and needed funds. He told me that, as a small boy, he'd seen his father occasionally start the car and let it run in the garage. To the son's knowledge, the car had not been on the road since 1945, when it first arrived on a ship.

I made an appointment to see the car the following day. Meanwhile, I read everything I could find about Alfa Romeo. This was done in an era lacking computers, the Internet, even the all-but-appendage we now call cell phones. The results of my research left more questions than answers. One fact, however, had been confirmed. Alfa Romeo *had* constructed four cars on special order for occupying German generals in 1941. These cars were built by hand in what remained of the destroyed Alfa factory. All were 6C2500 models, with six-cylinder, 2.5 liter motors. Importantly, the vehicle number supplied by the car's owner from its title indicated his car was a convertible. If so, it was the first of the four cars built.

After work the next day, I aimed the Volvo wagon west for Providence. A half hour later I was roaming from street to street in a dense, run-down residential area of the city. I finally found the correct street and met the owner, a man about my age. We walked to the detached garage at the rear of the property. As the doors were unlocked and opened, there sat one of the most unusual automobiles I'd ever encountered.

The Alpha was larger than expected. It appeared even more so with its white exterior, and due to the bulbous 1930s styling by Italian coach-builder, Touring Superleggara. Nonetheless, it was as impressive as it was unusual. The interior was finished in red leather, dried out but serviceable. The car sat five, three in the rear. I was surprised to see the steering wheel, shifter, and foot controls on the right side, but later confirmed that all pre-war Alfas were right-hand drive (RHD).

The motor was a massive, in-line six cylinder. It filled the space under the hood completely. As with the rest of the car, nothing appeared to be missing. Everything was in its place. As expected, given storage conditions, the tires were rotted and the exhaust pipes and muffler had deteriorated. Helpfully, there was no evidence of damage, rust, or repair anywhere on the car. I was looking at a time capsule built four years before I was born.

I decided on the spot to purchase the car. Who would not? I offered about half the asking price, then gave back enough to secure the sale. By the following weekend, the car was paid for, delivered to our home, and sat in one of our garage bays. Seen within the larger space, and with better overhead light, the stylish class of the rare car became apparent. The large vertical Alfa grill, rounded windshield, and the extendable "trafficator" turn signals on the car's flanks, all brought the curvaceous Italian lines of the car into perspective.

A new battery, a change of motor oil, the addition of several gallons of fresh gasoline, and several hours spent learning, slowly and carefully, how the car preferred to be started and operated, found the Alfa running smoothly, if not quietly, in the garage. Within two weeks, and with four new tires mounted, the car was driven to a local shop for an exhaust and muffler. After adjusting to driving with right-hand steering, I found the Alfa handled responsively and was much peppier than expected. Everything worked: the long-shafted transmission shifter, the brakes, and the dashboard instruments. Like Rip Van Winkle, the car had been awakened from its long slumber, and seemed happy to be on the road.

I stopped the project as this point. My approach to old cars was to initially repair or replace faulty systems, ensuring that the vehicle operated safely and without problems. I found the ownership experience heightened by efforts needed to bring the vehicle back to standard. The 6C2500 was simply too well-preserved to consider even a partial restoration. Instead, I enjoyed the beautiful car as it was, driving weekends with the top down, enjoying the stares and questions of the curious. These were understandable, given the Alfa's unusual appearance.

There were only two surprises with the Alfa over the year we remained in Rhode Island. I considered this a tribute to the build quality of a car constructed in the chaotic turmoil of a world war, then subjected to decades of unprepared storage without benefit of temperature and humidity control. One surprise was that the water pump had a slight shaft leak, which was difficult to suppress. Every few weeks I replaced the packing, and tightened things up, trying to eliminate the leakage. But I was never completely successful. To its credit, the Alfa did not seem to mind, running smoothly and never overheating, even in the summer. Finally, I let the pump leak, but checked the coolant level more frequently.

The other surprise, however, was unsettling. Going over the

Alfa, I discovered, magnet in hand, that the exterior of the car was thickly layered in body putty. Alarmed, I shifted mentally to crisis control, wondering if my rare and unique find was instead the creation of shyster artistry. I'd heard of similar scams. Later, I learned from an Alfa Romeo historian, and to my great relief, that 6C2500s were shaped roughly in steel or aluminum by hand, then covered in putty. The putty was then sanded, using curved wooden battens as guides, to achieve the exacting lines drawn by the designer. This process was likely necessary due to the limited capabilities of the destroyed Alfa factory. It also explained why my measurements of opposing front and rear fenders had shown them to be curiously asymmetrical.

When our time in Newport and on Aquidneck Island ended, we moved to the Washington, D.C. area for our next assignment, and found a home near George Washington's Mount Vernon estate in a quiet suburb of Alexandria, Virginia. There was no space for the Alfa. I arranged with the Newport Car Museum to place the car on display. For several years it was prominently shown as "the Hitler car." This disinformation proved a small embarrassment. But I'd found secure, temperature-controlled storage for the car at no cost.

Due to that exposure, I was regularly contacted by interested parties wanting to buy the car. A gentleman in London wrote every month or two, each time offering more for the car. When his offer reached the unable-to-be-refused level, I sold the only known remaining 1941 Alfa Romeo 6C2500 in the world, the first built, and one of only four, to England. Did I miss that rare and trouble-free motorcar? Yes, I did. Do I wish now I hadn't sold it? Of course, though the proceeds were useful for a military family living in expensive Washington, D.C. Evidence of my mistake was clearly manifest three years later, when I read in a hobby magazine that the only 1941 Alfa Romeo extant, a cabriolet, now painted red and apparently restored, had sold at an auction in Monte Carlo for a sum almost one hundred times what I'd paid for the car.

By then, having gotten to know several car-collecting types who loved, and sometimes owned, arcane Italian automobiles, I had bought another 6C2500. This was a 1949 two-seater Super Sport (SS) model with an elegant roadster body by Italian coach builder, Pininfarina. The car was not running. But it was overwhelming to look at, as it sat in the garage, a static display, while its owner sought to find someone competent to rebuild the motor and sort through the mechanicals. But that expertise was not to be found. Parts were unavailable. After two years of searching, during a busy time in my professional life, I sold the 6C2500 SS roadster to a custom steering-wheel manufacturer in Nyack, New York, hoping he would succeed in bringing that stunning car back to life.

My ownership of the two, now highly valuable, early Italian motorcars, came at a time when there was little interest in European vintage vehicles. Some were rightfully termed "sleds" for their uninspired designs. And right-hand drive vehicles had little following in the United States. Other 6C2500 models, such as the remarkable Golden Arrow (Frescia d'Oro) coupe, best remembered when an example was destroyed in the film *The Godfather II*, possessed uncommon grace and alluring elegance. But in that earlier time, 6C2500s were considered barely collectible. For those with imaginations who could see past the disinterest and neglect, and ignore the more outrageous designs, the potential of these inheritors to Alfa Romeo's successful 1930s racing machines was captivating. With hindsight, I mourn what might have been, had I decided, against logic and reason, to keep one or both of those fascinating Alfas.

This regret might explain why I later spent three years attempting to purchase a rare, celebrity-owned early Maserati.

While searching for a competent restorer for the 1949 6C2500 Alfa Super Sport roadster, I'd come in contact with a number of knowledgeable people in several countries. One of these was an older Italian gentleman, a seller of fine art for decades. He did business from offices in Bologna, Italy, and Buenos Aires, Argentina. We became friends, and often corresponded, while I was seeking a reputable rebuilder for the Alfa's motor. His name was Bernardo.

When Bernardo's call came late one evening, it had been more than a year since we'd spoken or written, the sale of the '49 Alfa having ended my unsuccessful restoration search. Bernardo was calling from Argentina. He wasn't offering to assist me, however. Instead, he sought my advice and assistance in resolving a pressing legal matter in the United States. He had, as he explained, owned one of the rarest Ferraris of all time, a 1950s GTO. Only a handful were produced, and they were valued accordingly, in the millions. He had kept the Ferrari for years at his hacienda in the Argentine countryside, intending at some point to sell it as a sinecure for old age. On returning from Italy to his Argentine home recently, he discovered the Ferrari was missing. It had been stolen.

The Argentine police offered solace but little concrete assistance. They had assured the owner that the Ferrari was no longer in the country. At that point, Bernado had turned for help to his world-wide network of art collectors, many of whom were also collectors of vintage cars, and to Enzo Ferrari, whom he knew on a personal basis. Soon this global search party discovered the location of his missing car.

The car was in the possession of a wealthy and well-known international fashion designer, and was being kept in New York City, as part of his private collection of rare supercars. Bernardo was seeking strategic advice to help recover his car from a billionaire, whose legal and financial resources were, in a practical sense, unlimited. I suggested he hire a reputable NYC law firm, on a contingency basis if possible. But I was not much help to the distressed Italian. I suspect that his 1950s Ferrari GTO still remains in the fashion designer's collection, having been defended by the best legal minds, and kept securely beyond the reach of Argentine and Italian law in the United States.

In trying to draw me in to his campaign to recover the Ferrari and also, as he admitted, as an initial step to build sufficient funds to finance a recovery effort, Bernardo suggested I might purchase another car he owned, which he stored in Bologna. It was a very early Maserati, an A6, one of the first street cars produced by the Maserati brothers in the late 1940s, building upon their earlier racing successes, and after the widespread destruction of the war had been followed by reconstruction. He described the car as completely original, a somewhat primitive fixed-head coupe, built upon what was essentially a race car's chassis and drivetrain. It was, however, the Maserati's provenance that caught my attention, driving my imagination into overdrive.

Bernardo had purchased the Maserati A6 in Argentina, then shipped the car to his home in Italy, where he secured it on his property. This decision seemed to mimic his failed strategy to locate his valuable Ferrari thousands of miles from Italy in Argentina, until he decided to sell, only to have it stolen. The A6 was originally purchased directly from Maserati by a well-known Argentine Grand Prix race driver. In the grandest of theatrical gestures, he in turn presented it as a gift to Eva Peron in 1951. Eva was the wife of Argentine president and strong man, Colonel Juan Peron, the founder of *Peronism*, a political movement still alive in modern Argentina.

Eva Peron was the subject of the successful play, and later movie, *Evita*, seen by millions worldwide. The theme song, *Don't Cry For Me Argentina*, which remains on global playlists, is known to the entire world. So is the story of the Perons, but particularly Eva, whose success was seen to be based upon having had "all the right deprivations" before her meteoric rise from poverty to the presidential domicile, Casa Rosata. It was the ultimate rags to riches tale.

Eva owned the car less than a year, dying of cancer in 1952. Her ownership of the car was well documented. Her use of the vehicle was not. Bernardo had purchased the car from an elderly Argentine collector who had, quite practically, hidden the coupe away as political winds blew to and fro in that country over many years, and as the Peronist movement rose and fell. There were only a few thousand kilometers on the car. Bernardo had cleverly named the A6 "Maserita," combining the Maserati marque with Eva Peron's popular nickname —"Evita."

Bernardo mentioned the price he expected for Maserita, a sum at the very outer reaches of our resources. We were interested, knowing of Peron's global notoriety, and of the premium often attached to celebrity-owned cars. As it happened, a Virginia neighbor had invited us the following month to the wedding of his daughter to an Italian businessman in northern Italy. We were traveling to Italy, and could visit Bernardo and see his Maserati at the same time.

The wedding was lovely. But, throughout the two days of dinners, festivities, and socializing, my mind was elsewhere. Bologna was less than an hour away. Finally, the rice was thrown, the last hand shaken, expressions of thanks given and received. We were soon driving on the Autostrada, hoping to see an interesting old car with a fascinating history.

Bernardo was a pleasure to meet in person. Upon our arrival in the city, we enjoyed a long afternoon lunch together, during which our host presented my wife with a kilogram (2.2 lbs) of the finest local Parmigiana-Reggiano cheese. Then it was on to the Bologna Convention Center, where the Maserati was the central display amidst a collection of art objects being sold by Bernardo. There, prominently posed in the center of the lobby, was Eva Peron's A6 coupe.

We spent two hours with the Maserati, and concluded that we'd found a rare motorcar so perfectly preserved that there should never be a question of its restoration. Were there visible flaws? Yes, a few, but they were no more noticeable than the changes which take place in people across their lives, respectable amulets of age.

Painted a metallic blue, the coupe's body contours were poorly shaped, its sheet-metal work primitive. In fact, the car was primitive throughout. That characteristic, we decided, was its charm, and inevitably, its claim to value. Despite the lack of finished crafting, and an awkward design which, though oddly attractive and purposeful, could never claim itself a pinnacle of quality craftsmanship, the car spoke loudly to us. Maserita was exactly what one should expect in a true 1940s Italian race car, masquerading as a boulevard two-seater.

As my wife, a blonde like Eva, sat in the Maserati for photographs, I found myself wondering if Evita, perhaps aware of her illness and its likely consequence, might have enjoyed driving such a unique and personal gift, finding in its raw power and agile responsiveness a respite, however brief, from the fate which awaited her. We'll never know.

We left Italy having committed to purchase the Maserati at an agreed price close to Bernardo's expectation. We needed time to gather funds and conclude the sale, while at the same time researching further the car's origins and the Peron connection. Maserati's records confirmed the sale to the Argentine. The connection to Eva Peron's ownership was well established. As we evaluated the prospect of purchase, success seemed imminent.

But Maserita was not to become ours. It took a combination of factors to undo what had seemed done. The central difficulty was that the price was well in excess of established values for the few early A6 Maseratis extant. There were very few A6s in the world, which itself made proper valuation difficult.

We persevered. For an additional year, I was in regular communication with Bernardo. Each of us kept trying to find a reasonable compromise that would allow the sale to go forward. Meanwhile, my efforts to get closer to Bernardo's priceless stolen Ferrari GTO bore no fruit at all. The supercar did exist, and its body and engine numbers matched those Bernardo had provided. But the security surrounding the car and the collection, and the insularity of its wealthy owner, proved an impenetrable combination. I felt sad for Bernardo, but also for myself. My success helping my friend might have helped us find agreement on the Maserati.

Then, Bernardo seemed to have second thoughts. Perhaps the connection to a world-famous person, still much in the news, had more importance in valuing the car than he'd earlier concluded. His original offer, which was beyond the upper limit of other A6 valuations, had been presented in U.S. dollars. Aware that he had offered the car at a firm price not subject to change, Bernardo wrote us, advising that his offer was in euros, not dollars. His offer letter argued otherwise in print. U.S. dollars, it said. At the time, the currency shift increased the price by about thirty percent, a level now beyond our capability.

The issue was decided. We withdrew.

I recently learned that "Maserita," the 1946 Maserati A6 Coupe once owned by Eva Peron, is now on display in a vintage automobile museum in northern Italy. I do not know if Bernardo remains the owner, if the car has been sold to the museum, or to another private owner. I do know that its current value would be several times the figure I was once offered — even in Bernardo's euros.

Now and then, I recall the little blue coupe, its famous owner, and reflect on what might have been had it come to our family. But I'm at peace with that adventure, and with its outcome. We did everything within reason to acquire a very rare car. In the end, our efforts proved insufficient, given circumstances beyond our control.

You can't win them all.

If "Maserita" was to be ours, it would have been.

It wasn't.

So, "Don't cry for me, Argentina ..."

8

Doc Hudson's Legacy

*The perfection of Zen is to be perfectly and
simply human.*

In the three animated *Cars* movies, all of them children and car
collector favorites, the late Oscar-winning actor and professional race
driver Paul Newman provided the audio for the Doc Hudson character, a wizened, gravel-voiced, mentor to younger hotshot characters
like Lightning McQueen. The collectors aside, few enjoying those
movies would have recognized the name Hudson, a company which
last produced automobiles in 1957. But very few car collectors would
have known that, in 1929, the year the Great Depression began,
Hudson was considered one of America's finest luxury automobiles,
a solid favorite of gangsters toting their "Tommy guns" through
America's city streets. Hudson's production in that year ranked third
behind Ford and General Motors.

Those knowledgeable about America's history of auto racing
might also recall Hudson's sheer dominance of stock car racing in
pre-NASCAR days. Post-war, slope-backed Hudsons were built close
to the ground, creating a low center of gravity that required little
braking in turns. Their reliable straight six-cylinder motors, equipped
with "Twin H-Power" dual carburetors, competed successfully against
bigger, stronger V8s, winning the great majority of stock car races
until Ford and GM conspired successfully to have Hudson banned
from racing, allegedly because of declining production numbers.

My late father, a man ecumenical, even random, in his family transportation selections, was one of those who had knowledge of Hudson's history and its reputation for quality. On a weekend afternoon in 1957, our family's string of pedestrian Chevrolets and Fords ended abruptly, when he drove a 1955 Hudson Hollywood coupe into our driveway.

It was a stunning car, very different from other cars our family had owned. Its bold egg crate grille announced its racing heritage to the world. Chrome trim abounded. The sensually curved body had been designed in Italy. Bright white paint on the upper exterior gleamed. The teal green on the lower body accentuated the car's beautiful lines. The Hudson's mileage was only about twenty thousand. Almost new. The Hudson fairly shouted, "See *me!*"

Two unique amenities captured a restless fourteen-year-old, already dreaming of his driver's license. The first was an adjustable radio antenna, mounted on the roof above the windshield, and hand-operated for fine tuning, using an overhead knob between the two sun visors. The second was a metal-shrouded continental kit for the spare tire. Mounted on an extended deck above the rear bumper, and painted in the contrasting colors of the car's exterior, the rear-mounted spare was the most eye-catching feature on the car.

As we gathered to explore the Hudson's interior, it was obvious that its external luxury was matched within. The seats and side panels were finished in plush, two-tone materials. As on the outside, bright chrome trim was everywhere. The "Magic Air" heat and ventilation controls, located beneath the push-button radio, looked like an airliner's instrument panel. In the rear, a thick cord stretched across the back of the front seat. This allowed children, before the era of seatbelts, to stand, holding the cord, and watch their parents and the road ahead. Decades earlier, the cord had been added to hang lap robes in cars not equipped with heaters.

As the only car in our family, we enjoyed owning such a noticeable vehicle. There wasn't another Hudson in our town, or in those nearby. Over the two years the Hudson was with us, however, it developed a recurrent mechanical problem. The iron block for the six-cylinder motor had a lightweight aluminum head, which tended to warp, losing compression and power. Our mechanic was convinced the problem was due to the motor's insufficient cooling capacity.

Whatever the cause, the repair involved removing the head every few months, machining it level, then reinstalling it with a new head gasket. Each of these operations slightly raised the motor's compression until, finally, the motor would not run reliably, an intolerable state for a working man owning only one vehicle. As this was happening, the Hudson company announced that the firm and its manufacturing facility were closing. The beautiful teal and white automobile would need to be sold.

My father traded the Hudson, presumedly just after another head planing, to the local Chevrolet dealer, and drove home in our family's first new car, a grey and white 1959 Chevrolet Brookwood station wagon, with its now-famous batwing rear fender line. The vehicle suited our family. Being new, it carried a certain cachet. But we all missed the unmistakably head-turning flair of the 1955 Hudson Hollywood coupe with its continental kit.

Even in his mid-nineties, my father would recall the Hudson, and remark that it was the finest car he'd ever owned, his personal favorite as well. I remember being crushed by the Hudson's departure on the eve of my sixteenth birthday, and of my much-anticipated drivers license. I had discovered that the levers located on either side of the driver's bench seat operated what Hudson poetically termed its "Airliner Reclining Seat." This device almost instantly turned the vehicle's interior into a large bed. My youthful imagination had been in overdrive at the mouthwatering prospect of dating in an automotive boudoir. But it was not to be. I was reconciled to the prospect of dating in a station wagon which, as it turned out, had rear seats which conveniently folded flat.

The family's sale of the classy Hudson in which we had taken such pride, and the personal loss of such a richly-imagined dating environment, never left me. As I began collecting and restoring old cars in my twenties, I always kept an eye out for fifties Hudsons, particularly the 1955 models. But, even then, Hudsons were scarce, as orphan marques tend to be. And those I did come upon were either rusty, a serious challenge for a unibody automobile, or too worn out through long use to warrant restoration.

Forty-five Hudson-less years passed. Then a friend living in northern California wrote to tell me he'd spotted a 1955 Hudson parked in a neighbor's back yard. We conferred on the details and I learned that the owner's price was of the "I'd-like-it-out-of-my-yard" variety, a bargain. Well aware that old car bargains seldom turn out to be bargains in the end, I had an inspection done. It revealed no serious problems and established that the Hudson could be started and run. I bought the car, had it shipped to Virginia, and was pleased by what I saw rolling off the transporter two weeks later.

This vehicle proved to be my "learner Hudson." The car was complete and without rust. It ran and drove acceptably for a long-dormant automobile, especially after new tires were installed and a brake job completed. The mileage at seventy-seven-thousand seemed appropriate for the car's condition. I saw no reason to restore the Hudson. Spit and polish would render it acceptable for everyday use. Driving around, listening to the quiet-running six with its "Twin H-Power" dual carburetors, I reveled in the memories of our family's Hudson, almost fifty years in my mental rearview mirror.

Then disaster struck. In order to avoid offending neighbors in our residential area by having too many vehicles in the driveway, I'd left the Hudson parked and locked at my business, three miles from my home. There was a fenced parking area, night lighting, and a retail store on each side, open around the clock.

What could go wrong? I was about to find out. Arriving at work on a Monday morning, I was stunned to see that vandals had attacked a dozen cars in the area, one of them the Hudson. The windshield was smashed, leaving hundreds of minute glass shards throughout the vehicle's interior. Worst of all, the human wrecking balls had stomped on the roof with such savage force that it was completely caved in, the roof left within a few inches of the front seat backs. I was heartbroken, and very angry.

After making a report to the police, I went over the Hudson to assess repair possibilities. I decided that it was better to sell the car as it was, probably for parts. I put an advertisement in the local paper. While waiting for a prospect to respond, I found and installed a replacement windshield to protect the interior, now vacuumed free of glass.

An interested party called, then made an appointment to see the car. When he arrived, I was as surprised to find him wearing a clerical collar, as he was to see the flattened roof of the Hudson, though I had described the damage over the phone. Our conversation focused on the question of whether it was possible to straighten out the roof without first cutting it free of the body, a costly process, not to mention one requiring an expert in the welding arts.

As our discussion continued, I found myself looking at the depressed roof. Suddenly, I had an idea. Excusing myself, I opened the Hudson's left rear door and crawled, bent-backed, across the rear seat. I twisted my body to position both feet flat on the floor just behind the front seat, then tried to push myself upward against the collapsed roof. My hope was that the roof might raise slightly, creating a more straightforward repair option that kept the roof intact.

I pushed upward without exerting much force. Nothing happened. I tried again, this time adding more force, as I straightened my back and pushed. Again, nothing. But I did sense the roof give slightly. The minister, meanwhile, kept cautioning me to not hurt myself. We agreed on that advice. I turned my face away from him, resumed my cramped stance, pinned beneath the roof as I was, and pushed rapidly upward, exerting all the force I could manage in such an awkward posture.

Crack!!! A deafening sound echoed through the car, like a cannon shot. This was followed immediately, though I could not swear to this on a bible, with an almost equally loud exclamatory "F__k !" shouted from somewhere in the vicinity of the minister.

I relaxed my back, arms, and legs, and looked up. The Hudson's roof, with headliner in place, had snapped back to what appeared to be its normal height. Could it be? I climbed out of the Hudson, spent by the exertion, and looked at the roof. It had resumed its proper shape. It was as if the vandals' attack had never occurred.

The roof's curves had fully reformed. Closer inspection showed that the stomping had left heel marks at the roof's edge just above the windshield, a minor problem, easily repaired.

Within fifteen minutes, the minister and I, who had just shared the only automotive miracle either of us was likely to experience in our lives, reached purchase terms. He parted shaking his head, but smiling. The Hudson was paid for and driven to its new home three days later, a sudden and rather unexpected end to my Hudson ownership. But I'd gotten to relive my memories and, however accidentally, resolved the worst of the vandals' carnage.

Sometime later, through a collector friend, I learned of a family in Ohio that had recently lost its elderly patriarch. They were interested in finding a home for a 1955 Hudson that had been in the family since new, almost fifty years. It was reportedly a much-loved and well-cared-for automobile, but now lacked anyone in the younger generation willing to assume responsibility with the grandfather gone. I bought the car sight unseen, something I very seldom did, and would never recommend to another collector, but for a very reasonable price, and after receiving a satisfactory inspection report from the collector friend who'd brought the car to my attention.

When the transporter arrived several days later, the driver described an emotional scene as the car was loaded in Ohio. As he had driven the Hudson out of the late owner's garage, the family had surrounded the old car, patting it with their hands, some of them crying. Talk about well loved…

Getting my first look at the Hudson, I understood why it might leave a hole in someone's life. The car was a superior example, without rust or damage. Like new. The sought-after Hollywood coupe model gleamed in the afternoon sun. The exterior was a soft snow-shoe white over a stunning butterscotch cream, a living example of an era when stylish automobiles were painted in a full palette of bright, optimistic colors and not limited, as they are in the current era, to the boring basics of black, white, silver or tan.

But what had I spied behind the rounded trunk? It was a metal continental kit with the spare tire, adding class to an already stunning vehicle. This brought memories rushing back of a similar car, decades previous which also had a continental kit, though in teal, not butterscotch.

"But wait!" as the braying salesman on television shouts, "There's more!" The Hudson had only fifty-two thousand original miles. It was equipped with rare factory air-conditioning which, once serviced with R12 freon, worked as advertised. But the greatest surprise was hidden under the hood. This Hudson had been purchased new with an upgraded, factory-installed Packard V8 motor with automatic transmission, a combination which ran like a Swiss clock, and was almost completely silent when driving. While Hudson's famous "Twin H-Power" six-cylinder had memorably dominated the stock car race tracks for a decade after World War II, this rare and unusual Packard V8 option provided a higher, quieter level of automotive power.

The Butterscotch Bomb, as she became known, behaved as flawlessly on the road as her appearance suggested she should. In essence, this Hudson was that uniquely fortunate car that had lived a life of conservative use and coddling care in the hands of a single mature owner, committed to keeping the car to an exacting standard. The Hudson was always an attention-getter at area car shows, since many in attendance had heard of the marque, but never seen one. It was particularly welcomed at orphan shows, where it joined the ranks of DeSotos, Studebakers, Packards, Continentals, and other makes no longer in production.

The Hudson remained with us for several years. Though never used as a daily driver — how could an owner do that to a near-perfect half century-old car, a veritable time capsule? — the car accumulated three or four thousand miles each year and was a pleasure to drive, the kind of driving that keeps a smile fixed on a driver's face.

Then, as happened to me several times over my collecting career, the Hudson become better known when it appeared in a magazine article with photographs. An automotive museum in the northeast had long sought a similar Hudson in top condition, and promised the exposure and level of care the car deserved. She remains there on display in the museum, perhaps the best unrestored example of one of the final model years of Hudson.

Am I sorry I sold her? Yes, I am. The Hudson remains one of the few collector cars that I would like to have back, an exceptional example of original and unrestored 1950s automotive splendor. That rarest of collectible cars.

On the other hand, her sale to the museum allowed a collector with limited resources, but almost unlimited collecting objectives, to seek another challenging project. More importantly, it gave the 1955 Hudson the chance for a longer and higher quality life than I could have provided, a life in which other car collectors and interested people would get to see an almost seventy-year-old vehicle still very much in its prime.

Anyway, that's the way I see it. I think Doc Hudson would agree.

9

Lincoln Continental Mark II: Personal Luxury at its Finest

In Zen, the artistic technique is a discipline in spontaneity, reflecting a spontaneity in discipline.

I worked summers in the late 1950s as a caddie at a local country club in coastal New Hampshire, carrying one or two golf bags on my shoulders for eighteen holes. It was outdoor work and paid well, certainly better than my paper route. Many of the golfers, particularly those who could play on weekdays, were professional men — doctors, lawyers, car dealers, company owners — those in a position to set their own hours and recreate when they wished.

We caddies learned a lot from the conversations we overheard from the golfers. Finance. Politics. Local news and, of course, scandals. We often heard things one would never find in the newspapers. These years were the high water mark for fascinating automobiles. The men who played golf drove cars out of reach of average families. While playing, they often discussed at length the various makes and models: the car they now owned or thought to buy, or the one their neighbor across the street owned, which they appeared to envy. But nothing stimulated a long and animated discussion, one that might continue as we walked and played several holes, more than an interesting car driving by on a road fringing the golf course. Each man had an opinion. We caddies listened and learned.

I remember one particular day. Four attorneys were playing

together in a foursome with two caddies carrying their bags, myself one of them. All of the players seemed interested in automobiles. Each had a favorite, and explained to the others why his choice was superior to the competition. As the round continued, the group stopped its play several times to watch and comment on a passing car. They discussed its merits, and sometimes the merits of its driver, as they walked the fairway and approached the next green. These players had a heightened interest in automobiles in general and luxury automobiles in particular. They reacted noisily to any Cadillac, Lincoln, Chrysler, Thunderbird, Corvette, or foreign sports car that came in sight.

Then something unusual happened. We were on the tee at the eleventh hole, which was wedged into a corner where two country roads met. The men were still engaged in their animated banter about favorite cars, as the first attorney stepped up, teed his ball and prepared to drive. Just at that moment, a long, black automobile drove slowly by, stopped at the corner, then turned left and passed behind the tee where we were standing.

From the first sighting, all eyes remained on the car as it drove up to the stop sign, stopped, then turned and passed out of sight. No one spoke a word. From a cacophony of shouted opinions back and forth to complete silence, a silence unbroken for some time after the car disappeared. More strangely, after the players teed off, and were walking to their next shots, not a word about the black car was spoken.

I was dumbfounded. I couldn't fathom what had happened, though I knew that *something* had happened. I wanted to ask one of the two attorneys, whose bags I carried, for an explanation. But they were not regulars. I didn't feel comfortable asking. So I kept walking with my mouth closed.

I've never forgotten that day. Later, I asked another club member, one I'd known for some time, what the car might have been. "Oh," he answered, "I suspect that was a Lincoln Continental Mark II, a new and very expensive, limited-production car, so limited that only famous or really wealthy people are able to own one. I'm told they cost two or three times what the finest Cadillac Eldorado or Chrysler Imperial goes for, and that, even at such a price, Ford loses money on each one it sells."

I found two of the cars parked in the country club lot as I finished work one day. One was black, like the one we'd seen earlier, perhaps the same one. The other was white. They were beautiful cars, imposing, sleek-sided and richly finished. They commanded attention. I walked home to our family dinner. Life went on. Since that day I've had sixty years to reflect on the scene when I first saw the stately Continental Mark II approaching, and our golf group stopped what it was doing, and stood silently, spellbound, as the car drove past and out of sight.

I've owned and restored four Mark IIs over the years. All were 1956 models. Two were black, one white, and one seafoam green. These were unique motorcars, essentially hand-built and hand-assembled. Produced at great cost by Ford's Lincoln Division, the three thousand Mark IIs built in 1956 and the first months of 1957 were actually completed by Lincoln's new Continental division, which did not survive the Mark II's demise. The Continental Mark II was Ford Motor Company's attempt to win back the executive car sales leadership from Cadillac. Though the Mark II was not to endure, the campaign succeeded

The Mark II is among the most complicated of automobile restorations and, at a certain level of wear and deterioration, probably impossible to restore unless cost is of no concern. It is not a project for amateurs to consider. But driving a six-thousand-pound Mark II is a completely unique experience, like being the captain of an ocean liner directing a great ship's progress over the sea. The experience leaves little doubt that those privileged to own and drive these remarkable cars when new found themselves cocooned in a level of perfected luxury, thoroughly convinced their money had been well spent.

America has produced many of the world's most beautiful and compelling automobiles over the last century. In terms of blunt impact, none have the remarkably compelling presence of the

1956-1957 Lincoln Continental Mark II. I have long believed, probably since that first sighting on the golf course that, from a purely aesthetic standpoint, the Mark II with its simple, yet breathtakingly elegant, design is the finest-looking automobile ever produced in America.

Returning to the golf course scene, I still wonder what happened there. What was really going on? That golf foursome was made up of seasoned professionals, men of the world, successful, and well-informed about automobile makes and models. Why the fascination? The silence? What caused those four men to follow the Mark II as if spellbound.

Was it awe? Envy?

I think not.

It was reverence.

10

British Cars:
Proper and Improper

Zen creativity: painting by not painting;
playing the stringless lute.

Decades ago, in a moment of electrifying mental weakness, I bought a British sports car, a 1966 Austin Healey 3000, from a university professor in Nashville, Tennessee, sight unseen, while living overseas. The Healey was red with black leather. It was the same car my college roommate had owned. I knew the 3000 to be a true sports car in every sense of the word, great fun to drive, powerful and responsive, with an exhaust note rumbling with testosterone.

The "Big Healey," as they were called, had two well-known flaws, major or minor, depending upon your risk tolerance. On a road slick with water, snow or ice, the grabby brakes had a tendency to keep you going forward after a firm application, and at the same speed, but with the front end of the car now following its rear. This was nothing that an experienced rally driver couldn't handle. But my hands still get clammy when I recall the wrenching sense of losing control in such a fashion at speed.

The second flaw, less threatening, was somehow more insidious. This involved the two British companies, Lucas and Smith's, which together monopolized British automotive electrics over many decades. The almost legendary lack of reliability produced by this combination was stunning in breadth and scope. Anything electrical could fail at any time, and without warning.

One summer evening, I loaded my brother-in-law and five of our children in the Austin Healey for a ride to buy ice cream. What could be more American, even in a British sports car? Midway down a narrow country road with no streetlights or lighted homes, everything electrical on the car, headlights, taillights, instrument panel, everything but the motor, suddenly went dark. Nothing could be seen, not even the road ahead. Nor would we be seen by an approaching car. Scary, particularly with the youngsters along. We crept home slowly, groping more than driving and, with God watching over fools as he sometimes does, made it safely home without seeing another car. The evening could have ended much differently. The problem? A rotted battery grounding-cable had separated.

I know about British cars' unreliable electrics not only from hindsight, but also from my next foray into things British, a 1958 Rolls Royce Silver Cloud I. This was a beautiful automobile finished in sand and sable. It captured hearts wherever it appeared, and drove powerfully with its massive six-cylinder motor. The Silver Cloud's interior leathers and wood were so luxurious that my standards for such things have been unrealistic since. I even enjoyed the oddity of the right-hand drive arrangement until, one day, pulling out from behind a large truck to pass, I found an oncoming vehicle dead in the middle of my windshield and coming fast. We learn and, as the pundits say, whatever does not kill us makes us stronger.

One night, we returned home late along a darkened southern Maryland highway after attending a performance of the musical *Hair* in Washington, D.C., a trendy play with full nudity on stage, a well-advertised fact which guaranteed that every seat in the house was filled. Motoring quietly, we were the last in a row of six or seven cars pulled over by a Maryland state trooper, who did not turn on his flashing lights, but instead signaled to each car to pull over with a hand-held flashlight. The drivers responded by moving over to the shoulder and stopping. Parking to the rear of the Rolls, with his emergency flashers now turned on protectively, the trooper walked past the row of cars to the head of the line, and began processing tickets. This was going to take some time and we knew the babysitter was expecting us.

About an hour later, as the occupants of each vehicle received counsel and the dreaded ticket, then pulled onto the highway and went on their way, the state trooper finally arrived at our car. He stopped at the window on the left side. My wife pointed across to me sitting behind the steering wheel. He walked around to my window, which I lowered. There was no request for license and registration. Instead, in his soft, slow southern drawl, he looked over the polished Carpathian wood dashboard and its lighted instrument panel.

"Is this a real Rolls Royce?" he asked.

"Yes, sir." I replied. There was a lengthy, uncomfortable silence. The trooper said nothing more, but let his eyes roam over the car's leather interior.

Then he asked, almost shyly, for someone at least six-and-a-half feet tall and in uniform, "May I sit in it?"

What choice? "Yes, sir." I said again, opening the door and stepping out. The policeman moved past me and, very gradually, stooped down and bent his tall frame into the car. He sat back in the seat, both hands on the wheel, looking over the instruments, and, through the windshield, down the long hood to the Flying Lady mascot posed atop the louvered chrome radiator.

"A Rolls Royce, huh?"

"Yes, sir."

"Well, thank you for letting me sit in it. Quite a car. You know, when I pulled you over, you were going just a bit over the speed limit. I'll just give you a verbal warning tonight. I guess if I ever needed to find you or this car here in tobacco country, I wouldn't have much trouble." He put on his hat, then touched it with a forefinger. "Night, folks."

With that, the state trooper walked back to his car. We continued home.

Soon we moved again, this time to California. A doctor from Montana had seen our ad in *Hemmings Motor News*, flown east, bought the Silver Cloud and drove it home. A few weeks afterward, our household packed up and gone, we followed his path west in our

Volvo 145 wagon. A week before our departure, I'd been offered a turbocharged four-cylinder Lotus Esprit by a recent widow, anxious that her two teenage sons would take her late husband's sports car racing when she was at work. Under some neighborhood pressure to be helpful, I purchased the car, but owned it less than a week. The first person who responded to the newspaper ad, bought the car after an inspection and test drive. In that short interim, I took the opportunity to air the car out on a nearby highway, and learned what light but powerful sports cars can do, given opportunity. With wings installed, that little Lotus would have flown.

Settling into our home on California's Monterey peninsula, I felt certain that my British car collecting was concluded. British cars simply didn't move me. But, as we all come to know in living our lives, sometimes things just happen. A few weeks after our arrival in California, I received a weekend call from an old friend, whom I knew had owned a Triumph TR-3A sports car for many years, possibly from new. It was, effectively, one of his children. He was calling to ask if, as a friend, but also as a car guy, I would accompany him to "the scene of the crime" which, as he explained, was only a few miles from my home. His much-loved Triumph, a car he'd commuted in for years, had been stolen several weeks earlier from a parking lot. It had just been found by the police, badly damaged, parked behind a local motel. My friend said he could not go to see the wrecked car alone.

Could I refuse such an emotional request? I couldn't, and agreed to meet him at the motel. An hour later, we arrived there at the same time, and checked with the motel manager, who had notified the police after discovering the vehicle at the rear of the property. We walked to the rear of the building. I was glad I'd come along as we reached the Triumph. The police had not exaggerated. The sports car had been savaged. Evidence of mindless fury was everywhere.

The battered TR sat in a circle of its own bits and pieces. Metal shards, broken glass, and various chrome parts, lay scattered on the ground. The car's windshield was smashed, and had been ripped from the vehicle. Its convertible top was shredded, the support bows bent and tangled. Glass fragments were everywhere. The hood, trunk, front fenders, and both doors had been kicked in. The seats and door panels were torn, and the gauges' glass faces were all cracked. The scene was stomach-wrenching for me. I could only imagine what my friend was feeling as he surveyed the carnage through tears.

Neither of us could grasp what possessed someone to steal the Triumph, then destroy it. It was sickening to think that someone could do such damage to a beautiful vintage automobile. We walked away without deciding what had to be done, the car's owner numb from what he'd seen. It had only been a few months, he said, since he'd pulled and rebuilt its engine, using a chain fall and convenient oak tree in his back yard.

He stopped and turned to me. "I'd like you to have the car," he said. "I know I can never take it back. And I couldn't bear parting out what's left of it."

Sensing his distraught state, I took a moment, then answered carefully. "I'm so sorry that this has happened to you. It's a tragedy. But with two project cars in my garage, I'm really in no position to purchase another car."

His pained look told me more than words could say. "I didn't mean I'd sell the Triumph to you. I want to give you the car. The title is clear. Perhaps you could park it in your driveway, remove whatever can be sold, then send the remainder to the crusher. I don't care. I just know I can't do it myself, not after all our years together." Then he added, "If you'll agree, I'll sign over the title and drop it by. Please understand. You'll be doing me a great favor and I'll never forget it."

There was only one answer to such an emotional plea.

The next day, I drove the Volvo wagon to the rear of the motel, filled it with broken Triumph pieces, then backed the car close to the TR's nose. A rope was attached to the car's tow ring. With a sympathetic neighbor driving the Volvo in first gear, I put an old pillow down over the glass shards on the front seat, climbed in, shifted the transmission to neutral, and released the hand brake. The caravan crawled the three miles to our driveway, where the TR-3 sat for several weeks, as I thought out the unwelcome process of stripping and parting out the car.

It was a quiet Sunday morning as I went up the driveway to retrieve the morning paper. Walking back, I paused, looking at the crumpled vehicle with new eyes. Would this little Triumph want another chance at life? I debated with myself. Before breaking the car apart, why not invest a few hours, clean up the mess, and find out if it could be brought back, thereby cancelling its date with the crusher? By the following weekend, several evenings of effort after dinner had wrought significant change.

The interior, filled with glass and metal fragments, was swept out and vacuumed. Broken items were gathered on my workbench, their nomenclature and part numbers listed. The seats and door panels were removed for further cleaning and eventual recovering. Not unlike a vandalized Hudson you read about earlier, the pushed-in hood and trunk, doors and fenders, were made of quality sheet metal. All were returned to their original shape using a rubber-headed hammer.

It became obvious that those who caused the damage had concentrated their energies on the sheet metal and interior. The engine, transmission, rear end, tires, wheels, brakes, steering and suspension were all in good order. Lacking a key, we hot wired the ignition. The motor fired up. Its sound signaled that the exhaust and muffler were not damaged.

The next afternoon I took a victory lap around the neighborhood, sitting on a temporary driver's seat. With the original seats already removed for repair, six pieces of seasoned red oak firewood piled together, and covered with two old patio chair cushions, served. The TR-3A all but snorted its approval rounding the final turn into our driveway. Having proven her will to live, she was covered with a tarpaulin to protect her from rain. The comeback had begun.

Much work remained to resurrect the Triumph, and get her back on the road, reliable and safe. It would take most of the winter to complete the work and reassembly. I sold one of the project cars to make room in the garage. By this point, our list of replacement items was complete. Due to the popular appeal of early Triumphs, and the numbers on the road in the United States, a strong aftermarket existed. Several suppliers could provide almost any item needed. I found Moss Motors to be especially helpful, and leaned heavily on them to replace items destroyed or damaged beyond repair. Though most of the parts were reproductions, they were of uniformly high quality, with excellent fit and function.

Content that I had the basic supply system in place, I gave thought to the possibility of using supplemental labor to augment the few hours each week I had available to work on the car. Ultimately, I "hired" our two teenage daughters, Noelle and Christine, believing that, though they were unlikely to enjoy the grinding, pounding, patient work required, they wouldn't object to doing so for pay. I also thought that their participation in the restoration work, and in seeing a car taken apart and reassembled, would stand them in good stead later, putting them in that rare class of adult females who could deal knowledgeably with automotive maintenance and repairs, as was later proven the case.

On a clipboard, I listed various tasks I believed within the girls' competence, given instruction and some supervision. On another clipboard was a labor record. Each girl recorded hours worked on given dates and on specific tasks. In this way, fenders were removed, the replacement interior was installed, and many new parts found their way onto the car

By spring, a dashing dark blue TR-3A, with lighter blue interior and black vinyl top, sat in the driveway. As the project concluded, we splurged a bit to bring added panache to the little sports car. A young attorney responded to our newspaper ad and agreed to purchase the car at the listed price. With a certified check in hand, and the Triumph gone to its new home, I sat down with our daughters to determine their earnings. In accordance with our agreement, all costs of the project were subtracted from the proceeds. What remained was divided between the girls in proportion to the hours each had recorded working on the car.

I often recall how close the Triumph roadster came to being

taken apart, crushed into a small steel block, and having its tough little automotive soul extinguished. Having helped her avoid that fate, I now imagine her enjoying the winding back roads of coastal northern California and no longer call to mind her sad appearance as she sat, forlorn and in pieces, behind that motel.

11

The Immutable Joy of
Station Wagons

*Zen training can begin only when it is
finished.*

Back in the day when dinosaurs roamed the earth, from the end
of World War II in the 1940s until the doubtful miracle of the first
SUV appeared toward the end of the last century, a harbinger of the
countless swarms to follow, the station wagon was the quintessential
car of the American family. Roomy, useful, flexible, campy — even
without fancy wooden panels on sides and rear, the family wagon
was ubiquitous from coast to coast.

Until the station wagon's popularity placed them in every American driveway and garage, only a few earlier motor vehicles were configured to provide services other than passenger carriage. The British
created the "shooting brake," a vehicle which supported the gunning
parties of the landed aristocracy. Similar creations appeared in the
garages of Indian maharajas, and for similar purpose. Rolls-Royce
seemed to own the patent for these specialized vehicles. America's
commercial businesses, particularly those involved with deliveries,
converted automobiles or trucks into station wagon equivalents in
the decades before delivery vans and other alternatives evolved. In
the 1930s, the Stout Scarab and Buckminister Fuller's Dymaxion
car were America's first station wagons, minivans, or perhaps both.

Growing up in the 1940s and 1950s, the era when these unique
vehicles went from interesting and noticeable to necessary, my family

133

did not own a wagon. They were too expensive for our family budget, until my younger sister started school and my mother returned to teaching. Soon after, a new grey and white 1959 Chevrolet Brookwood station wagon, the infamous batwing model, with wing-like styling flairs extending out over the rear fenders, became our family car. It was still in use when I received my driver's license. This forces me to admit that I did my high school dating behind the wheel of a station wagon. The utter shame. Later, our family bought another vehicle, as there were two working parents. It was a used Volkswagen Beetle or "bug." You understand, of course, a teenager's predicament in this revelation.

So it should come as no surprise that, having graduated college, begun a profession, and married a sensible, conservative young lady, our first new car would be a sensible, conservative station wagon, a dark green Volvo 122 Amazon from Sweden. The car went with us to Japan for two years and, despite being run on gasoline with negligible octane ratings, made it back to the USA not long after man first walked on the moon. Our second Volvo was a turquoise 1971 145 model. It had air conditioning for our new baby and, of course, for her parents. The Volvo yearned to travel and went with us to Italy for three years, never to return.

We drove Volvo station wagons exclusively for the next three decades. Safe and reliable, they'd lost their exclusive Nordic panache and become ubiquitous on America's driveways. They could be driven hard for hundreds of thousands of miles with minimal problems and expense, the stolid 240 models in particular. We drove a yellow 240 for eighteen years, and over 300,000 miles. My mother would cry on the phone when told we were coming to visit in "that decrepit old yellow car."

"Doesn't it have a million miles or so?" She'd ask, voice wavering. When later sold to a graduate student, he trumpeted as he departed that he would return at 400,000 miles just to say hello. My mother would have fainted at those words.

Other Volvos followed. All were great cars. Our dark green 1988 turbocharged four-cylinder 760T wagon was surpassed in its elegant toughness only by our final Volvo, a six-cylinder baltic blue 1998 V90 wagon, a car so unusually sporty for Volvo that its door handles and roof rack were painted in the car's bright coloration. Surprisingly, a Volvo collector bought the V90, having declared it a future collectible.

This ended the Volvo line in our immediate family, though our daughters, Noelle and Christine, and several of our grandchildren, later drove Volvo 240s for years. But Volvo had changed. Motors and transmissions were coming from Asia. Interiors grew smaller, some uncomfortably so, even as I was growing larger in middle age. Claims for safety and reliability, once a trademark strength, became hollow in the face of contrary statistics. We agreed to look for a suitable replacement but, after driving Volvo wagons for forty-five years, a new car took time to find.

We ultimately selected Cadillac's small SUV, the SRX. Built from 2004 through 2009, this unusual, sharp-edged, long-limbed "Art and Science" design became the aesthetic parent of a generation of Cadillac models. Its influence can be seen a decade later in many of the division's offerings. The SRX was roomy, capable, reasonably luxurious, and just big and yet also small enough for our needs. Helpfully, it was a car, not a truck, and had a car's comfortable driving characteristics.

We were fortunate to find and buy a used, well-kept, low-mileage 2008 SRX, equipped with the dependable 32-valve Northstar V8 motor. Only two percent of the SRX production came with the V8. The rest were equipped with a serviceable but under-powered six cylinder. Finding an SRX with the V8 motor and all-wheel drive (AWD) was an added bonus. We've enjoyed two of these cars for more than a decade, and over 200,000 miles, and have yet to find a new or used replacement SUV that meets or exceeds its qualities.

Our family commitment to station wagons, and my avocation to find, restore, and enjoy interesting vintage vehicles, was eventually to find a nexus. This first occurred in the mid-1970s, when I found a 1951 Ford Country Squire "woody" station wagon with Ford's famed flathead V8 in Maine. The dark-green nine-seater was in excellent condition, ran well, and was used summers in New Hampshire, where earlier these cars were known as "beach wagons."

Beach wagons were used to ferry children and their paraphernalia to and from beach playgrounds in the summer. Often the sand-covered youngsters were allowed to ride home sitting on the lowered tailgate at very low speed. Oh, the horror! Our "woody" spent several years with us. Its regular use drew collector interest and purchase offers. Finally, we received an offer so unrealistic it had to be accepted. The Country Squire was returned to Maine.

Several other Ford Country Squire wagons followed, none as nice as the first. They remained with us for a time, then found new homes. I'd always favored the 1955 and 1956 models. I'd been a twelve-year-old newsboy when they were new, and I saw them daily on my paper route. Those images were frozen in my memory. The later Ford wagons ran well and looked solid from twenty feet. Up close or behind the wheel, however, it was clear that more investment was needed, more than the vehicle's value warranted. Rust was a common problem, particularly if the car spent time in road-salted New England winters. Wagons were heavily-used vehicles, compared to sedans, coupes, and convertibles. They tended to be worn, inside and out. Thus, the effort and investment to bring them back was greater.

As a boy I was a loyal fan of television rancher and pilot Sky King, my interest a harbinger of my later becoming a Navy pilot. Sky King and his daughter, Penny, rode around in a 1955 or 1956 Chrysler New Yorker DeLuxe Town & Country station wagon. I sensed, even when young, the special allure in its lines. Over the years, I found two examples of these wagons, apparently an attempt to resolve my wish fulfillment. The first was a handsome 1959 DeSoto wagon, white with green trim, a chromed roof rack, and a 318 cid V8 that ran, but barely. The DeSoto was complete, also barely.

This activity took place before the sudden rise of station wagon values. When wagons became collectible, prices soared. I had paid little for the DeSoto, bought as a used car through local advertising. I assessed it as a possible restoration project. Looking back, then forward to today's eye-popping wagon values, the car would have been suitable to restore. But based on market realities at the time, my two months of driving and working on the car suggested that I would have to spend approximately twice as much on the car as it would be worth when completed. Knowing through experience a car project's practical limits, I donated the car to a veterans' charity. Naturally, it remains on my I'd-like-to-have-it-back list.

My second attempt at wish fulfillment went better. Much better. I bought a 1956 DeSoto station wagon with a Hemi V8 out of California. The situation involved a medical hardship and, for whatever reason, the car had not sold, though nationally advertised. The photos and professional inspection report suggested an excellent original vehicle. The owner claimed it had been in his family since new. I made a low offer which, after some pushback, was accepted. When the DeSoto arrived, its off-white body and salmon roof a perfect compliment to its high styling, I was stunned. The car was perfect.

The Hemi V8 motor and its bay were as spotless as they were period correct. The underbody, frame, and exhaust reminded me yet again that purchasing cars long resident in California tended to be a successful strategy. The interior, headliner, dashboard, and gauges were the equal of the rest of the car. Even the tailgate, rear window, and rear storage area, which receive the heaviest use and ill treatment, appeared undamaged and without noticeable wear.

Such a result only occurs now and then, the surprise of a semi-blind purchase turning out better than imagined. More often, the experience runs in the opposite direction. But it does happen. The items needed to improve the car were minor. Both bulky bumpers were fogged, and the car's overall appearance was improved by having them re-chromed. The chrome hinges that supported the tailgate were also fogged and were sent to the chrome shop at the same time, along with four door sill plates. The carpet was passable, showing no wear or discoloration. But it had a moldy smell, probably from long indoor storage without ventilation or dehumidification. Its replacement cleared the air. The DeSoto was a gleaming jewel.

My bringing the DeSoto wagon easily — *too* easily? — to its lustrous best left a kind of unexplained emptiness in me that I found bothersome. It took time to come to grips with this vague discontent, and summon enough personal honesty to reason out my negative feelings. Finally I saw it. I had sold out. Intent for many years on finding my own version of Sky King's Chrysler Town & Country, I had settled. Twice. And gotten exactly the dissatisfaction I deserved, even from a nearly perfect car.

The DeSoto Hemi was a beautiful executive station wagon. Anyone would be proud to own it. Its condition suggested whoever bought it would have a positive experience for many years, assuming proper care and maintenance. I had many inquiries about the car, several from those who had contacted the former owner after I'd purchased the car. One or two of them had that slightly choked, needy sound on the phone that made me consider raising my asking price to take advantage. Soon an acceptable offer was presented. I stopped playing the naysayer and accepted. Only then was I told of the DeSoto's destination — Dubai, of all places.

I was content. Though the DeSoto was a stunning old car, and possessed all the right attributes, the highly regarded Hemi engine foremost, it wasn't *the* car I truly sought. There must be one out there somewhere. Hopefully, I would connect with it one day. Perhaps Penny King might join me for a ride.

It seemed that, absent my continued search for El Dorado, the conquistadors' "Lost City of Gold," that perfect 1955 Chrysler New Yorker DeLuxe Town & Country station wagon, available at an embarrassingly reasonable figure, my decades of connection to the American station wagon had come to its end. But events had proven my assumptions and suppositions incorrect so many times that turning my back on these unique vehicles had a certain air of halfheartedness. And a good thing, because an interesting project was probably out there searching for me. And it found me just two months later.

Oddly, the vehicle was nothing rare or high end. Certainly not a Town & Country. Quite the contrary. Perhaps that was what captivated me. It was a 1953 Ford Country Sedan station wagon, not a top-of-the-line Country Squire. No woody or faux wood side panels. No fancy signal-seeking radio. No fancy origin story. No fancy anything. The station wagon had been in the same family in Ada, Oklahoma, for three generations. It had no rust, damage, or extensive wear, the latter confirmed by its original mileage in the low sixties.

Every record, beginning with the original sales documents, came with the wagon, which had the much-loved and enduring flathead V8. It was also a Ford fiftieth anniversary model, as indicated by the gold "50" on the steering wheel's plastic center hub. Most importantly, the car drove as one would expect of a lightly used and well-cared-for vehicle, despite its age, and won me over completely with its easy drivability and handling. Even the electric overdrive worked, reducing the motor revolutions and cabin noise levels at higher speed. I was in love.

The initial plan was to go over all mechanical systems and ensure the Ford was safe and reliable. But the more I drove and enjoyed the station wagon, the more I thought it deserved a full restoration. My theory was that, with everything complete, working properly, and undamaged, the Country Sedan could be easily restored at realistic cost. We embarked on a six-to-eight-month restoration project. Fortunately, the key cost assumption proved correct.

Two months into the restoration project, the wagon body sat stripped down to bare metal on four sawhorses. The motor, transmission, and rear end were out for rebuilding. I had delivered the seats and side panels, then the exterior chrome including bumpers, after long distance drives in the Volvo, to upholstery and plating specialists I'd used in the past, eliciting promises for completion in two or three months.

Five months along, it was coming together. The brakes had been renewed, the steering and suspension gone through, and the shocks and springs replaced. A new wiring harness was installed. The drivetrain elements, now rebuilt, were installed, and a re-cored radiator sat in front of the V8 motor, which had a new stainless steel exhaust. The body was painted in a soft seafoam green with contrasting oyster white around the windows. The original glass appeared as new. The reinstallation of exterior chrome, reupholstered seats and side panels, and a new set of wide whitewall radial tires, nicely set off the completed Country Sedan. She looked as if she'd just rolled off the production line.

Everywhere the car traveled, she drew appreciative smiles and kind words. The fact that the wagon was not a top model seemed to raise, not lessen, interest. Not unlike the positive impression she'd made when first found, the Country Sedan seemed to be so comfortable in her skin that she was appreciated for just what she was. That impression was heightened by the high quality of the restoration. We had not stinted. Common she was, but uncommonly beautiful nonetheless.

As the Ford became known in the Washington, D.C. area, we received an invitation to drive the car in a movie, *My One and Only*, being filmed in Baltimore. The film was set in the early 1950s. It was paid work for the car, and for my wife and me as well. On the appointed day, we drove over, arriving at the film location in a worn-down section of the inner city. An hour later, we were dressed in period clothing and hats. The car had been sprayed with a liquid dust to appear a bit careworn, and sported a vintage Maryland tag.

For two hot and humid days, we filmed street scenes. Each "take" was repeated until the director was satisfied. Then the cars were moved to another shooting location for the next scene and its multiple takes. The weather made the work grueling for everyone, actors and walk-ons like us, film crews, cameramen, lighting and filter techs, food and costume caterers, but more so the vintage automobiles operating for long hours at slow speeds in such intense heat. Everyone needed to drink water continually. Ice bags were routinely placed on film car radiators between takes. Our wagon's new radiator kept the coolant temperature within limits.

On the final day of our participation, a neighbor called my wife Nancy on her cell phone to see how we were doing in the heat. She joked that our hope to see stars Renée Zellweger, Kevin Bacon, and Chris Noth had probably not worked out. In response, my wife quickly took a photograph with her phone of a powder blue 1953 Cadillac convertible parked directly in front of our Ford. Behind the wheel sat Chris Noth, playing Zellweger's son, while Renée herself sat in the passenger seat. Both were being sheltered under umbrellas to keep their makeup from melting.

Though exhausting due to the weather and non-stop, twelve- to fourteen-hour shooting schedule each day, being part of a film-making experience was an eye-opening glimpse into a unique and fascinating world. The paychecks at the end were a bonus. We'd probably have paid for the experience. Film crews are always looking for reliable cars for period films in locations where they intend to work. Driving one's collector car in a movie is a demanding but rewarding way to expose your car, earn a fee, and get an inside look at the film industry doing what they do. Our takeaway was that everyone on a movie set earns every penny they're paid.

Over the years, there were offers to buy the station wagon. But it seemed she'd found a home, and so, to buyer after buyer, it was always thanks-but-no-thanks, and we continued to enjoy the simple perfection of a classic 1950s station wagon, whose three seats for nine passengers could convey the whole neighborhood on a joyride or to events.

One day a letter arrived from California. It was on official Toyota stationery and was written by a lady who signed the letter as a vice president of the Japanese automobile company. She was the company's only female vice president, she later told me. She had seen a photo of the car in a magazine and wished to purchase the wagon for a particular reason.

That reason was made clear by a small color photograph included in the letter, apparently taken by a Kodak Brownie camera. Remember those? Though the color in the photo was faded, the car in the picture's background was obviously an exact copy of our 53 Ford. Even the exterior paint colors were the same. In the foreground were two children, a girl and boy, perhaps eight or ten years old. The writer identified herself as the girl in the picture. The boy was her younger brother. The picture of the children, and the family's all-time favorite car, had been taken in California in the late 1950s.

In a declaration most car collectors would readily understand, the woman wrote that her desire to acquire the familiar station wagon reflected her wish to have a possession that, whenever she drove or looked at it, would allow her to escape her stressful corporate existence and, instead, return in a reverie to the safety and simplicity of her childhood years. Do we all not at times in our adult lives feel the same, wishing to elude the grip of responsibility and complexity, and return to those "thrilling days of yesteryear"? Of course, we do.

Something has always whispered to me that every old car has a final destination, a final owner. Well, not really final. We older collectors realize that well-kept, valuable old cars will ultimately leave us and go on to other owners. Many of our old cars will outlive us, their unrestored and un-restorable human owners. This is as it should be. Sad perhaps, but simply the way things are.

The writer's offer was generous. But her well-expressed, personal reasons for wanting to buy the wagon, reasons that I understood and which reached deeply into my heart, were decisive. And so, as had happened before, I sat down with a folder of bills and notes to determine what I had spent on the car. This took a good part of an evening. Finally, I had a total for the original cost, transport, and restoration work. The result made me smile. It was essentially the same number as the offer. As the philosophers try to tell us, some things are intended.

So the 1953 Fiftieth Anniversary Ford Country Sedan was driven into an enclosed transporter, chained in place, covered and locked-in, and then it departed on its journey to warm, sunny California, and out of our lives. That remarkable sixty-year-old faded photo of the two children and their family station wagon had done its work. Watching the transport's door secured, getting my final look at the classic simplicity of the wagon's rear end, an image seen on this book's back cover, and considering all the adventures I'd had with various station wagons across the decades, I found myself wondering:

Was the Country Sedan's departure, however benevolent, the end of an era? I just hated to ask myself such questions.

You would want to know the answer, dear reader, having followed me through my carnival fun house of old station wagons, and new or nearly new as well. My answer? Yes. I *did* find the car. Early in 2018. And, fortuitously, again in California. A gorgeous coral-colored 1955 Chrysler New Yorker DeLuxe Town & Country station wagon with modest original miles and every option but factory air-conditioning, including the famous Hemi V8.

Move over, Sky King. We're coming through.

But it was not to be. The owner, a retired business executive who owned an eclectic collection of rare and valuable 1950s Chryslers, each nearly perfect, reacted to every question about the station wagon, however diplomatically put, as an insult. Discussions regarding price were strictly off-limits, which seemed strange in light of the fact that the owner's asking price was about twice the current market value. It was a beautiful car. But not *that* beautiful.

The matter resolved itself after I had a professional inspection completed. The report and photos identified a lack of proper care and maintenance and an extensive list of items needing repair. None were major. Together, however, they suggested a philosophy of car ownership lacking in care and quality. I sent the report to the owner without comment, hoping for some kind of reality check. He reacted by criticizing the inspector, a non-Caucasian as he insultingly put it, and by attempting to minimize items on the discrepancy list. An owner should never expect to sell for top dollar, however nice-looking a car might be, without repairing, or at least revealing, such problems.

I wished the man luck with his sale and thanked him for his time, and for accommodating my inspector. He became more courteous and sounded as if he might be discovering an interest in negotiation, and to having a more open and civil discourse. But it was too late coming. As on several other occasions, the small fee paid for a professional inspection, test drive, and highly detailed photographs, were worth many times their cost. In this case they had helped prevent a decision that would likely have brought a disappointing ownership experience.

Will I, years from now, as an elderly car collector — a hoary-haired Don Quixote, still tilting at vintage automotive windmills — be seeking a 1955 Chrysler New Yorker DeLuxe Town & Country station wagon to fulfill my dream?

Part of me, the wiser part, answers "I certainly hope not."

The other, still dreaming, ever hopeful, brashly retorts, "I sure hope so!"

I guess we shall see.

"Patience, Penny. Patience."

1966 Pontiac GTO Convertible, first new car.

1934 Dodge Brothers Sedan, first old car.

1966 Pontiac GTO Convertible, fourth and fifth, and "Last."

1934 Packard Model 1100 Sedan.

1929 Packard 640 Custom Sport Phaeton, fresh from Portugal.

1929 Packard 640 Custom Sport Phaeton, as restored by current owner.

1936 Cadillac V12 Turret Top Sedan.

Studebaker family mansion, Rye Beach, New Hampshire.

1966 Lamborghini 400GT V12 Coupe, original.

1966 Lamborghini 400GT V12 Coupe, as restored by current owner.

1941 Alfa Romeo 6C2500 Cabriolet Touring by Superleggera.

1949 Alfa Romeo 6C2500 Super Sport, by Pininfarina.

1946 Maserati A6 Coupe, "Maserita," and author's wife, Nancy.

1970 Fiat Cinquecento 500L Microcar.

1955 Hudson Hollywood Sedan.

1956 Lincoln Continental Mark II.

1965 Austin Healey 3000 Roadster.

1971 Triumph TR-6 Roadster.

1959 DeSoto Station Wagon.

1951 Ford Country Squire Station Wagon.

1956 DeSoto Deluxe Station Wagon.

1953 Ford Country Sedan Station Wagon.

1959 Chevrolet Fleetside Pickup Truck.

1955 Chevrolet Cameo Carrier Pickup Truck.

1958 Dodge Sweptside Pickup Truck.

1954 Chevrolet Corvette and author's daughter, Noelle.

1954 Chevrolet Corvette, author and wife, Nancy.

1956 Ford Thunderbird and author's wife, Nancy.

1956 Ford Thunderbird Roadster.

1958 Mercedes Benz 220SE Cabriolet.

1973 Mercedes Benz 450SE Sedan.

1973 Mercedes Benz 450SLC Coupe.

12

Pickup Trucks: "Nice Truck! . . ."

With a sincerity neither studied nor contrived, Zen stresses naturalness and spontaneity above all.

Having always seen myself as a car collector, it was difficult to understand why I'd pulled off a country road in rural Crozet, Virginia, to stare at an old truck, all but buried in the high bushes and weeds, far across a pasture on which a small herd of black and white cows were doing whatever it is that cows do. I could feel that old relic beckoning to me. We were in the south central part of the state for a weekend visit with our eldest daughter, a student at the state university in Charlottesville.

The truck was a Chevrolet, probably from the late 1950s, given the twin headlights. The paint color had once been blue, now just a suggestion. But what I found most appealing, even from a distance, was the front bumper and grille painted white. This spoke to me of an unadorned working vehicle, and soon led me to the front porch of a nearby farmhouse.

The owner, a bushy-eyebrowed retired veterinarian, answered my knock. As an equine and large animal vet, he had used the old truck for years to transport his charges. The wheel wells in the bed, he said with a laugh, would offer mute evidence of use with their many hoof marks. When the six-cylinder motor became unreliable at about the time he planned to retire, he'd pushed the truck into

145

its present location, planning at some point to make repairs and get it back on the road. But that thought was a decade in the past. If I wanted, I ought to walk across the field, and have a look at the old girl. If still interested, I was welcome to return and make an offer.

I did as the man suggested. The truck certainly showed its history, hoof mark indentations included, but it was all there, and without obvious rust or collision damage. How difficult would it be to rebuild or replace the motor? I paid pocket change for the truck. The owner told me he was happy the truck had found a home, and was no longer a part of his backyard panorama. I arranged for a flatbed to bring the truck to my northern Virginia home, confident that in a few months I'd have her running and, with a budget paint job, looking decent as well.

Two years later, I somehow finished the project with a fully restored 1959 Chevrolet 3100 Fleetside short bed pickup. She was a beauty, and turned heads everywhere she went. But what had gone wrong? Nothing really. My intention to get her running, and slightly prettied up, had simply given way to my usual penchant for perfection. In sandblasting the exterior sheet metal, both front fenders were found to be badly damaged, needing extensive metal repair. Replacements were needed. The cab needed patch panels for its rear corners and entrance steps, though the floor was solid. The worn-out tailgate couldn't be used. After several trips to area junkyards, we had the sheet metal needed to do the welding. We moved on to reassembly and finishing. By then, the rebuilt motor and standard transmission with granny gear, the rear end, steering, suspension and brakes were all renewed and waiting.

I loved that old truck. Painted in a light blue-green, I'd kept the bumpers and front grille in white. Underway the drivetrain was noisy, like most working trucks tend to be. But the truck was reliable, and quickly proved anew the old adage that uses can always be found for a pickup truck. Being a short bed, driving on anything but prepared surfaces was bumpy, and sometimes teeth-rattling. But we weren't running a limousine service with that old pick-me-up.

She stayed with us for a year or two. A neighbor, handy in

wood, offered to construct stake bed rails out of white oak. Upon installing them, he refused to take a dime. He simply wanted to see the old truck looking proper, as he put it. I was grateful, and had to admit that, with the stake bed slats in place, no doubt remained that this truck was available for work. And work she did, hauling two cords of seasoned firewood home every fall for our fireplace and wood stove, handling pickups and deliveries for my business, carrying everything needing transport that wouldn't fit in the back of our Volvo wagon.

One of our sons-in-law fancied the truck. His thought was to use it lightly and keep it up, then have it ready when his oldest son turned sixteen. Looking to begin another project, I agreed and the truck left for a new life in North Carolina.

* * *

Over the next decade, we owned several 1970s Ford trucks, standard models with 360 V8s and Fordomatic transmissions. They were fun. They were handy. And they were simple to maintain. But they weren't memorable, with one exception. This was a white 1972 F-150 in good used condition. For whatever reason, it captured our family's hearts. Everyone wanted to drive it, especially our recently-licensed daughter.

In time, it came to be called "Moby Truck" after Melville's great white whale. It needed nothing, but we added Sears seat covers to mask some fabric tears, and the infamous "Yosemite Sam" mudflaps behind the rear tires. Their "Back Off!" legend became a neighborhood conversation piece. One day, as I worked in the front yard, I watched my wife and youngest daughter wave as they climbed into Moby to go to a violin lesson. I waved back and watched them go.

Minutes later, the truck returned, parked in the driveway, and my wife hurried into the house. Apparently the instrument had been forgotten. I continued with my work, then looked up and raised my hand to wave, as the truck rolled back down the driveway toward the road. My wave froze as I realized there was no one in the truck. It had been left in neutral without the emergency brake on, and with the driver's door wide open.

A concrete culvert ran alongside the road at the bottom of our long, descending driveway. A moat bridged the culvert, with low concrete walls for safety, and overgrown plantings to shield the unsightly concrete. The truck gathered speed as it rolled backward. There was no time to take action. Suddenly, there was a crash. The truck stopped abruptly between the moat's walls, its engine stalled. I ran over to see what had happened.

The driver's door had saved the day, in a manner of speaking. Bent awkwardly out of shape, it lay flat on the driveway, having been ripped free of the car when it made contact with one of the low walls. Happily, the rest of the truck had suffered no damage. The door hinges were still attached. A replacement door would be needed but, thankfully, nothing else. As anyone responsible for such circumstances would be, the truck's driver was properly penitent.

South of our Alexandria, Virginia home was an extensive junk-yard and body shop in Dale City. Banks Auto Body had been owned and operated by a local black family for several generations. Three generations were active in the business. I knew the family well, having made many visits to search out parts for old cars or trucks I was working on. I called the office to ask if they could pull a '70s driver's Ford truck door out of their yard, paint it white, and install it on our truck.

They were happy to help, estimating $50 for the used door and $100 for the paint. I delivered the doorless truck the next day. The work was estimated to take about a week.

A week went by. Two weeks. No call. Finally, after three weeks, I called myself. Banks the Younger answered. He was about my age. I asked if there was any problem with the truck repair. He hedged a bit, then told me he needed to get his dad or granddad to speak with me. Uh, oh, I thought. What could have gone wrong? A minute later, the grandfather was on the line. There must be something serious to involve the grandfather who, on all my earlier visits, spent his time quietly reading from his bible, as he oversaw Banks family members doing the daily tasks of the business he'd founded decades before.

We exchanged greetings, then I asked whether the used door had been found, painted, and installed. "Yes, it has," he replied in his quiet way.

"Are you ready for me to drop by and pick up the truck?" I asked. A long moment's silence. Finally, he responded, though not by answering my question.

"We've had a small problem, and the family hasn't been able to decide what's to be done."

"Mr. Banks, would you like me to drive down to discuss this?"

"That would probably be best," he allowed, "How about tomorrow afternoon?" I agreed. We ended the call.

As it turned out, a contractor had delivered three work trucks, all white 1970s F-150s, the same day I'd dropped off Moby. They were to have light bodywork and fresh paint in an effort to keep them in service an additional year or two. Somehow the wires got crossed between the front office and body shop. After the replacement door had been found and installed, four white F-150 work trucks, instead of three, were run through the bodywork and paint process. Moby had been mistakenly painted, and now looked like new.

The long silence from the Banks family had been caused by their understandable concerns about how to bill for the work done, which in our case had not been ordered. Relieved at the news and happy that our favorite truck had not been stolen, destroyed or further damaged, I asked the grandfather what he thought a fair solution might be.

He thought awhile, then said, "Well, the bodywork and paint for each truck came to $450. We gave a discount because a regular customer needed several trucks done, and we ran the work like an assembly line. Somehow, your truck got put in that line. Your work was $150, which is all I can honestly charge you." I looked at this good man I'd done business with for more than a decade, and who let me visit, now and then, not to find parts, but rather to walk through his hundreds of old cars and trucks, and commune with them for an hour or two.

"Split the difference?" I suggested.

"My very thought." answered Granddad Banks.

I drove a spanking clean Moby Truck home late that afternoon, a truck made new for $300.

* * *

Owning those Ford F-150s, particularly Moby, and having earlier restored the 1959 Chevrolet Fleetside, whet my appetite for trucks. Like station wagons, they're genuine American icons. I'd been reading *Hemmings Motor News*, and other old car publications, about the increasing collectibility of certain old trucks. This brought to mind that, about twenty years earlier, I had bought a 1954 Chevrolet Corvette in Cucamonga, California, just east of Los Angeles along historic Route 66, to work on, then use as a daily driver for the five years we expected to remain out west.

When backing my purchase out of the mechanic's garage, I recalled that the vehicle parked in front of my vintage Corvette was a white 1950s truck with a bright red bowtie on the tailgate. From my reading, I knew that Chevrolet had produced the Cameo Carrier Pickup, also known as the "Corvette truck," in very limited numbers from 1955 to 1958. The Cameo, with its sedan-like interior, 265 (later 283) cid V8 motor, available hydramatic transmission, and unique but fragile fiberglass rear fenders, was an expensive "no-go show boat." But its rugged beauty, and limited production numbers, had captured the car hobby's attention. This sought-after vehicle was now rapidly increasing in value.

Hmmm. Was it a Cameo I'd glimpsed as I drove away in the old Corvette all those years ago? My imagination captured, I sat down after supper with my "old car file," a square cardboard box into which I'd tossed ever scrap of paper with names, addresses and phone numbers I'd kept, pack rat style, in my pursuit of old cars over the years. Actually, *decades*. I emptied the pile of papers onto the kitchen table and began sorting, reading, then tossing pieces of paper back into the box. An hour went by. Then two. My neck was getting stiff. My interest was flagging.

Then there it was, a torn fragment on which "54 Corvette #777,

George, and a 213 area code phone number" were written. I picked up the phone and dialed the number, which rang several times. Then someone answered.

"Hello."

"Hello, is this George in Cucamonga, California?"

"The same."

"Would you happen to recall selling a white 1954 Corvette to a young fellow and his family, who arrived in a yellow Volvo wagon from the east coast, bought your car, then drove it north to Monterey."

"Yes, I do. You came back a year or two later, and showed me what you'd done to the car. The sidedraft carburetors had replaced the twin two barrels sticking up through the hood, and you'd even managed to find a replacement steering column and an original steering wheel. That Corvette had been used for dirt track racing up around San Jose, and the driver had shortened the column and installed a small racing wheel for that purpose. Now that I think about it, the car even had Offenhauser valve covers and some kind of special crankshaft."

"You have a great memory, George. I'm that young guy from all those years ago. I have a question. Was the white truck parked in front of the Corvette a Cameo? And, by chance, do you still have it?"

"It was and I do. I bought that 1955 vehicle for my son to drive in high school. But he told me he wouldn't be caught dead in that old white dinosaur. Broke my heart. Why? Do you want to buy it?"

"Yes, I do." Twenty minutes later we'd agreed on a price and that, over about three months, George would get the vehicle running and reliable, for a second fixed price. I'd ship radial whitewall tires to his business, which he would install. Then my wife and I would fly out and drive the Cameo back to Virginia together.

That's *almost* how it worked.

Six months later, we flew out to California, and were pleased to find the Cameo parked out front and ready to travel, or so we thought. It seemed that George had kept his commitments. Instead of heading directly east to Needles, and into the unforgiving desert, we turned south to the San Diego area, only an hour or so away. There, Mike Stansel, a good friend and knowledgeable old car expert, had asked — well, actually demanded — to look over his friends' truck before we began a three-thousand-mile journey back to the East Coast.

We arrived at our destination without incident. For two days, the truck was driven and gone over with care. As it turned out, there were ample reasons for my friend's concern. Some were safety-related. Others, mostly leaks caused by the truck's having sat for several decades, were less concerning. It was unlikely, Mike observed, that we would have made it up and over the Guadalupe Pass east of El Paso in Texas. The brakes needed work. The leaking hydramatic transmission needed a professional rebuild. The V8 motor ran well, but required adjustments, a carburetor rebuild, and new gaskets. Mike suggested we leave the truck with him. He planned to have it ready for a cross-country trip in a month or two.

The estimate proved correct. Late one night, Mike picked me up in the much-improved Cameo at San Diego's Lindbergh Field. It turned out that my wife was not available for the adventure, and Mike volunteered to take her place for the long trip to Virginia. Loaded with tools, a spare gas container, and some extra parts, plus our own scant belongings, we set out on I-8 at dawn, the early sun just rising above the mountains to the east. It was to be an old truck trip for the ages, filled with wonderful experiences and, thankfully, no problems or emergencies. Just two old friends enjoying a beautiful old truck, the open road, and each other's company for eight sparkling days. On each day of the trip, strangers would walk up to us, smile, and look the Cameo over. They each said the same thing. "Nice truck."

Well, it *was* a nice truck.

The trip didn't start out well. Our first stop, after crossing the Borrego desert, was Yuma, Arizona. It was a hot day, bone dry, with temperatures exceeding 115°F. The truck had no air conditioning. We rotated the flipper windows forward, as we had seen our parents due in the hot summers of our childhoods. That helped. But

George had missed installing rubber grommets to block openings in the firewall. We had missed this as well. Thus, the motor's heat was directed back into the truck. By the time we got to Yuma, Mike, at the wheel, was suffering from heat exhaustion. In a dehydrated daze, he unintentionally ran the truck over a curb, and onto a lawn at a military air base outside Yuma.

Sitting under a misting lawn sprinkler, lots of hydration, and some spicy Mexican food, brought him back. But the experience led to a change of plans. We decided not to continue on the southern route through El Paso and Dallas. Instead, we turned north from Phoenix to Flagstaff, then eastward on I-40. This proved a saving decision for the two drivers, as temperatures were consistently fifteen degrees cooler on the northerly route. And we had the added pleasure of visiting Route 66's historic sites along the way.

Driving through Alburquerque, New Mexico, after an exceptional lunch in a tiny Mexican cantina on the edge of town, we pulled up beside a Checker cab at a red light on the main drag. The cab driver looked over at us, smiled, and offered to trade us straight across, our "ratty old pickup" for his "almost new" taxi, the two gawking fares in the back included. Somehow we were able to fight off the strong temptation, smiled and waved, and continued eastbound. As we pulled away, we heard again that oft-repeated compliment. First, that admiring glance. Then, "Nice truck ..."

One of the interesting events we encountered, while crossing the Panhandle, was a gathering of Route 66 aficionados in Landergin, Texas. Located west of the famed Cadillac Ranch sculpture, a row of old Cadillacs buried vertically in a row beside the highway outside Amarillo, Landergin was a ghost town with blocks of empty residences, a row of closed commercial buildings, and empty grain elevators sitting beside the road, a deserted community amidst endless miles of flat land.

Locals had recently opened and spruced up several of the derelict buildings, and created a boisterous, two-day event for all things "66." There was great food, lively entertainment, and what the organizers called "down home Texas hospitality." Hundreds of old cars

and trucks, and dozens of motorcycles were drawn to the "happening," with license plates from Maine to California, and from Florida
to Washington state. The Cameo fit right in, its white body, and its
red bed, tailgate bowtie, and interior, declaring its "66-ness." We met
lots of nice folks, and ate well. But we decided to pass on an invitation to participate in a "the fastest eater of an enormous, three-inch-
thick, porterhouse steak" contest. As the sun went down across the
prairie to the ageless sound of a small country band playing the Texas
Two Step, the late-stayers dancing, clapping, and laughing together,
we smiled our goodbyes, walked over to our old truck, and pulled
out onto the dark ribbon of highway eastbound.

Years later, driving another old car coast to coast, I passed again
through Landergin, and stopped beside the road to survey the former
site of the Route 66 celebration. The ghosts had returned. The town
was deserted. A dry wind blew the tumbleweeds across the parking
lot, where country music once played, vats of barbecue and tubs of
iced beer were consumed, and hundreds gathered to happily celebrate
the Mother Road. Staring up at a grain elevator, leaning slightly as
if against the wind, I was glad for my memories of that lively, earlier
visit. Then I drove on.

As the Cameo crossed the tableland of the west's open spaces,
we often passed the time by estimating distances and driving times
to a distant topographical feature, objects such as a butte or a range
of hills. We consistently underestimated both distances and times.
Unlike our homes on the two coasts with large populations and limited perspective, our route across the broad, flat stomach of America
allowed us to see great distances in all directions. Often we'd drive
for an hour or two, and see only a solitary roadrunner or shy coyote.
We drove past or through towns, or former towns, like Landergin.
Silent, overgrown, played out, sad. Along the coast, populations feel
the constrictions of dense living. Out on the plains, where you could
see as far as your eyes would focus, it was the opposite. Relaxing into
those great distances, and into the blanket of silence broken only by
the wind, listening to the constant rumble of the Cameo's V8, the
steady hum of the tires winding down the miles, we felt something

of the peace many feel entering a church.

In *Zen and the Art of Motorcycle Maintenance*, the late Robert Persig commented on the sense of openness and space when traveling in the West. He wrote that: "We seemed to meet so many lonely people, in the supermarket, at the laundromat, and when we checked out at the motel. Those pickup campers and RVs rolling through the redwoods, full of lonely retired people looking at trees on their way to look at the ocean. You catch it in the first glance of a new face, that searching look, then it's gone. We see so much more loneliness around today. It's paradoxical that where people are the most crowded, in the big coastal cities of the East and West, the loneliness is greatest. The explanation, I believe, is that the physical distance between people has nothing to do with loneliness. It is rather the psychic distance. In the West, the physical distances are big but the psychic distances are small."

At the friendly gathering in Landergin, where fans from all over the country gathered to celebrate Route 66 as the Mother Road, the sense of psychic distance was all but insignificant. Driving across the expanse of the former Republic of Texas, a land of great physical distances stretching to the horizon in every direction, it was even more so.

We stopped in Oklahoma City overnight. Mike had in-laws there, and had grown up in the area. We'd been well-treated by strangers we'd met throughout our journey. But it's always special to relax with family. After dinner, we went out together to a minor league hockey game. Lots of fun, though the players seemed more focused on fighting than playing. Before thanking our hosts, and getting on the road the next morning, we performed the only maintenance of the trip on the Cameo, gapping and installing a fresh set of R-44 spark plugs, a gift to our pickup, after days of driving at highway speeds on a half-century-old motor which had, until recently, slept for three decades in east Los Angeles.

As those who have driven between coasts know, the scenery east of the Mississippi River is a pale shadow compared to the American West. President Eisenhower's broad highway system, the shortening of visual perspective, and the increase in humanity, both on and alongside the road, are very different from rolling along alone for hours surrounded by great natural beauty or endless flatland. By now, we had settled into a routine, getting up a little later, eating a full breakfast, changing drivers more frequently, and stopping well before dark, catching a nap, relaxing in the pool or hot tub, eating a leisurely dinner, often in diners or small cafés, and getting to bed early. The Life of Riley.

Everywhere we went, we were treated well. Often, we felt as if we made lasting friends in those brief moments off the road. The Cameo remained the subject of interest whenever we stopped, even when we did not stop, and was sometimes given special treatment. Arriving at a Days Inn or La Quinta, the manager might invite us to leave the truck parked under the bright lights at the lodging's entrance. Good for business, she'd say. Good for security, we thought, heading off to the hot tub to loosen up.

On our last day, as we drove through the quiet rural beauty of southwestern Virginia east of the former railroad hub of Roanoke, we stopped for an early lunch at a small family restaurant, located at the crossroads of two busy rural highways. Stepping inside, the smell of coffee and hot food was captivating. A number of farming types were tucked into their meals, bent low in conversation, coffee cups in hand. We found a quiet corner and took our seats. An attractive young lady brought menus, then returned, coffee urn in hand, for refills and our orders. The food was country plain and plentiful.

Paying our bill and rising to depart, we thanked the young woman for her friendly service. She surveyed the two of us with a sly smile in her eye, and declared, "Gentlemen, here in the South, we women know how to take care of our men." That remark, sincerely delivered, whatever its intent, remained the topic of conversation from our restaurant exit to our next stop after several hours on the road. It's often come up in discussions down though the years. "Yee Haw!"

We stopped in the afternoon to visit Appomattox Courthouse, the closing scene of our nation's Civil War. It was a warm, sunny day.

We both sensed the gravity of a place so important to our country's history, and discussed the complex feelings that must have welled up in Generals Grant and Lee, victor and vanquished, as they met on July 9, 1865, their inner relief that the long and bloody conflict was finally to end.

By nightfall, the Cameo was parked safely in our driveway, no worse the wear for her three thousand miles. After a few day's visit, Mike flew home. The truck joined our family but, in recognition of its condition and rarity, never took on working responsibilities. Instead, she made the circuit of parades and car shows, and various weekend old car gatherings. She was a fine specimen and mostly original so, almost inevitably, an automotive publication wrote to ask if one of the best Cameo Carriers in the country might be available for a photo shoot. We agreed with both the assertion and the request. The location selected was a nearby home on the Potomac River, almost two hundred years old, and built to resemble George Washington's Mount Vernon estate, which was on the Potomac, about a mile distant.

The photography took the entire day, over 400 pictures in all. Every hour or so the truck was repositioned on the property to better view details of interest, or place the sun at the proper angle. or include an old rail fence or flowering bush in bloom. Far from being bored by the long day, it was fascinating to see how hard the photographer worked to completely blanket the Cameo with photographs. Months later, when a courtesy copy of the coffee table book about vintage Chevrolet trucks arrived in the mail, I was pleased to see how accurately the photographs had captured the truck.

Others reacted similarly, something I had not anticipated. Soon, the letters and phone calls began. It seemed that everyone wanted to buy our old truck. Our initial response, with well-practiced gruffness, was "not for sale." But interest did not wane and, in time, an offer from Tokyo, Japan, was received that couldn't be refused. A month later, the Cameo was loaded into a transporter, and left for its new home halfway around the globe. Having lived in Japan for two years in the late 1960s, I like to imagine that most distinctive of 1950s

American vehicles driving around Tokyo or on the Kanto plain near Mount Fuji, a huge white pickup truck in a sea of small Japanese automobiles. What a contrast.

And to think that this most unlikely of journeys began late one evening on my dining table, as my fingers filtered handfuls of paper scraps, seeking a number for George in Cucamonga.

* * *

The departure of the 1955 Cameo seemed the time to re-direct my attention to the old car collecting that had long been my focus. I began to look more closely at car publications, and the usual sources I relied upon, to find candidates. One of those sources was a local advertising pamphlet, the Weekly Want Ad. I sometimes bought a copy at Seven-Seven. It came out every week, and cost a dollar. One evening after dinner, I sat down to go through the daily mail, then picked up a Want Ad I'd bought a week earlier but not read. There were always lots of interesting old vehicles in the small publication. Most were worn out or required repairs exceeding their potential value. Now and then I found something for sale that had potential, an air of mystery, or both.

So it was that evening. A small ad under Trucks 4 Sale stated: "1958 Dodge truck. Painted Sunoco colors. Illness forces sale." I ruminated. Weren't 1950s Dodge trucks sort of pug ugly vehicles? Good reliable performers, but hard on the eyes? And what's this about Sunoco colors? I guessed that the truck must have been used at a gas station. But weren't Sunoco's colors bright yellow and blue? Even the mental image seemed hard on the eyes.

Setting aside my reservations, I dialed the phone number in the ad. A friendly feminine voice answered. I introduced myself, and established my interest in the old Dodge truck advertised for sale. She replied that her husband would be able to answer my questions, and that she'd have him on the phone presently. A harsh and repeated throat-clearing followed. Then a voice with little strength came on the line.

"How may I help you?"

"I'm calling about the '58 Dodge truck. What can you tell me about her?"

"Well, I bought her in 1963. She'd been little used. I owned a Sunoco gas and service station in rural Maryland. Just sold it a year ago, in fact. At that time Sunoco would paint any service vehicle in those bright company colors, for the free advertising, I guess. She's been used regularly at the station for decades, and parked there in a spare bay at night. Never damaged and never rusty. She's kind of ugly and, with that yellow paint, a bit hard on the eyes. But I kept her when I sold the station. She's parked out back in our garage. Anything else?"

"Yes, I'd like to come by this afternoon to see the truck, if convenient. And I'm wondering why, if you'd grown so attached to the vehicle, you'd now decide to sell her?"

His answer took a while. Finally he responded, "Because I'm dying in a month or two. It's the cancer. I want the truck gone, so my wife doesn't have to deal with it. You're welcome to come by this afternoon. Earlier would be better for obvious reasons." We agreed on a time. He provided his address, and several landmarks, to help navigate the rural Maryland countryside.

Arriving an hour later, I was invited into the kitchen by the owner's wife. The man was sitting at the kitchen table, an oxygen bottle by his side. Speaking slowly through oxygen inhalations, he bid me take a seat. I did. We introduced ourselves, then covered the Dodge and its history in greater detail than earlier on the phone. The effort of talking tired the man, whose pauses grew longer as his speech slowed. I asked if I could have a look at the truck, then take it for a short ride. The owner was amenable, and pushed a set of keys across the table to me. His wife led me the door, and explained how to enter the garage through an unlocked side door, then to open the locked garage doors from inside, bringing light on the Dodge. I followed her instructions.

There she was. Parked beside the couple's passenger car, the strong colors immediately caught my attention. How could they not? A Sunoco truck it definitely was. Then, my eyes focused on the truck's bed. What was that? I walked over, and put my hand on the odd addition to the upper edge of a rear fenders. It was the Dodge designer's insightful borrowing from a Dodge sedan's upward swept tail fin which, unintentionally, created one of the rarest and most collectible of trucks, the Dodge Sweptside. Unmentioned in the Want Ad advertisement, or in my kitchen conversation with the owner and his wife, I couldn't believe my good fortune finding such a rare truck.

I started the Dodge, which ran smoothly and quietly, then took her for a short drive, which confirmed that the well-kept appearance throughout was matched by obvious care taken to preserve the truck's running gear. Everything worked as advertised. The instrument panel showed about sixty-six thousand miles, which the truck's appearance and driving manners confirmed as likely original. What a pleasure to operate. As I shifted through the gears, backed up, tested brakes, and put the vehicle through its paces, I knew I'd found a rare automotive gem. Returning to the owner's home, I backed the truck into its spot, and closed up the garage, I knocked on the back door and rejoined the owner at his kitchen table, returning his keys. It was time for a price discussion.

Though his price was fair for the model in original condition, I attempted to reduce the figure. I told the owner that his truck was solid, that it performed well on the road, and that I would like to buy it. I offered roughly half of the price he'd asked. He looked at me, a crinkling around his eyes betraying a slight smile, then said, "I assume you've heard the phrase, a snowball's chance in hell." We both laughed, and soon found agreement at a price closer to his original figure. I left earnest money as a deposit, and arranged to return the following day with a certified check for the balance. That done, I said goodbye to the couple, and drove home.

The drive was routine. I felt the truck gradually loosen up as it rolled down the road, happy to be in use after being stored for a year. But I felt bittersweet about the purchase. I purchased old vehicles because I felt a personal affection for a certain make or model, and an intention to keep and improve the vehicle as I learned about it, until some circumstance called it on to another owner. While I appreciated the tough reliability of the Dodge, and definitely the surprise in discovering its sweptside rarity, its appearance did not appeal to me. It wasn't only the distasteful exterior paint, which was correctible, but a certain crudeness in the overall design. This spoke strongly to utility, but without a whispered word for aesthetics.

But I did "get it." Trucks are about utility. Any design appeal one finds in a truck ought to be counted as accidental. A bonus. My memories of the 1955 Chevrolet Cameo reminded me of how appealing a truck could be, if the design intention was there, without sacrificing utility. What I decided as I drove the Dodge home, was that I would find someone who held a Dodge Sweptside truck in the same esteem I'd held the Cameo. Within two months that man had been located in the Chicago area, and the Sweptside was on its way to join him. It would soon undergo a full restoration, including a different paint scheme. The Dodge Sweptside pickup would ulti-mately become the valuable vehicle it deserved to be.

Should I have felt ashamed at having "turned over" the Dodge as a speculation? I did and I didn't. In time, I came to consider myself the agent who found a rare old truck, well off the beaten path, and got it to someone who could and did insure its future.

* * *

Was this the concluding chapter of my foray into old trucks? Not hardly! Within three months I'd bought a turquoise and white 1971 Ford F-250 three-quarter-ton Custom Camper Special from its orig-inal owners in Oregon, an older couple who needed funds for a relative's operation. The Ford had only 27,000 miles, and had been purchased new to try out "the camping life" at nearby Crater Lake, a total failure according to the wife. I could only imagine! Subse-quently, the F-250 had seen only intermittent local use over the years, and was kept under a carport. It had a 360 cid V8 motor backed by a 3-speed Fordomatic transmission, and a Dana rear end. It also had rare Ford factory air conditioning, an auxiliary gas tank, a mechanic's tool storage locker on a rear fender, original split rim wheels, and a huge 8-foot bed.

From its delivery to Virginia, the F-250 never needed anything but oil and filter changes. It was used for local work, including picking up and delivering orders for our family business. Occasionally it drove farther to pick up deliveries at airports an hour or more away. Its single flaw was the Dana rear end's gear ratio, installed to help the truck carry heavy loads onto uneven, muddy construction sites. It put the truck at a disadvantage on the highway. At speeds above 50 mph, the low gear ratio had the motor begging for relief. We soon installed a "boulevard" rear end, which brought a relieved smile to the V8 at those higher speeds.

The F-250 remained with us for over fifteen years, its mileage finally passing 34,000, as it arrived at forty-one years of age in 2012. Our eldest daughter, Noelle, who lived in Roanoke, Virginia, with her husband and four children, also happened to be a 1971 model, who would turn forty-one that year. With the closing of our business, and my retirement a year earlier, the truck had seen less road time. Because of its size, the three-quarter-ton vehicle was kept outdoors, though on pavement, behind a fence, and under a waterproof cover.

Knowing that a vehicle tends to go downhill without regular use, we decided to deliver the truck as a birthday gift to our daughter at midnight on her birthday. I would've liked to have been there, and seen the entire family rousted from their beds, to find this huge turquoise and white truck perched on a rollback at their front door. The passing of the truck down through the generations seemed a fitting conclusion to my years of enjoyment in that quintessential American world.

So trucks are gone from my life. But the memories? The memories will always be with me.

"Nice truck ..."

13

1954 Corvette: America's First True Sports Car

*Zen is not merely a cult of impulsive action
but, similar to free association, a technique to
get rid of obstacles to the free flow of thought.*

Once upon a time, perhaps fifty years ago, I was a far greater
car-collecting risk taker than I am today. Some of those chances,
made sight unseen, and on the weakest evidence, resulted in purchases that turned out just as one should expect — disasters. But
some worked out well, proving again that even blind squirrels find
a few acorns.

Such was the case with a 1954 Corvette I purchased in southern California while living in Maryland. In my defense, I did know
at the time of purchase that I would soon be moving the family to
Monterey, California. A weak justification? I'd have to agree.

You read about this car briefly in the chapter about old trucks.
I'd picked up the Corvette east of Los Angeles in Rancho Cucamonga,
then followed the family Volvo north to Monterey. Departing, I'd
noticed an old white pickup parked in front of the Corvette, a red
Chevrolet bow tie on the tailgate. Chasing that memory to earth,
twenty-five years later, resulted in my purchase of a rare 1955 Cameo
Carrier pickup, a one-for-the-ages, cross-country road trip, and a
great deal of fun, until the pickup's eventual departure to a collector
in Japan.

The Corvette left the Cucamonga garage on a dry and dusty

163

summer day, and drove in the wake of our 1971 Volvo 145 station wagon several hundred highway miles to Monterey, without complaint or ceremony. Do not the gods protect fools? Yes, they do. But there is something special, even enervating, about climbing into an old car you have never seen before, and do not know, then driving it for hours on a lonely highway. If only from the need to pay the closest attention to the vehicle, probably out of fear, you come to know a great deal about the vehicle in a very short period of time.

This wasn't your grandfather's Corvette. It was #777 out of about five thousand 1954 Corvettes produced in the car's second year. Counting the three hundred cars manufactured in 1953, this was the 1077th Corvette produced. But it was considered just another used car at the time. Corvettes could be found everywhere in 1974, particularly in sunny California. Typically, they cost no more than a couple thousand bucks. The fiberglass body had been tidied up and repainted the original polo white. The car had spent years as a dirt track racer near San Jose.

Most of the racing modifications were not obvious. The Corvette had a vinyl convertible top, which could be stored in its boot, as well as a rare "Plasticon" hardtop, an aftermarket accessory, which was only slightly more protective than the ragtop in the rain. The steering column had been shortened in order to mount a racing steering wheel close to the dashboard and firewall. The standard steering wheel on early Corvettes, taken from Chevrolet's full-sized sedan, was too large for the car and limited the driver's ability to change direction quickly.

The second modification was all too obvious. The three original side-draft carburetors, designed to fit inside the confined engine compartment, and under the low hood, had been removed. In their place, with a different intake manifold, were two two-barrel carbs mounted vertically. This had required cutting a rectangular hole in the hood. No one could miss this, nor could they miss the sound of a six-cylinder motor modified to provide maximum power and torque. I'd taken friends out in the Corvette and been told that there was no way a Chevrolet Six was under the hood. There was just too much "giddy-up" in that old girl.

The carbs helped, of course. But, opening the hood, one quickly saw that, whoever raced the vehicle in the past had put money in the motor. A 235 cid Stovebolt Six it was. But there the similarity ended. Motor internals were all Offenhauser, as announced by the valve covers. This was definitely the secret sauce for whatever success the former owner had enjoyed on those dusty dirt circles. The "hopped up" Stovebolt was backed by the standard two-speed Hydramatic transmission, widely used by Chevrolet. Together, they definitely got that little white car down the road. The Corvette behaved well when driven normally. It got decent gas mileage and had a comfortable interior with useful instruments. The noise level — the late Ross Perot's "giant sucking sound" comes to mind — of those thirsty upthrust carbs, staring back at the driver though the windshield, invited occupants to wear ear protection.

In Monterey, the car assumed a secondary role, serving as my commuter to work. The weather was generally mild, so the top was always stowed. What the little roadster did not know was that it was about to become a project. My friend Mike and I had decided to un-modify the Corvette's obvious race modifications, leaving the "Stovebolt on Steroids" as it was. We'd locate and acquire an original intake manifold and three original side-draft carburetors. This would allow us to repair or replace the fiberglass hood and re-create the Corvette's original appearance. The car's internal fierceness would remain hidden.

The second modification was more complicated. We could locate a standard Chevrolet steering wheel. But there was no way to un-shorten the steering column. Months passed, as we looked for a replacement column, which was unique to the early Corvette. We considered a donor car, but one could not be found. In the meantime, as engineering types, we had studied the steps required to remove the existing column. It seemed we would need to remove the steering wheel, radiator, manifold, and carbs to gain more room in the limited space around the motor. The steering box would also need to be disconnected.

At that point, we encountered two problems. A thin retaining ring held the steering column in place beneath the dashboard. Made of fragile fiberglass, it would easily break if pressure was exerted. We had to be careful with that support. Also, on the lower end of the steering column, even with the radiator, carbs, and manifold removed, there did not appear to be sufficient space to rotate the steering box, and free the column for removal through the dashboard and firewall, unless the left fender was removed or somehow leveraged aside to create more room. We stewed over this challenge for weeks.

Finally, I wrote a short letter to Ed Cole, Vice President of Chevrolet Motors, one of the key executives who had fostered the idea of a Chevrolet sports car, and whose strong leadership saw the program through to production. Think what the automotive world would have missed over the past sixty-six years, had he failed in that mission? My letter described our project and the steps we believed were needed to replace the shortened steering column.

I stressed that we were uncomfortable levering the fender several inches laterally in order to rotate and free the steering box. I closed by noting that, while we wanted to bring the car back to its original appearance, we were concerned about permanent damage to the fender. I noted as well our lack of expertise removing a fender from the car. In an attempt at humor, I closed by asking if the problem we faced was caused by Chevrolet having assembled the car around the steering column, and that, by design, it therefore could not be removed.

To our surprise, we received a reply within two weeks. Cole was very encouraging. He joked that our surmise about the Corvette being built around its steering column was close to the truth. Importantly, he agreed that our approach for levering the fender outward to produce more working space was the correct solution. Done with care and patience, he wrote, the fiberglass fender would not be damaged, and would return to its shape when released. He wished us luck getting our Corvette back together.

To say we were encouraged would be an understatement.

We were ecstatic. The corporate father of the Chevrolet Corvette confirmed and supported our theories. By then, I had located and purchased an original manifold and the three correct side-draft carburetors, though the latter needed rebuilding. Our search for a donor car intensified. Two weeks later, a 1954 Corvette was listed for sale in the local paper, not running and available for parts. The price was right: a few hundred dollars. We drove over to inspect the car, and found, to our surprise, that everything we needed was on or nearby the vehicle. The owner wanted his garage back. By the following afternoon, the donor car was parked in my garage alongside its beneficiary. At the next opportunity, we planned to do some serious "shape-shifting" with the two Corvettes.

Mike and I shelved thoughts of academic work for several nights the following week. We spent many hours following through on our plan to "original-ize" the Corvette. The old hood with its carb opening came off. The two carbs and intake manifold were next. Then the radiator. Accessories on the left side of the motor were removed, as we worked to create as much maneuvering room in the motor compartment as possible. Finally, the steering wheel was removed from its column, and the steering box was disconnected from its attachments to the steering system, at the column's lower end. When this was accomplished, there was definitely more room for the operation blessed by Chevrolet Vice President Cole. But was it enough?

To provide the desired leverage, I'd purchased a heavy duty garden hoe, not for its functional purpose, but for the thickness and length of its wooden handle. Nicknamed "Farmer John," it lay propped against a wall near the Corvette's front grille. We took our time, carefully maneuvering the steering box and column, while watching for stress on the frail fiberglass column support. Finally, we'd shifted the column as far as it would move, without being able to rotate the steering box. It was time for Farmer John.

While one of us held the column and steering box immobile, the other inserted the hoe handle between motor and fender, so that its lower end could be levered against the garage floor and left front tire, exerting pressure on the inner side of the fender. It was the ultimate trial and error escapade. With each increase in pressure on the hoe, the fender shifted slightly away from the motor. But the required effort seemed to double. Would the fender or the man break first?

Very slowly, and without cracking the under-dash support, we managed to wedge the fender away from the motor until, on our fourth attempt, the steering box could be rotated vertically 180 degrees in the direction of the stretched fender, so it was now on top of the steering column. With the radiator previously removed, an angle was found to pull the column gently forward through the dashboard and firewall, and free of the car.

We'd done it. The near impossible. Though it was 10 pm, the evening's work was not completed. That came two hours later, when the steering column from the donor car was installed on #777. This required us to perform each of our previous steps, but in reverse. It was time to call a halt to the evening's work, before exhaustion set in and we began to make mistakes.

The remaining re-assembly of the Corvette took several more weeks. We were no longer struggling to turn our theories into repair realities, so our progress was steady. There were the usual moments of anguish and hilarity, and sometimes both together, all accepted parts of any car restorer's palette of practical experience. Some of these moments come easily to mind.

As we got to a point where almost everything had been reas-sembled but the carburetors, we remembered that the latter required rebuilds. Rebuild kits were readily procured but, late on another night, we realized the kits did not include the leather replacement diaphragms for the accelerator pumps inside each unit. Mike asked if I had any soft leather that might serve, so we could finish the job. Leather from one of my old flight boots was sacrificed. Three rounds were cut out from a boot tongue for that purpose. Within another hour or two, the Corvette was running, smooth and strong. Success!

After installing the standard steering wheel, we lay together on the garage floor in front of the Corvette, trying to determine how best to reconnect the steering controls to the steering box, so that the car would turn left with a left turn of the steering wheel, not the opposite. Lacking a tech manual or schematic, we drew out the system on the garage floor with a bright-red "Marks-A-Lot" marker, then eyeballed the connections so that they replicated our homespun diagram. After some checking and rechecking, the job appeared to be done. But a test-drive remained for a little sports car which, now complete and running, was as anxious as we were to hit the road.

Outside the garage, rain was pouring down. We got in the car, started up, and backed slowly out of the garage, then up the steep driveway, instantly wet. The brakes worked. I turned the wheel left, and touched the accelerator slightly to overcome the driveway's steep grade, and to back us onto the road. The Corvette did the expected, not the opposite. Laughter, cackles, even screams resounded as we took a victory lap, getting almost airborne over a small bridge while driving around the neighborhood. As we reentered the garage, the car and its two hooting occupants were soaking wet — but victorious.

Such moments are indelible and live forever. Any effort, however complex, that is conducted with care and discipline, and where objectives include a reverence for quality — for doing it right — brings rewards that cannot be expressed in words. Instead, those events and accomplishments live on within us, and within our friendships, deeply buried and never lost, a cause for recollection and smiles through the years.

When it was time to leave Monterey for an assignment in San Diego, Mike's wife Rita drove the Corvette south, where it became my commuter vehicle again, always top down in the warm and constant sun of southern California. Now and then a rare afternoon shower would leave the car's interior soaked, puddles on the carpeted floor pans. When this happened, knowing I had an hour or two left in the workday, I would open the doors wide, and leave them open. When I left work, the sun had done its work. The car was dry for the ride home along the Silver Strand.

Eventually, the car was sold to another collector in California. He loved the car. I could tell from his reaction to the Corvette that he'd give her the best of care. I still have a memory that as I drove the car to the new owner's home, I couldn't stop crying. Why would a grown man cry his eyes out over a car? You and I know the answer.

I flew for a few years after the Corvette was sold. When I sat down to pull on my flight boots before a flight, I'd look down, shake my head, and laugh at what I saw. There on the left boot tongue were three holes, each about two inches in diameter, where we'd cut out the diaphragms for the side-draft carburetors' accelerator pumps years before.

Each time this happened, I sensed that my connection to the little Corvette — the special bond we shared — was still in place. I'm grateful for that. Some say the old cars we pour our sweat and treasure into never really leave us, even after they're sold — that instead, they live on forever in our hearts. On the evidence, I'd have to agree.

14

1956 Thunderbird:
Fun, Fun, Fun!

In Zen, trying to be natural is an affectation.

Bob and Kay Patterson were our neighbors in Virginia for over thirty years. In World War II, Bob had been an Army Air Force fighter pilot in Europe. Shot down over France in his second year of combat, he became a prisoner of war in Germany until the war ended. Later, he flew for more than thirty years as a pilot for Eastern Airlines, the last few as captain of a 747 on international routes. Bob had uncommon skills in wood and metal work. The fully-equipped shop in his basement would have paid tribute to a commercial enterprise.

The couple never had children. Kay had flaming red hair, a personality to match, and was a born leader in committees and community projects. She'd spent the war as a volunteer. The Pattersons were known for their contributions to local schools, churches, clubs, and other community organizations. They were known in our neighborhood as "The Indefagitables."

That was in their sixties. As the couple aged through their seventies, and into their eighties, both became crotchety. Social skills and interests waned. Bob began to show signs of wartime PTSD and, later, dementia. As a friend and neighbor, I frequently helped Kay repair household systems, and begin the process of cleaning out decades of accumulation in their basement, attic, and garage. While organizing their over-filled garage one weekend afternoon, I saw two

171

items that interested me. One was an upright player piano with exquisite hardwood carvings and dozens of piano rolls. The other was a vintage Ford Thunderbird, covered in dust, and buried under a pile of blankets and boxes.

Months went by. I continued to be helpful. One day, Kay told me she'd heard I worked on old cars, and wondered aloud if I might get her car running out in the garage. I asked her what it was. She told me it was a Thunderbird, but could not recall the year. I asked how long it had been stored. She thought for a while, then replied that it was in the late 1970s, some twenty years in the past. Had Bob or some service stored the car properly to protect it? "No," she answered, "I drove it into the garage, turned off the key, left it in the ignition, and got out." Trouble right there in River City. I managed to dodge her request for assistance with the vehicle and, though I continued to help the aging couple, the subject did not come up again.

But then it did. One Sunday afternoon, just as a Washington Redskins-Dallas Cowboys football game was about to begin on television, I got a panicked call from Kay. She needed me to come right over. "Why?" I asked. It turned out that several houses on their street were holding a multi-family yard sale. It had been advertised in the *Washington Post*. The ad drew large numbers of buyers. Unfortunately, Bob had left the garage door open. The rear of the old Thunderbird was seen by the bargain hunters. A number of people were now ringing the doorbell, and knocking on the door, wanting to buy the car. With all the racket, Bob had suffered a panic attack and locked himself in their bedroom upstairs.

Kay was obviously highly stressed. But what exactly could I do? Come over and tell everyone to leave? Kay had a better idea. I should come over, give her a check for the car, then tell those waiting on the front lawn that the car had been sold, and ask them to leave. What is it about women with red hair? I asked what she wanted for the car. The figure she mentioned would not have bought an early Thunderbird parts car. I agreed to her request, quickly wrote the check, drove to her house, presented the check, closed the front door and pulled down the garage door. Then, waving the signed-over title and handwritten bill of sale in the air, I told the gathering the car had been sold and that the yard sale, at least for that address, was ended.

It took a few days to get a friend to help me unload the dusty boxes atop the car, then push it out of the garage and down the driveway, where it was hooked to his pickup truck and towed the few blocks to my driveway. There it sat for about a week, while I earned a living. One day, walking down the driveway to pick up the morning newspaper, I took a rag and stopped to wipe down a rear fender on the car. Why, the car was white. Who would have guessed?

The next weekend I had time to do some cleaning. I put everything outside on an old card table: hoses, soap, cleaning solvents, sponges, brillo pads, towels, and rags. Then I went to work. Three hours later a different 1956 Thunderbird sat in the driveway, spiffy as could be, paint cleaned, chrome shining and, after lowering the ragtop and scrubbing the interior with strong solvents, it no longer smelled of mold. Isn't it a wonder what "elbow grease" can do?

Encouraged by the improved appearance of the long-hibernating vehicle, which showed a modest seventy-three-thousand miles, I began to work on getting the car running. A new battery and fresh gasoline were purchased. The motor turned easily with the new battery, a step in the right direction. But it wouldn't start. The four-barrel carburetor was checked and cleaned. Next the plugs were removed. They were old, of course, but still clean and correctly gapped. I reinstalled them. Later that night, frustrated, I took tools and a drop light with extension cord, and crawled under the Thunderbird's rear to examine the gas tank and fuel line.

Seeing no obvious problem, I disconnected the fuel line to confirm fuel flow forward to the motor, while my wife turned on the ignition. Voilà! The wire mesh filter between tank and fuel line was completely blocked with desiccated, greenish mold. It was removed, thoroughly cleaned, and reinstalled on the fuel tank. The starter barely made contact when the engine came to life. It ran roughly for a few minutes, then smoothed out. The blocked filter had obviously been the problem. Replacing the fuel filter and adding fresh gas to the tank, brought added life to the motor, which now sounded like the Thunderbird Special V8 that it was.

It was satisfying to see the old car come alive, and to drive it into our garage for the night, the top still down. We were feeling festive. A glass of wine was in order. But I'd seen something unfamiliar while under the car. I wanted to get back underneath with a drop light to see if my initial sense of alarm was overblown. Unfortunately, it wasn't. I moved the light around for several minutes, while inspecting the frame on both sides, just inside the quarter panels. What a shock. The longitudinal frame members were almost gone, all but rotted away. I doubted that the Pattersons, always finicky to a fault with details, had known of this. They had long ago bought an attractive used sports car, and never looked beneath it.

Had they done so, they would have been dumbstruck. Some clever welder had installed two small steel beams, one on each side of the car, running from the front wheel well to the rear. This strengthened what remained of the two main frame members. It was a crude but effective piece of work, and was probably holding the car together. In the space of ten minutes, the vehicle had gone from a potentially restorable collectible to a worthless relic, except for its parts. I closed up the garage and went into the house, feeling empty inside.

We enjoyed the Thunderbird for a week or two. Carefully. Pictures were taken. I spent time learning more about original Thunderbirds. Their custom bodies, but not apparently their frames, had been provided by the Budd company, a taxi manufacturer. The T Bird was definitely solid and well-made. It deserved the growing attention it was receiving, and its rising values in the old car market.

But this was not a car to keep. I placed an ad in the classic car section of the *Washington Post*. The phone was ringing off the hook by 8 am the next morning, despite my detailed explanation of the frame rot and welded-in steel supports. Three men came by that afternoon to see and drive the car. One made a cash offer that balanced out the payment I'd made earlier to the Pattersons.

The buyer lived nearby, and his older brother was a fellow

boater and friend of mine. He told me he felt the car could be enjoyed locally, and at modest speeds. At his age, that suited him perfectly. He did not intend to change or repair anything, though he nodded agreeably when I suggested he change the oil and oil filter, something I'd not gotten done.

For the next three or four years, until we retired and moved back to New Hampshire, I enjoyed seeing the white Thunderbird driving slowly through our neighborhood, and on local roads, always with the convertible top raised. An old man was enjoying his dream car, and was obviously unworried about what lay under it.

A decade or more passed. Though I no longer felt particularly attracted to the model, something about the early Thunderbird remained with me. My tracking system still looked for nice examples and evaluated them. While I didn't consider the welded TBird a bad experience, it was definitely a disappointing one. I was probably looking for a good vintage Thunderbird experience, so these roadsters would end positively in my memories. But the years kept rolling by without finding what I was looking for — until, quite suddenly, I did.

I found the ad in *Hemmings Motor News*. It was another colonial white 1956 Thunderbird. But there the similarity ended. This example had both the convertible top and the porthole hardtop, as perfectly memorialized in the mythic film, *American Graffiti*. Informative emails and phone calls heightened my interest. The owner was a retired career airline captain, who lived in California, born and raised. He had bought the car from a Los Angeles used car dealer in 1958, when it was two years old. It had been kept in the family garage ever since. For the past decade, the TBird had been relegated to weekend driving, an excellent way to keep an old car running well, but not becoming worn out. Could there be a better provenance? I doubt it.

This car also had a clinching factor that weakened my usual reserve. Most 1956 TBirds came with one of two interior colors, black and white, as had our earlier example, or a more garish red and white. I understood and remembered that strong colors, reflecting our country's burgeoning post-war optimism, had been a trend in the 1950s. This was also the era of extended tail fins and other visual automotive celebrations. I thought the Thunderbird's interior color choices harsh, not in keeping with the plain, attractive lines of its roadster body. The discovery that the interior of this California car was a subdued turquoise blue and white was welcome. It looked beautiful in the photos, definitely "in keeping." I was sold. So was the car.

This 1956 Thunderbird experience was the exact opposite of the short-lived, welded example. As it arrived in Virginia, placed high on the open transporter, I was able to see the undercarriage and frame. No undercoating. No rust or discoloration. No evidence of leaking oil or grease. Just clean white sheet metal and a black frame, proof of why so many collectors look to the west for the old cars they seek. This well-cared-for California Thunderbird, owned for almost sixty years by someone knowledgeable about mechanical systems and committed to a high standard of preservation, was the kind of car any collector would be proud to own.

The pleasurable ownership of this roadster needs no lengthy description. Except to mention that owning a well-maintained, perfect old car fosters a sense of confidence and reliability we typically expect only of new or late model vehicles. Unlike many collector cars, a high quality old car can be taken anywhere. An owner can relax while driving, and not have to keep one eye always on the gauges, and one ear listening for an unwelcome sound.

The Thunderbird made the rounds of shows and rallies in northern New England. At one of those events, a man came up to me and asked if the car might be for sale. A second-generation Portuguese-American from a Cape Cod fishing family, he had been the first in his family to go to college, had found his start in business managing a Dunkin' Donuts store, and now owned three Dunkin' franchises himself.

I love that kind of story. They give us hope for our nation's future. But I told the man that the car was not for sale. He said he'd been looking for a Thunderbird with an interior other than red or black for years. He confided that it had taken twenty-two years for him to bring his businesses to a level where he could afford to purchase an early Thunderbird, the car on mental display in his personal American Dream.

"He had me from hello!" If there was ever someone to whom I'd want to sell the Thunderbird — and the car, of course, would eventually be sold to someone — it would be someone like this man. A self-made, hard-working, enterprising sort, who knew exactly what he wanted, and was prepared to pay for it. Our price negotiation took less than five minutes, and was sealed with a firm handshake, followed by his bear hug. He arrived at my home the next day, followed by a commercial rollback driven by a friend. The Thunderbird sat in the driveway, its porthole hardtop cinched securely in place. We exchanged the certified check and necessary paperwork. The broad grin never left the new owner's face. The car was pulled onto the rollback and secured. Another bear hug followed. The two vehicles left, taking the Thunderbird to her new home in western Massachusetts.

There are moments in the old car hobby when the planets are all in their proper places and perfectly aligned. This was one of them. The sun was high in the sky. A warm breeze passed over the land. I felt privileged to participate in one man's well-deserved attainment of his cherished symbol of success. And the purchase price had made me whole after an enjoyable three years with a beautiful vintage sports car.

What more can someone ask?

15

America's Junkyards: Sacred Ground

Zen's sense of detachment, of seeing all
things as happening by themselves, brings
a deep, illimitable quietude, like the gentle
ceaselessness of falling snow.

For many who noted the question on the movie poster, "Where were you in '62?" not with humor or ambivalence, but with keen interest in the soulful "memory lane" that was the cult classic *American Graffiti*, there were several scenes in the movie so touching that they reached deeply within, almost painfully, to a hidden reservoir of personal nostalgia.

For me, one of those scenes was the beautiful blonde in the white 1956 Thunderbird sought so avidly throughout the film by actor Richard Dreyfuss. Such a symbol of unavailability, so near and yet so far. This painful experience was shared by almost every male teenager, and certainly this one, in the 1950s and 1960s.

But the scene that forever lingers in my mind is not that one, nor is it Mel's Drive-In with its fabulous 1950s cruising machines and memorable music playing as the opening credits roll, or the Saturday night high school hop with Danny & the Juniors singing "At the Hop," or even the fateful drag race, where a brash outlaw, played by Harrison Ford in his first movie role, loses to the yellow deuce coupe and sees his hot rod '55 Chevy destroyed. It was none of these.

The scene that most moved me in *American Graffiti* takes place

178

when hot-rodder John Milner, played by actor Paul Le Mat, walks quietly through a local junkyard at midnight with MacKenzie Phillips, playing a preteen who, embarrassingly, has accidentally become his passenger on a night when everybody is watchfully cruising the main drag. There, among the wrecked and worn-out automobiles piled one on top of another, Milner points out the hot cars he'd raced and seen wrecked, the station wagon filled with teenagers, all lost in the heartbeat of a terrible head-on collision, a sober recitation of cars he'd known in the valley that had, in the end, all found their way to this lonely automobile graveyard. The scene had a solemnity completely out of character with that ultimate coming-of-age film.

I loved that scene. It brought me back to Ralph's Truck Junkyard in my hometown, to Banks Auto Body and Junkyard in Dale City, Virginia, to the dozens of junkyards I'd roamed, here and there, looking for vintage car or truck sheet metal or mechanical parts. Or not looking for anything at all, except the experience of being alone among the old vehicles, feeling the solitude and the sadness, the extinguished lives of the vehicles and, sometimes, those who rode in them. One can find peace walking in junkyards, a placid calm among acres of abandoned cars and trucks, their stories showing plain or long forgotten.

Once, living in southern California, a few of us took a weekend drive to a business billed as the biggest junkyard in America. It was located in southern Arizona, near the old mining town of Bisbee. There, on thirty flat acres, over 7,000 old cars sat in the open, their paint slowly fading in the hot sun. The cars weren't stacked. Instead, they were set in rows by make and model. How would you feel walking down a row of more than one hundred 1949-1951 Ford coupes, sedans, and convertibles? Another even longer row of 1955-1957 Chevrolets? The vehicles, all from the sunny Southwest, had bodies and frames the nation's salt-deploying rust belt could only envy. But the same hot, dry weather and bright sun that preserved the sheet metal, had baked and shredded fabric or leather interiors, and canvas or vinyl convertible tops.

It was awe-inspiring, looking at those rows and rows of similar cars as far as the eye could see, lined up like a mighty army massed to take the field. It was something every car collector should see. But it left me cold. Too organized? Too sanitized? Or just too much of everything. Too endless. I don't know. But the experience never let me get out of myself, as was so often true in other junkyards.

That weekend in Arizona occurred many years ago. More recently, I had a second experience involving an aggregation of old cars that time had forgotten. Hidden in plain sight on Route 117 in Pikeville, North Carolina, its American Motors sign still mounted on a showroom roof now partially caved in, sits an AMC dealership that closed abruptly, decades ago. A chain-link fence with padlocked gate was installed around its perimeter. And there it sits today, over one hundred cars left exactly where they were the day the dealership closed.

The "why" of how this happened is, as you might expect, complicated. The family that owned the dealership had owned car businesses down through the decades, favoring smaller independent manufacturers instead of the Big Three. Studebaker. Willys-Overland. Mercer. Kaiser. Frasier. And finally, in the mid-1950s, AMC. American Motors was formed from the merger of Nash-Kelvinator and Hudson, each barely clinging to life. The merger worked after a fashion. Until it didn't.

In 1973, the dealership was moved to the Pikeville location along Route 117. Selling the respected AMC models brought success. But in 1979 AMC partnered with Renault. Later, Renault bought a major stake in AMC, then introduced an American-built version of the Renault to be sold by AMC. The cars sold well at first, but proved highly problematic over time, so much so that dealerships could not keep up with repairs.

The Pikeville dealership reacted by refusing to sell the Renaults. They'd joined AMC, confident of Nash's strong engineering culture and respected build quality. Eventually, Renault sold AMC to Chrysler Corporation, producer of today's successful Jeep line. The dealership responded by shutting down and fencing off the property. The legend of a mythic ghost dealership began to make the rounds.

But the dealership never completely shut down. Rather, it went inactive. Moribund. And nature took over, as it always does. The cars are still there. And the dealership and surrounding outdoor parking, once macadam and mowed lawns, now wildly overgrown by tall grass, high bushes and even trees, is open by appointment.

A captivating vision, it was impossible to resist. My good friend, Mike Stansel, and sons-in-law, Tom Milam and David Marr, agreed to mount an expedition to explore this "lost city of old car gold." Our Friday night rendezvous was in Roanoke Rapids, somewhat north of Pikeville, at a Motel 6 just down the road from Ralph's Barbecue, a famous down-home eatery off I-95, where we would later gather, break cornbread, and discuss our adventure.

Early the next morning we set out. An hour later we were parked outside the dealership fence, staring at the foliage-shrouded cars within. We called the dealership owners to gain entrance. What followed, as the padlock was removed from the gate, was a unique if somewhat sad adventure. It had rained overnight. The ground was saturated and boggy. It was summer, hot and quite humid, conditions guaranteed to bring out all manner of persistent insects, including the largest and most avaricious mosquitos ever seen by our party.

But there they were, AMC cars of every type and description: Hornets and Ambassadors, Ramblers, Pacers, and Spirits. The front and one side of the showroom building had rows of display cars, arranged as they'd been parked before the dealership closed. It was a struggle to get close to the cars, because of the water, but also due to all the overgrown grass and bushes everywhere. We spent an hour or two struggling through the forbidding acreage and its jungle-like environment. No one got lost, a near thing perhaps, but we were all wet. Almost without exception, the cars were complete and technically restorable. In practical terms, however, few would ever be claimed, as the costs to overcome years of exposure to weather and benign neglect would significantly exceed the value of a restored AMC car.

A possible exception were the sought-after muscle cars, the AMXs and Javelins. These performance models had a collector following and rising values. Later, as we ventured carefully into the ruined showroom and service area, we came upon several of these models, rainwater trickling on them through the missing sections of roof. Two of the Javelins were rare Mark Donahue editions. These cars were technically new, never registered or delivered, a stunning discovery. But even a new car would require a complete restoration after sitting unattended in the elements for over thirty years.

The service area to the rear of the showroom had an intact roof, and housed 1964 presidential candidate Senator Barry Goldwater's personal 1969 AMX. More notably, there were four Nash-Healeys stored in the service space. A sports car sold as both roadster and coupe, these were rare collectible cars. About 500 were produced from 1951 to 1954. The condition of the Nash-Healeys varied widely. Two were definitely restorable, another possibly so. The fourth had been damaged and appeared to have spent time outside as well. At best, a parts car.

Our guide reminded us several times that "everything was for sale." Earlier, we had inquired about prices on the muscle cars. These proved higher than warranted, given their forlorn condition, ending any interest we had in purchasing. Finally, tour complete, we were escorted through the soaked foliage to the gate. We thanked our host, then got in our car to depart, as the gate's padlock clicked behind us. Though the stories about the dealership had romanticized the place, and suggested there were bargains available among the deteriorating inventory, these fictions took nothing away from a morning's exploration of a unique automotive entity frozen in time, the kind of old car adventure best undertaken with family and friends.

An hour later, our quartet was at Ralph's trough, drinking sweet tea, and snorting down North Carolina barbecue, stewed tomatoes, collard greens, and pecan pie, with all the fixins'. We regaled each other with the strange things sighted at the dealership. A tree growing up through the shredded remains of a convertible top. Cars left on wet ground slowly submerging in the earth, their wheels already sunken and disappeared. Brand new vintage muscle cars sitting in the showroom, the rain dripping down.

A unique experience for each of us? Sure 'nuff.

The visits to Arizona and North Carolina, each unique in its own way, and not to be missed, were nonetheless not the type of experience I'd sought from the junkyards I'd visited through the years. Those were like going into a church. Solemn. Peaceful. Quiet, except for the buzzing of the bees. A place to get in touch with yourself, to let the mind wander, to commune with the old cars and trucks piled indiscriminately around, waiting to tell their stories, wishing to feel the road under their tires again.

Junkyards are, in their own way, sacred ground. A place to think your thoughts and let memories linger. A place to appreciate what has gone before.

16

Mercedes–Benz: A Century as the World's Standard

In Zen, superior work always has the quality of an accident.

Owning Mercedes-Benz automobiles for over fifty years does not make one an authority on the marque. But it does suggest a certain depth of knowledge, made credible by the fact that those Mercedes were each more than twenty years old when acquired. Getting to know a vehicle toward the end of its statistical life is revealing. The strengths have endured, or they have not. The weaknesses are obvious, and often perturbing.

My first Mercedes was an accidental acquisition. While living and working on Florida's panhandle during the late 1960s, I traded in a late model car without air-conditioning for a 1963 Mercedes 220SE four-door sedan with Behr a/c so frigid it would freeze Coca-Cola bottles solid on the car's front seat. These 220S or SE models were called finback or pontoon cars, the latter term derived from the "pontoon-like" body styling. Sturdy and reliable, if not aesthetically creative, they suited a professional owner class who wished to demonstrate success, without appearing to be doing so.

I loved the car. Its subdued appearance in pale yellow was seductive. I was sold on its teeth-clenching a/c frigidity in the unrelieved summer heat and humidity of Florida, conditions so different from my native New England. My wife disliked the car, so be forewarned about how this story concludes. The 220SE managed to survive more than a year with us, serving without incident, though the failure of two retreaded tires required new rubber all around.

The "E" in 220SE finally brought down the house. "E" stood for fuel injection, and when the car's fuel injection pump failed, we learned to our dismay that its replacement cost was more than three months of my salary. My wife's position had won the day. We were in the market for a new car with a warranty. This turned out to be a dark green 1967 Volvo 122 wagon, a car so safe and reliable that it earned the moniker "Amazon." Our Mercedes brought more in trade than we'd hoped, reducing the monthly bill, and the discord.

A Mercedes-less decade followed. The nation prepared to celebrate its bicentennial in 1976. I was honored that my small New Hampshire town asked me to be the guest speaker for the event. I spent months anguishing over what to say, unable to decide what topic to speak on. Unwisely, I spoke at length on several subjects, thereby delivering one of the longest, most convoluted, presentations ever heard by the once tolerant townspeople. It's telling that I was asked to speak again only after a hiatus of thirty-six years.

For all Americans the nation's bicentennial was a high point in their lives. The honor given me created an even higher high for me. With my head still spinning from those ready smiles and firm handshakes, I fell for another pale yellow ("harvest gold") Mercedes sedan on a used car lot in a nearby town. It was a 1973 450SE in like-new condition, with very low miles. The price was surprisingly low. Mercedes were not yet common on America's roads and highways. I convinced my wife to support the purchase by selling the 1951 Ford Country Squire "Woodie" station wagon we'd used for family vacations.

The 450SE sedan was the finest modern automobile I have ever owned or will own. It was the smoothest, most powerful car on the road, with a cabin more silent than any vehicle in my experience. Over the three years we owned the car, it did nothing but impress. Succeeding years of this model, or its extended wheelbase cousin, the 450SEL, suffered due to U.S. import regulations. A catalytic converter was added in 1974, reducing performance and gas mileage. The bumpers and rear-view mirrors became heavier in appearance, clad in thick unsightly rubber. The 1973 450SE was the perfected beauty of the 220 series, the first model in Mercedes' line of luxury "S" models.

Some weekends we took off for Las Vegas or Phoenix, less to see the cities than to experience the car crossing the desert at significant speed, while we remained in the cocoon of that eerily silent cabin of leather and burl wood. The rapture ended when our family moved to southern Italy for several years. I sold the Mercedes to a collector friend in Los Angeles.

If I could have one car in my life, the 1973 450SE would be the one. A perfect car by any measure, I occasionally check to see if one might be available. They are, but very few. Most need restoration, always expensive on highly engineered cars. Convertibles and coupes tend to be valued more highly by collectors, while sedans and wagons are consumed and forgotten. This suggests I will never have another 450SE, though I keep searching as the years go by.

About the same time we owned the 450SE, in the late 1970s, I found another interesting Mercedes prospect. It was a white 1958 220SE four-seat cabriolet (convertible), with red leather interior and black canvas roof. It was being sold by a foreign car dealer in Phoenix, Arizona. By this time, I'd allowed myself to develop the mistaken notion that I knew something about buying vintage cars. This led me to qualify the car by phone and letter, then fly to Phoenix intent on making the purchase, and driving back to San Diego.

In Phoenix, I gave the Mercedes a complete inspection, and reviewed its documentation. Then I put it on a lift, and went over the undercarriage, or so I thought. I drove the car in the city and on the highway. It was a beautiful machine, and passed every test. I was surprised to find the car equipped with a rare Hydrac transmission. This involved a standard shifter without a clutch pedal. The clutch was a flexible joint on the steering column's shift lever, unusual, but simple to operate. I came to admire its functional simplicity.

I went ahead and bought the car, filled the tank, and set out for San Diego as evening descended across the hot, dry desert, arriving before midnight after a stifling but uneventful trip. The car was used regularly, particularly for weekend family adventures, and never caused a problem. Two years went by. One day, my wife called in the late afternoon. She'd used the 220SE to pick up our daughters at school, stopped for groceries, and was driving home when, passing over a rain drain, the Mercedes dipped into the depression, then recovered — except for the left rear, which remained lowered. Since the car seemed to drive normally, my wife took it home, parked in the garage, and called me to describe her experience.

I told her not to worry. I'd look the car over after dinner. My guess was that one of the rear main springs had bounced out of its retaining saddle, passing over the rain drain, and could be re-seated with a jack and crowbar. My guess was nowhere near the reality. I crawled under the car that evening to inspect the undercarriage, using a garage light to see what had happened. It was immediately clear that the car had *no* frame behind the rear axle. It was rusted away, then covered with various metal scraps, wire mesh, and gallons of "Bondo" body putty. Later I learned that the car had lived most of its life not in Arizona, but in Minnesota, where salt is spread heavily on winter roads, much as in New England. It was a clever job, including enough metal content in the fakery to fool my inspection magnet — *and* me.

When you make a mistake on this scale, the remedy is to admit the error, then develop a plan to repair the damage, and recover as much as possible of your investment. An expert welder soon re-created the frame and undercarriage, over-strengthening to such a degree that the repaired car was probably stronger than the original. It drove as before. I took the opportunity to repaint the exterior in a lustrous black, which set off the red leather interior. Ironically, by the time the 220SE was repaired and repainted, we were preparing to go overseas for several years. Only one vehicle could be shipped. As usual, it was our reliable Volvo wagon.

I was in a quandary about the Mercedes. Even though I'd

completed an expensive repair to insure the car's integrity and crash-worthiness, I was loathe to sell the vehicle without revealing what had happened. Several fellow car collectors, seeing the quality of the repair, advised otherwise. They were probably correct in their advice, but that course wasn't for me.

Instead, I ran the car through a reputable West Coast auction after taping a 4"x5" card to the windshield. The card described the structural failure, the repair work completed, even the welder's contact information. The car sold quickly on the auction's first day but, predictably, for much less than those somewhat rare models were then bringing. I was undeterred, poorer financially, but confident that one seldom goes wrong doing the right thing.

My years in southern Italy were spent searching for a vintage Ferrari or Lamborghini to bring back to the United States. Success never capped that effort. I did, however, come upon many intriguing cars while traveling — pre- and post-war Fiat 500 "Topolinos" (little mouse), surely one of the world's cutest vintage cars; a decidedly un-cute, ultra-lightweight, and scary-fast Fiat Dino Spyder (convertible) sporting a six-cylinder Ferrari motor, and a 1960s Mercedes 250SL "Pagoda" roadster converted to liquid propane, an exceptional, priced-right car, except that the propane tank filled the entire trunk and raised concerns about a rear-end crash. Returning home three years later, we were unable to welcome a European automobile to American roads.

Inevitably, one's searches lead to other, sometimes richer, opportunities. In the chapter on the 1936 Cadillac V12, for example, you may recall our starstruck discovery of a Mercedes 450SLC coupe in a California dealership window. We fell hard for its unique design. As the coupe's price exceeded our annual salary at the time, thoughts of purchase were deferred, though a vow was taken that, one day, we would own an SLC, whose louvered rear-pillar opera windows not only improved the driver's vision, but provided a trademark identification feature.

We owned five SLC coupes over the next three decades. The first, a stunningly original, one-owner 1973 model, in sand beige with palomino leather, came from Palm Desert, California, and remained with us over thirty years. The car's original owner and I corresponded until he passed away a few years ago. A rare 1981 500SLC in teal with aluminum body panels and ABS brakes was with us almost twenty years. Its buyer in Oslo, Norway, was so pleased with the car, and how it was represented, he invited us to spend a summer at their family's second home in a small village beside a fjord, and to use our former coupe to tour Norway. The resulting visit to that country was a singular chapter in our traveling lives, creating an enduring friendship between the families. Many people we met in the old car hobby became fast friends.

Other SLCs wandered into, then out of our lives. An oil executive did not want to take his '74 model to a Key West salt-air retirement. A local Iranian family, returning to their country, saw our SLC, and asked if we might buy theirs. Several diplomats in Washington, D.C., had these coupes as personal cars, which they advertised in local classified ads when they were reassigned. The cars were offered well under value. It was simple to make necessary repairs, then put an attractive Mercedes back in circulation at an affordable price to a new owner.

I will always have a special feeling for the Mercedes 450SLC coupe. Few collectors know of the cars' international road-rally triumphs, or the homologation process for Formula One Grand Prix qualifying that resulted in the creation of the limited production, lightweight 1981 500SLC at the end of the 107 series. For whatever reason, the collecting community never came to value the car. Possibly, it was seen as a changeling, a by-product of 107 roadsters. But SLC coupe owners knew what they had, a personal performance car in the grand-touring tradition. The lines of the coupe body, particularly the C pillar, were Teutonic perfection with a dash of Italian elegance. The SLC's twelve-inch-longer wheelbase made driving more comfortable, particularly on poor road surfaces, while the occasional rear seat for three, and enlarged trunk, created more room compared to its sister roadsters.

We approached the present without a Mercedes project, but not for want of trying. I had purchased a new S430 sedan for my wife in 2003, eliciting her promise that she'd drive it for a minimum of ten years. Instead, and perhaps to prove a point, she's now driven it for seventeen years. It's still going strong. Who knows? In a few years, it may become a collectible!

In time, I began to look more vigorously for another Mercedes project. I finally settled on the 560SL roadster, the last of the 107 series SL roadsters produced from 1971 (1973 in the U.S.) to 1989. In its rugged German simplicity, the 560SL was the culmination of series development, a complex, highly engineered vehicle, which sold when new for over $60,000. Most of the production was sold in the United States.

When I began my search, there was a surfeit of 560SL examples for sale, most at very reasonable prices, given mileage and condition. This suggested that the collector community had yet to develop an appreciation for the model. Such a situation offers visionary collectors an opportunity to purchase before recognition of the car's collectibility drives values higher.

Three decades after production, I reasoned that the cost of repairs for such a complex auto, let alone the chilling thought of a restoration's expense, was likely a factor in deterring interest. The successful professionals of the 1980s, then in their forties and fifties, who had the chutzpah and financial wherewithal to purchase these cars when new, were by now in their seventies and eighties, and had long since sold these attention-grabbing, high-end steeds from their salad days. If I was correct, these factors accounted for the large numbers of 560SLs available, as well as their lower values. Typical examples sold routinely for about one quarter of their sticker price.

I sought what collectors would term a "nice driver," a complete car, without damage or rust, good to look at from a distance, and safe and reliable on the road. I began my search on Web sites, such as Autotrader and CarGurus, which advertised classic car categories, as well as later model used cars.

Soon, with all the digital information now available, I'd completed two tasks: construction of a pricing model by year, condition and location, and an outline of trade-offs I'd be willing to make in purchasing a 560SL. I spent time kibitzing online auctions for 560SLs that met my criteria. This familiarized me with the market, particularly the differences between asking and selling prices, a helpful negotiating tool, but also of importance determining demand for the 560SL.

I looked into the model's problems, weaknesses, and eccentricities. Online blogs were helpful. I also interviewed owners, including a local 560SL owner who'd owned his car since new. Before buying an old car, it is useful to know the cost of frequent failure items, also to establish that those items remain available from the OEM (original equipment manufacturer). Fortunately, while supply sources existed for Mercedes models going back decades, including the 560SL, the vintage Mercedes owner's "ace in the hole" was available — Mercedes' Classic Car Center in Irvine, California, which twice each week flies parts orders direct from Germany.

My final effort before preparing to buy a car was to estimate future collector interest and predict future value. If done exactingly, this establishes a budget floor for purchase, and for the repairs or restoration efforts that may follow. If the estimates are accurate, actual costs over the ownership period will be roundly known, and may be recovered when the vehicle is sold. Experienced collectors know the importance of making well-reasoned estimates of collectibility and future value as a primary means to reduce risk and uncertainty.

By all measures, the 560SL showed future promise. It was an impressive vehicle, almost prohibitively expensive when new, a powerful, responsive driver, and the inheritor of three decades of model development by a world-renowned luxury marque. Delivered with both a canvas convertible top and removable hardtop, it was a highly regarded automobile, although not limited in production. My analysis suggested that a driver-condition example ought to bring twice or more its present value within ten years, a reasonable timeframe for my ownership.

The 560SL roadster was produced for four years, from 1986 through 1989. I did not consider the first two production years, 1986 and 1987, because, as with any new model, there were learning-curve issues. The bugs had to be found and slain. Studying the model's evolution, a number of improvements were made in the 1988 model. I also left the 1989 model out of consideration. Collectors often pay premiums for the initial or final production years of collectibles. The first 1953 Corvette or 1955 Thunderbird, the last 1976 Cadillac convertible, as examples, which brought premium prices on resale. My observation has been that production premiums, with few exceptions, tend eventually to disappear.

My research revealed that the best-preserved 560SLs had already enjoyed some price appreciation: 1988 examples with 30,000 to 60,000 miles brought prices between $25,000 and $40,000, while rarer cars, with mileage between 5,000 and 30,000, pampered garage queens, much-admired, little-used "objects of art," brought $50,000 and, in several cases, $65,000. A few examples having sold at or above their sticker price was an indication that all collectible 560SLs should eventually see their values climb.

With my research completed, I determined to find a complete, original 1988 560SL, without rust or damage repair, and with mileage in the 60,000 to 85,000 range. My study suggested an expected price range of $15,000 to $22,000 for the car. A number of 1988 examples were on offer in various venues, particularly online. I watched carefully, waiting for something special.

I hoped to find an example near the bottom of my estimated price range, with appropriate mileage, but in above-average condition. After months of searching, I found a candidate 1988 model in an auction online. Located in the mid-Atlantic area, it was a one-owner vehicle offered from the estate of an elderly couple by the executor, a relative. The 86,000 original miles were appealing, as was the exterior color, a metallic tan-grey "smoke silver," with a light-tan interior. Detailed photographs of the car revealed only minor body or interior flaws.

It appeared I had found the clean, affordable, well-maintained driver I'd sought. I found reinforcement in the auction's boldly written claims. Little used in recent years, the car was reported in excellent condition, with several thousand dollars recently spent to upgrade brakes, struts, and exhaust, fix minor leaks, and add premium radials to insure safety and reliability. Repair and maintenance records would be included with the car's paperwork. If all proved true, I anticipated possible savings, based on the list of completed repairs I'd not have to undertake.

Here I pause the story to conduct a discussion with you, dear reader. This book spans many decades of a car collector's experiences. But it almost never happened. Though the concept had been in my head for years, one objection stood in the way. Though I've been a writer throughout my life, I'm a reserved person, who has become more reserved with age. Writing in the first person and describing personal experiences, some embarrassing, was out of my comfort zone. The obvious conundrum: it's difficult to tell a personal story without being personal.

This cautionary tale you're now reading about the 1988 560SL offered an opportunity to balance the ego you may find shining through in earlier chapters. Its facts should counter whatever unruly hubris escaped through my pen, as it is impossible to brag about failure. Most poignantly, this story should remind you that even experienced car collectors, having spent decades buying old cars, can still get it completely wrong. I offer this story as a reminder of the need for due caution in the purchase of *any* old car or truck, boat or house, or any valuable asset. If this chapter prevents a single reader from falling prey to those few predators in our hobby, and instead encourages more risk-averse, defensive buying strategies, then the unsavory revelations soon to appear will have been worth whatever weight I might bear.

Let's now continue the 560SL story.

As the online auction ended, I was the highest bidder for the 1988 560SL at $12,600. But I was not the winner, as my bid didn't meet the seller's hidden reserve price. We began phone and e-mail correspondence, common in these situations, in an effort to find a middle ground and conclude a deal. The seller revealed his reserve had been $18,000, based upon an appraisal made after recent repairs were completed. After further discussions, a compromise was found, and a price of $15,000 agreed on. This was at the low-end of the range I expected to pay for a car in this condition and mileage range. The seller agreed to pay for the $450 transport fee to New Hampshire. I wired payment for the car per the auction's terms.

Despite all the "green lights" in the purchase process, I broke a fundamental rule of car collecting by failing to put "boots on the ground" — hands, eyes, and feet directly on the car before making *any* payment, even a deposit. This principle required that you travel to the location of intended purchase and carefully inspect the vehicle, especially the undercarriage, and on a lift if possible. Then the car must be driven to confirm its road-worthiness, and each of the car's systems operated to determine proper functionality. Finally, the car must be proven to be the one depicted in photographs and descriptions.

If the car is too distant for cost-effective travel, there are expert professional evaluation services at your disposal, some certified as appraisers. These, for a modest fee, typically a few hundred dollars, will visit the seller, inspect, evaluate, photograph, and drive the vehicle on your behalf. They provide a detailed report within a day or two, which includes dozens of close-up photographs, systems evaluations, and test-drive results. I used auto-inspection services a number of times and, in all but one case, the evaluations and photos were decisive in *not* purchasing a car that I'd hoped to buy. In this case, I failed to follow my own standing rule. The information was so consistent and positive, so completely convincing, that I bypassed the one step that might have saved me from myself, by inspecting the car myself or paying for an expert on-site inspection and appraisal. Hell, I blew it!

Almost predictably — one might say, deservedly — breakdowns began after payment was made. Communications became erratic. Answers to questions became sketchier. E-mails went unanswered. More pointedly, the car wasn't delivered in a few days, as is customary in the hobby. A month went by, as my concerns steadily rose. Finally, on a rainy afternoon, the transporter arrived, and the car was deposited in my garage. I turned on the lights, and walked around the Mercedes, soon realizing the differences between the photographs and the imperfect car before me.

Sobered, I asked myself, "Could this be the car I'd seen, then bought, in the online auction?

It wasn't.

Wear showed everywhere. The clear coat on the upper surfaces of hood, trunk and all four fenders was de-laminated. There were dings and defects on every body surface. The "like-new" brown canvas convertible top was decrepit, its seams shredding apart. The steering wheel's leather cover had split, and was held in place with electrical tape. The right front bumperette had been shorn off, leaving only its mounting bracket. This was but my initial assessment. One thing was clear. A significant misrepresentation had taken place. I had facilitated the fraud by not following long-established procedures.

I spent a weekend going over the car, then drove it to assess performance and reliability. Forgivingly, the drive revealed few other problems. One of the positive surprises was that there was no evidence of rust or damage repair on or under the vehicle. On the road, the car drove tightly, powerfully and responsively, just as a thirty-year-old, low-mileage car should. After the bitter initial discoveries, the roadster was a pleasure to operate. I began to wonder if the troubled vehicle could be resurrected.

Two other mysteries were discovered which added to the car's enigma. Shockingly, the vehicle identification number (VIN) plate wasn't the same as that on the bill of sale or other paperwork. It was close, but had two unmatched numbers. The mileage shown on the instrument panel was about twenty thousand miles *less* than that listed in the auction *and* in the documentation which came with the car: 68,000 instead of 86,000. A recording error? Surely a one-in-a-million occurrence in the history of automobile sales. Mileage errors, real or "rolled back," are more typically altered in the opposite direction.

What to do at this point?

I got in touch with the seller. He responded. Leaning heavily on his responsibilities as estate executor, and its burdensome demands, and his job, which required frequent travel, he attempted to explain the car's delivered condition, an explanation which was pure nonsense when measured against the incongruities. You need not be bored with the details. Meanwhile, the personal check he'd provided for the car's transport was returned for insufficient funds. A promised replacement never arrived. Promises of restitution were made, some by the seller's attorney, but nothing was ever received.

I contacted the police department in the owner's location, presenting the facts, forwarded photos and documentary evidence, then waited while an investigation was completed. Months later, I received a phone call. A detective team had surfaced additional complaints of auto-sales fraud involving the person who sold me the 560SL. Other unspecified legal matters were also involved. The investigative file was being forwarded to the city's prosecuting attorney for possible legal action. I'd be informed of results. That was two years ago. Knowing something of the seller's location and its "*Sopranos*-like" reputation for widespread crime, I'm not surprised. They likely had bigger fish to fry.

I realized I had two decisions to make. The first, whether or not to take legal action, using the police's investigative report as a means to seek justice, and, hopefully, financial restitution. This involved finding, interviewing and hiring a lawyer or law firm hundreds of miles away, and spending money without a guarantee that the expenditure would produce anything in return. From what my life had taught me about the law, it seemed that people often won judgments in court and were awarded damages, sometimes substantial, yet never recovered the first penny. Why? Because the person or entity that had been clever enough to illegally damage them, was also smart enough to avoid the reach of the justice system. I decided not to seek a legal solution, nor to dwell in the past.

The second decision was more difficult. What should be done with the 560SL? I could cut my losses and sell the car "as is" locally in New England, where few 560SLs are seen, or possibly in Germany. I'd learned that the model was now being imported by its country of origin.

In the meantime, I grew to enjoy driving the car, despite its unwelcome flaws. Its heart beat strongly, and it wanted to please. I'd developed a wistful desire to put the car right. To support that somewhat irrational thought, the roadster had a solid body, and a drivetrain that would pass anyone's test for performance and responsiveness. All systems worked properly, or what was needed to make them so was known and affordable. I settled upon a light restoration, bringing the 560SL to a reasonable standard of appearance, and ensuring its reliability.

The decision to keep the car and make improvements surprised no one, including you, dear reader. I seem to have a certain history. The project was divided into three parts: replacing the desiccated convertible top, exterior bodywork and repaint, and mechanical and systems work. With winter arriving, the need to remove the hardtop to provide full access for the two more complicated work phases was obvious. Replacing the convertible top became the priority. A new ragtop would allow all-weather driving. But when stowed, it provided access for the other work. Fortunately, a top and interior business was located just a few miles away. They ordered a black German Haartz canvas top, and soon had it installed on the original frame. A perfect fit.

Next was bodywork to remove the dings, then repainting. After receiving recommendations from fellow car collectors in the area, I made an appointment to meet Matt Woods, the owner of Eastcoast Classic Auto & Restoration in nearby North Hampton, a body and paint shop which had specialized for years in refinishing Oldsmobile 442 muscle cars, gaining a reputation for award-winning projects. However, as Matt sheepishly admitted in our first meeting, they had never refinished a Mercedes. But I sensed he was interested. His crew were performance car guys who saw the 560SL as something of a supercar. It was also helpful that the roadster sat just outside the office window, quietly sending its message. "Let's get it on! Paint me !!!"

With both of us aware of the pushy Germanic presence peering though the window, Matt and I got down to business, established the scope of work, hours and materials required, timelines, and possible uncertainties. Having determined in our discussion that we both sought a finished product we'd be proud of, we agreed the car would be stripped to bare metal, while leaving the body assembled. Visible imperfections would be removed, and then the car would be painted and trim reinstalled. A detailed estimate came within a few days.

I found the hourly rates reasonable. The total hours, however, confirmed that we were definitely back in the restoration business. The smoke-silver paint alone, available only from Mercedes, cost almost $2000. I agreed to deliver a list of replacement fasteners and fittings, gaskets and grommets, new taillights and headlights, sill plates, and other body items, including badges and titling. Though still passable in appearance, most of the originals would look unacceptable when contrasted with fresh paint. A used fiberglass radiator air dam was found to replace the damaged original.

A week later, just before Christmas, the Mercedes was delivered to Matt's shop. As the crocuses rose through the melting New England snow in mid-April, the project was complete. A new car was born, in some ways better than new. I'd stopped by a few times to observe the work in progress, and to affirm my interest, believing that capable people are best left alone with their tasks. I was surprised at the level of effort and the steady progress being made. It's obvious when skilled professionals are deeply involved in their work. Progress payments kept everyone satisfied. Fortunately, the final invoice didn't require another mortgage.

The project thoroughly reanimated me, especially after the depressing experience of the 560SL's badly misrepresented — *and* managed — purchase. The car's exterior was now flawless, its paint deeper and more luminous than the original. The time and expense taken to get all the details correct were obvious. Finally, a car to be proud of, and one that could again be proud of itself. Everywhere the car went, fellow collectors raved at its finish, door and fender gaps, and the attention to detail shown in the finishing assembly. Matt Woods and his helpers could be justifiably proud of such a result.

As the car passed through the stages from beast to beauty, I received additional information from the police department, and learned more about the situation. The seller was, in fact, the executor of his late grandparents' estate, who were indeed the original and only owners of the car until they passed on. But there was more to the story. An attorney was now assisting full time with the estate settlement, not because it was complex, but because the executor, though not yet middle-aged, had suffered early-onset dementia, and needed written lists to remember who he was, and what he needed to do each day. I now understood some of the earlier confusion — the inaccurately documented VIN and mileage, for example. Over time, I felt some peace, realizing that what had occurred wasn't intentionally a crime. The detectives added that the attorney had asked for my contact information to arrange restitution for whatever "misunderstandings" had occurred. I'm still waiting for that call.

The 560SL project was concluded, except for providing additional mechanical assurance. For this, we turned to the local Mercedes dealership, which, fortunately, had a service manager with genuine interest in older Mercedes, and two mechanics who, many years earlier, had actually worked on the model. Selected repairs were completed — brakes, struts, radiator, the cabin's environmental system, and a head gasket replaced to eliminate a small but irritating oil leak. If your memory, loyal reader, takes you back to this 560SL's online auction, you may recall that these repairs closely mirror the list claimed as having been completed previously.

The work took several weeks, during which I was able to purchase four used but restored wheel rims, and a good used steering wheel, which the dealership installed. A Mercedes dealership conveys an unnerving image of eye-popping labor rates and staggering repair bills. Suffice it to say that they didn't give away their contributions. But both the work and parts were fully guaranteed. The mechanics took obvious pleasure in working on a favorite older model. The service manager went out of his way to provide good value. I was very satisfied with the outcome.

Hence, the finished roadster, its light-turned-moderate restoration now complete, returned home to take up residence with our family. It brought with it the same kind of fun and the same deeply satisfying feelings I'd had for more than half a century with other old cars returned to a semblance of originality. But was it perfect? No, it wasn't. Perfection is an impossible standard to judge anything made by humans or, more pointedly perhaps, man himself. As an engineer and former test pilot, my critical skills sensed several minor imperfections deep in the 560SL's drivetrain — small matters, entirely tolerable, and not safety-related. Perhaps, I thought, I should suppress my training and enjoy the car as it was, slightly imperfect. This I resolved to do.

Until Fate intervened with intentions of its own.

Two years passed. I enjoyed the Mercedes SL more all the time. It was a joy to drive, even the exhaust's subtle rumble struck the perfect note, and I had learned the habit, acquired with some difficulty, of being blind to her few minor flaws, some so subtle that I'd have difficulty finding the words to explain. Then one day, purely by chance, I met the one man who would understand my remaining concerns, and could do so without my saying a single word.

My best friend of some forty-five years, Mike Stansel, whom you met in earlier chapters of this book, always visited for a week, spring and fall. We went wandering through small towns and on back roads, looking for old cars and trucks, bookstores and antique shops, in no particular order. This tradition had been ongoing for thirty years. Initially, it was based in Virginia, which meant our wanderings encompassed that state and others nearby. We'd worn all those roads and towns, old-car places, small and large, and old-stuff shops, clear down to a frazzle.

Mike's initial trip to New Hampshire, after my wife and I moved back to our hometown on the coast in retirement, offered virgin territory. But was it? As the date for Mike's arrival fell due, I consulted an atlas hoping to find enough of interest to suit our intentions. There were few old-car places this far north, though there seemed to be countless antique shops and bookstores. By the time Mike arrived, it became apparent that the Granite State couldn't compete for the numbers of old-car locations we'd visited in the mid-Atlantic down through the years.

But we found an alternative. We decided to explore promising antique shops which, when lined up on the map, took us north near the Vermont state line and the Canadian border. We'd ambled about before. We enjoyed each others' company, and never failed to find interesting things to see and do. Once or twice, we'd come upon something so unique and unforgettable, that it could only have been found by someone *not* looking for it.

You are correct, loyal reader. That's *very* Zen.

On the second day of our adventure, we were having a relaxed and enjoyable time, as always. We spent the night in a highway lodging near Dartmouth College in West Lebanon, New Hampshire, enjoying the company of working men tired of the road. Dinner was served in a huge high-ceilinged room, filled with live bushes and small trees. A babbling brook ran between the tables. In a bar filled with men relaxing and drinking some of their day's pay, we were the only customers served solid food. Several empty tables surrounded us. In retrospect, the scene was surreal — and also very Zen.

Before turning in, we consulted our map, and decided to drive south the next day, along the Connecticut River, which forms the border between Vermont and New Hampshire. As we started the car and drove out in the morning, it was raining, off and on. After passing through several small towns, I began wondering if we'd planned a poor sightseeing route. We'd seen nothing worth our stopping. Then, as that thought sat just behind my eyes, irritating me, we came upon a fascinating church, one of the most unique either of us had ever seen. Mike wanted photos, so we pulled in.

The church was perfectly designed, though on a outsized scale for a town of perhaps fifty homes and a few hundred people. We later learned that a descendant of the eminent American sculptor, Augustus Saint-Gaudens, who had lived and worked nearby, and was famous for his statues of Civil War-era figures such as Lincoln, Grant, and Sherman, but much celebrated for his peerless designs for our country's early gold coinage, had given carte blanche for the church's design and construction.

The result was a borderline "wonder of the world." The aluminum roof was dark green. The structure's various sections were built to resemble a farming village. Here was the grain elevator. There was the quintessential New England covered bridge, set perpendicular to the main entrance, allowing cars to drop church attendees off under cover when it rained or snowed. It was altogether charming.

Mike left the car to take his pictures. I glanced across the church's broad south lawn, and noticed a small white building, apparently a car-repair business, given the three dozen European cars parked in rows around it, several in the latter stages of distress. I'd found my morning's calling. Calling to Mike to follow me when he'd finished, I drove over and parked, then got out to take inventory. There were several old cars, including a Mercedes 450SLC coupe, one of my favorites. Many were parts cars. None appeared restorable.

When visiting old-car locations for the first time, an unwritten protocol is followed: You can look at anything from a distance without disturbing anyone. However, if closer inspection is desired, and to an avid car collector, this is typically craved, it's wise to find the proprietor and ask permission to wander through his vehicles. This tactic not only wards off the threat of German shepherds and shotguns, it's also a surefire method to learn instructive things.

Little did I know.

I knocked and entered the building. The lights were on, but there was no sound, and no one in sight. To the right was a small office with a battered lunch pail sitting in the middle of a desk. The single chair was empty. A grey file cabinet sat nearby in a corner.

I ventured deeper into the working area, surprised to find a dozen cars there, both vintage and modern, all in decidedly better condition than those parked outside. They were British, German, and Italian. I noted a late-model black Ferrari 360 coupe in the middle of the work space, then saw a pair of legs protruding from under its left side. I'd found the proprietor or someone to ask permission to wander through the cars parked outside. For the fourth time, my "hello" echoed around, just loud enough to be heard but soft enough not to intrude or irritate. The legs began to move. Soon a man about my age was on his feet. He approached and introduced himself as the owner. I introduced myself and asked permission to walk among the vehicles outside, which he gave with a smile.

Mike joined me as I wandered through the eclectic group of over-the-hill vehicles, including a Rolls-Royce Silver Shadow sedan, its fabric roof material partially torn away and blown across its windshield, but its flying-lady radiator ornament gleaming and intact. I explained what I'd seen inside, all apparently under the care of a single fellow of about our vintage. The truth was I had become curious walking through the derelicts outside, and excited about all those expensive classics inside being cared for by one older man. He must be a "magus," I thought, a magician or sorcerer of ancient times, and perhaps a "vintage-car whisperer" in the modern era. After hearing my tale, Mike couldn't wait to go inside and see for himself. So we did.

His name was Craig Wehde. And he *was* a magus, at least with respect to the eclectic variety of expensive automobiles, old and new, in his care. He advertised for "European Auto Repair" at his business, Sports & Vintage Cars, in Plainfield, New Hampshire.

After introductions, the three of us had a chance to chat a bit. Mike and I tried to ask our questions sideways to avoid giving any sense of an interrogation. Craig had worked as a mechanic on high-end foreign cars in and around New York City for several decades. He'd enjoyed the work immensely, but the city eventually wore him down, leading him to seek a smaller, quieter place to work, far from the bustle and threats of New York's busy streets. Some of his former New York customers still sought him out. But other car collectors had also found him in his new location. As the proprietor and sole mechanic, he had all the work he needed, and none of the problems of his former locale — a man at peace with his work, and his place, and with himself.

Impressed with what we'd learned, we responded to his questions by telling him something of our backgrounds in aviation and engineering. We thanked him for his time, then said our good-byes. Mike walked out ahead of me. Then, I don't know exactly what happened, but I received some kind of mental message. How foolish. I ignored it and continued toward the door. Then it came again. This time much stronger.

I turned back to Craig, still standing there waiting for the two of us to leave, and asked, "Have you ever worked on a Mercedes 560SL?"

A broad smile. "That's absolutely my favorite car, the 560SL. They were a big hit around New York City and the Connecticut shoreline. I worked on them regularly from their introduction in 1986, until the original owners sold them off, perhaps fifteen years or so altogether. I haven't seen one around in years. But I've kept the technical manuals. And I still have a diagnostic machine that I doubt could be found today in a Mercedes dealership, or anywhere else."

"I believe I could work on a 560SL, even in the dark …"

There's no reason to consume more of your time with the remainder of this long and winding road of a story. You, gentle reader, *know* the ending. However, what you'll never know, nor will I, is what brought this unlikely gift into my life that day. Perhaps the late Robert Pirsig, who was once quoted saying, "The only Zen you'll find on the top of the mountain is the Zen you bring with you," could enlighten us, and provide an answer. Alas, he's no longer with us.

Within a week, the roadster had been delivered to Sports & Vintage Car. Craig had it about four weeks, much shorter than my expectation, given the exotic marques waiting for his attention at his business. We later agreed, based on the unusual range and depth of our conversations regarding the few slightly unkempt matters deep within the subtle core of the car, that each spring I would drive the 560SL to his business, leave to explore the great northern forests for several days, then return when the blowing winds and rushing creeks whispered it was ready, going home with my prize.

Robert Pirsig wrote in *Zen and the Art of Motorcycle Maintenance*: "Each machine has its own unique personality, which probably can be defined as the intuitive sum total of everything you know and feel about it."

With the car's return came a modest bill.

And the 560SL, you ask impatiently? How was the car after its visit to the magus?

I'll tell you exactly how it was.

It was perfect.

17

Conclusions, Illusions, Enlightenment

"You say a man can't love a material thing
With aluminum skin and a cast iron soul
But they never heard your engine sing"
— Jimmy Webb, *Too Young To Die*

Advertising for the 2020 mid-engine Corvette Stingray, *MotorTrend* magazine's "Car of the Year," suggested it to be "a device which measures precision." By what metrics does it measure? In no particular order, the answer, according to Chevrolet, was: innovation, performance, design, responsiveness, aesthetics, and driver engagement. This list approximates what most car collectors seek, along with restoration cost and future value, as we continue our illusive quests for that barn find, estate gem, or well-loved family favorite.

Thank you, dear reader, for coming on this multi-decade ride down memory lane. I hope after reading the introduction, you might consider Zen's unwritten principles a support system for the rigor of old car collecting, and perhaps for life itself. These car tales, victories and defeats, object lessons all, should better position you for success in old car collecting. If you're already a collector, perhaps a trick or two found within will support future quests.

In writing this book, I wanted to avoid the prescriptive "laundry list" approach so common in describing the car hobby. I didn't want to explain everything needed or compile a how-to list for acquiring old cars. Such books are readily available. A search on your browser should quickly answer that need. I believe that the journey is equally important to its end. As Robert Pirsig wrote, "Sometimes it's better to travel than to arrive." Part of the satisfaction found in developing a hobby is learning your way into it, so the accomplishment is your own, not following the dots provided by someone else. Every car, every seller, and every set of purchase circumstances is unique. Thus instead of "how to," I've tried through parable to explain how I survived and enjoyed the car hobby. These tracks you may or may not decide to follow.

To expand on that thought, since a collector's financial resources are involved when an old car is purchased, he must prepare thoroughly, and treat each element of the process, if not with outright suspicion, then with due regard for Ronald Reagan's maxim to "trust — but verify." Over the decades in pursuit of collectible vehicles, I've had the good fortune to deal, almost without exception, with honest caring people. The old car world is full of them. It's the greatest strength of the hobby.

But I wrote "almost." Exceptions to the rule of honesty, though few, can cause outsized problems and cost unexpected sums. The 1988 Mercedes purchase described in the previous chapter was the greatest mistake I ever made in the hobby. That story offers a stark lesson. The reader must ask the obvious question: how could an experienced, methodical hobbyist make such a mistake? Taken in by a practiced and professional shyster is the short answer. I was lured by expert misrepresentation to abandon my own tried and true rules. The critical error of judgment lies, however, at *my* doorstep.

What, therefore, are the tenets worth keeping in the car collector's mind?

The first: know yourself. What is your motivation? What drives you to enter the hobby and seek purchase of an old car? Is this about self-image? When I was engaged to be married, aged twenty-one, I recall listing the imperfections I recognized in myself, hoping to give my fiancé an opportunity to better understand her intended partner, warts and all. In doing this, I also mentioned a goal I'd had for years, to own and restore as many interesting and unique collector automobiles as possible in my lifetime.

After saying this, I probably winced inwardly at the likely reaction. Instead, I was rewarded for my candor with a simple smile and gentle nod. And here we are, more than fifty years, and almost seventy interesting old cars, after that conversation. I knew who I was and what I wanted. By sharing that objective with my future wife, and gaining her acceptance, an unspoken agreement was fashioned. It has provided thousands of hours of hobby pleasure. A single, brief, honest exchange paved the way to an important and enjoyable aspect of my life.

Three decades living in the greater Washington, D.C. region, as I worked toward retirement, was a halcyon period for my participation in car questing and collecting, as I had more free time and resources available. The area was remarkable for turning up original old cars available at reasonable prices. Fortunately, I located an honest and skilled automotive jack-of-all-trades in northwest Maryland, to aid and abet my efforts. Together, we brought back almost a dozen vintage automobiles over twenty years, including the full ground-up restoration of the 1953 Ford station wagon you read about earlier.

Dave Krolak was proprietor of Nostalgia Works in Sharpsburg, Maryland. He and I worked well together and understood each other, perhaps because we'd both spent years in the Navy. He was a deep-sea diver, while I was a pilot. One day, as I was preparing to leave his shop, he caught my eye and told me that he'd come to know me as someone who visibly lost interest once a project was completed. Instead, he observed, I seemed far more involved in acquiring and restoring. I said nothing, though his comment hurt. It took time for me to realize that Dave's assessment was correct.

I enjoyed the journey. The research, the questing, the negotiating and deal-making, the project analysis and, above all, the challenging and uncertain process of bringing a vehicle back to life. This process captivated me completely. It was necessary that I admit this to Dave, which I did, but to myself foremost. It wasn't that I didn't feel pride in ownership, or enjoy taking the restored vehicles to old-car events or simply driving them for pleasure. I did do and feel those things. But I found the greatest satisfactions in chasing a rare part, or striving to find a special tool. I loved most being a working part, a cog, in the renewal process.

When I recall those long-ago words to my fiancé, I recognize that my boyhood objective has never changed. In order to experience as many unique collector cars as possible, there was also a certain pressure to "round 'em up and move 'em out." For those with resources that allow unlimited acquisitions, varied storage alternatives, and full-time professional support, vehicle numbers aren't likely an issue. For the rest of us, who must live within our means, and consider ourselves fortunate to have an understanding spouse, a two-car garage, a waterproof car cover, a decent tool box, and a few bucks available to enjoy working on an old car or two, our hobby involvement must be carefully planned and budgeted.

Okay, you say: You were discussing rules. I was. But I believe that *how* we go through the process of learning about ourselves, and understanding the factors which compel us to enter the old car hobby, might have essential value. Why? Because if you don't understand what underlies your hobby interest, you're essentially a victim in search of a victimizer — and there are plenty of the latter about.

Assuming you're successful in understanding your purpose, the next rule is the Boy Scouts' venerable motto: Be Prepared. As with most things in life, solid preparation is the key to eventual success. A professional painter of expensive cars once told me he had his crew put 80% of their effort into preparing a car's surfaces for paint, and 20% or less on the final color and clear-coat applications. Half of the 20% for actual painting was fine sanding and polishing between coats to insure the final result was a surface as flawless as the rest of the car.

As Robert Pirsig aptly wrote in *Zen and the Art of Motorcycle Maintenance*, "You see a certain quietness in skilled mechanics and machinists, and you see it in the work they do. To say they are not artists, is to misunderstand the nature of art. They give patience, care and attentiveness to what they are doing, but more than this, there's an inner peace of mind that isn't contrived, but results from a harmony with the work in which there is no leader and no follower. The material and the craftsman's thoughts move together in a progression of smooth, even changes until his mind comes to rest at the exact moment the material is right."

You cannot know too much about the car you intend to buy. Its history, its documents, particularly the title. Current and past owners. Seller reviews, whether a business or an individual. Rust and repairs. Collision damage. Un-original items. Matching numbers for body and motor. But these considerations, while important, pale beside the need to put your eyes and hands on the car, or, alternatively, the eyes and hands of a professional appraiser, knowledgeable in your make and model, who can travel as your representative to see, drive, and photograph the prospective purchase, then forward a written report of his findings with photos, including an estimate of market value.

Apply Reagan's adage — trust but verify — to each step of the documentation and purchase process, including the inspection and driving test. In arranging for any service, as in purchasing the car itself, try to deal with reputable people, whose quality of service and integrity are well-documented. At each step, seek a quality product or service at a reasonable price. Consistent preparation will almost inevitably produce this outcome.

Let me share a different approach to questing for and finding a collector car, a method I came upon only after a lengthy transformation over many years.

The first two decades of car collecting were wonderful for me, pure fun. It was an adventure to pit my rank inexperience against the hobby's seasoned collectors and service providers. I was young and ambitious, but poor. This forced me to purchase lower quality cars. Sometimes, I spent a year or more learning how to make proper repairs, while waiting for funds to purchase a part or service. Projects were often delayed as a result, not to mention labor-intensive and time-consuming. Looking back, I see this phase as a kind of apprenticeship, forced by circumstance. Slowly but steadily, I acquired the knowledge and experience to do much of my own work, an invaluable asset in any field of endeavor.

Then, not quite forty, I had an epiphany. Zen's emphasis on mindfulness played a role. At that age, I found the commitments required of a professional career that fed and housed my family, when combined with long hours at night and on weekends moving the current car project along, wore me down mentally and physically. I experienced what many of us do in our working lives: burnout. I lacked capacity to carry such a load. A candle cannot be burned at both ends.

Needing a new paradigm, I eventually found it. I loved old cars, and knew I'd always want the experience that came with having them in my life. So I changed my basic approach to the hobby without altering well-established priorities. Previously, I bought the least expensive example of a model. The dirt track racing '54 Corvette with the shortened steering column, for example. Then I spent months and sometimes years doing the work to bring the vehicle to the desired level.

Instead, I chose to spend most of my time locating excellent examples of a sought-after collector car through extensive research. I negotiated glacially, and often at feigned leisure, to drive asking prices to a level I could afford. This was ages before the Internet, e-mail, and cell phones, all of which have magically enhanced this more practical process, making it faster and more efficient. The car hobby no longer wore me down. It had again become fun.

But it was the result that was the glittering jewel. At the moment I bought a car, it was immediately presentable and usable. I would still do necessary repairs, and make changes to personalize the project. But these were minor in nature, and not burdensome to carry out. This added to the fun because, in resolving problems on my own, the car performed better, was safer and more reliable, and had become more truly mine through my personal involvement.

I'd like to ask you a question, dear reader: Are old cars alive?

At the risk of damaging my credibility, I'm posing what I believe to be a serious question. I'm not asking if cars walk and talk, though current automotive design and development initiatives seem to be moving steadily toward transferring operating functions from the driver to the car itself. Automatic or autonomous steering and braking. Collision avoidance. It's a commonplace that government rules and regulations demanding improved safety and energy conservation benefit everyone. They save lives as well.

But, layered in the many thousands over decades, these legal strictures of rule, regulation, and law have boxed in car manufacturers to the extent that, striving to meet the countless requirements imposed, they can no longer produce truly beautiful or unique cars. Instead, most are big, plastic-laden boxes, with smaller engines and fewer cylinders, hyped, electronically and mechanically, to haul the behemoth's weight.

Is it any wonder that car lovers and collectors seek something of more compelling interest and value by their nostalgic pursuit of collectible cars from earlier eras? Paint schemes that aren't limited almost exclusively to black, white, tan and grey, but instead tease the eyes with hues like seafoam green, pink, coral, multiple shades of yellow and blue. Fenders, hoods, trunks, and rooflines shaped in beautiful, alluring, even sexy ways, which make the heart beat faster. Interiors that are spacious, and as comfortable as sitting in your den recliner. Visibility as broad and wide as today's surround sound. Heavy chrome bumpers requiring two men to lift, and able to sustain contact at speeds in excess of 5 mph, without leaving acres of plastic shards on the road. Finally, majestic V8 motors, whose resonant, throaty rumbles connote power, stirring your insides with their authoritative sound, their promise of genuine driving excitement and endless fun.

Owning a collector car is, for many, the opposite experience of driving a modern vehicle.

Collector cars are, in their own way, sentient, rewarding the owner who provides care and nourishment, loyal in their own way. When, late at night, preparing for bed and locking up, a car collector opens the garage door, flicks on the overhead light, and appraises that special old car, is it inanimate? No, it is not. That car knows you are there. It appreciates your appreciation. It senses an emotional connection and wants to please. It sees your smile as you gaze on its appealing lines, and returns that love. Have we not felt the strong bond, fashioned by the sweat and treasure which re-created something of such beauty, something which, in turn, asks only to be with you?

I confess that I've never watched a sold collector car leave my driveway without feeling a tinge of sadness that I somehow let down a friend.

Brian Wilson, leader of the Beach Boys, and their principal songwriter, penned many songs about cars in the 1960s car-crazy era of TBirds, Stingrays, 409s, 427s and 455s, deuce coupes, and Woodie surfer wagons. One of these was titled, *The Ballad Of Ole' Betsy*.

Wilson probably imagined Betsy as a 1932 Ford or Chevrolet deuce coupe, delivered by the freight train from Detroit to its owner in California. Somehow, Wilson's owner knew of the car's long history, its former owners, that she had "been around," and thus the plight and pain in her earlier life. But he also saw her classic beauty, outer and inner, and sensed the strong loyalty and love she felt for him, emotions that he returned in full. He and Betsy had a special bond.

As the simple, but beautiful ballad draws to its close, the owner is saddened by the realization that, though he sees the gold in her rusted iron, he also knows Betsy is growing old, as are we all. This thought deepens his feelings for the old deuce couple and brings his tears.

Nostalgic? Saccharine? Sophomoric? Without question.

Yet why do we get goose bumps when we hear the song or read its lyrics? Perhaps a tear in the eye as well? Why do we relate to Betsy's owner, as he expresses his feelings for the old car? Why do *our* old cars touch us so profoundly, often in surprisingly powerful ways, while our modern cars touch us only a little or not at all? Why does merely seeing a certain old car passing on the road instantly convey scenes from a distant time, when we were young and that car was new? There are no simple answers to these questions. Taken together, they suggest that those who love old cars find something in them to which they react with strong emotion.

Objects that elicit such a reaction are not inanimate.

For us, they live. They sense. They feel. They know. And we belong to them every bit as much as they belong to us.

Growing older, life often seems a process of letting go of our valued things. We know, of course, if only at some deeper level, that we must each leave the scene ourselves at some point. Some years ago, it dawned on me that a number of the cars I had owned and restored were likely to outlive me. I'm good with that. In fact, I like the thought, as it suggests that we're only temporary conservators of these old cars we own and restore, that they'll be around long after we're gone, and that we can take comfort in having known them in our turn.

There are cars operating and roadworthy today that were produced over a century ago. By extension, and assuming that fossil fuels endure for a few additional decades, it's possible to imagine cars of the 1950s and 1960s — Fords, Chevrolets, Hudsons, Studebakers, Nashes, Pontiacs, Oldsmobiles, Buicks, Cadillacs, Lincolns, MGAs, Austin-Healeys and Triumphs — still safely and reliably carrying their owners down the road a century after their production. It's not *that* far off in the future.

Over the past decade, there's been a standing joke in my family. My wife and daughters laughingly ask if each old-car acquisition is, finally, "the last car." Somewhere along the line, I must have foolishly suggested that a particular car might be the end of the line for me. Our eldest actually told me that the title of this book should be *The Last Car.* One day, there will be an actual last car. But in responding to the family's friendly barbs, I've become increasingly enigmatic about that august passage and its exact details.

The truth is, while I've let other lifelong interests in sports and music gently come to an end, foregoing further participation, even though I felt I was surrendering something irredeemable from my private store of treasures, I realized long ago that the old car hobby would be the most difficult activity to let go. It's possible I won't, while breathing, ever find the courage to do so. Instead, the car hobby may have to let me go — when I go. We'll just have to see.

Why resist the seemingly inevitable? Because old-car collecting and an affiliation with the hobby, provide gifts that cannot be put into words, exerting a comforting power over us through the pleasures they bring.

At the center are the relationships, hundreds of them over the decades, not only with other hobbyists, buyers and sellers, restorers and tradesmen, parts businesses, specialty providers, and especially the personal friends, like Mike Stansel, who suffer through the long nights and countless frustrations with you. The cars themselves bring a unique and fulsome richness into your life, something uplifting and magnificent, all out of proportion to the extracurricular status of a mere hobby. Something, in fact, very much like J.D. Salinger's "perfect horse."

On top of it all is the sought-after perfection, never quite achieved, of each old car project. The planning, the research, the expenditures, the hundreds and sometimes thousands of grease-covered hours invested in bringing the car back to its original state. And, eventually, the arrival at a deep understanding of why such projects are important to us on many levels.

There are satisfactions in the car hobby only rarely found in the normal working careers we are forced into by circumstance. A good part of the reason is that we've freely chosen to do what we're doing, knowing as we make the choice that we're not only embarking on an effort of uncertain length and undetermined outcome, but that there's also what economists call "opportunity cost" in the mix. Our decision to proceed invariably takes time and attention from other aspects of our lives. Thus, there's definite heft in making such a committment.

In all this complexity, in an old-car project's many false starts, its jarring bumps and grinds, the inevitable box canyons in which we come to realize that "the only way out is through," and in the failures endured throughout, thoughts of Zen arise. For it is through

Zen's mindfulness that complexity can be confronted, considered in its proper context, and subsumed. In Zen, there is no beginning, and no end, and thus no "last" — nor "last car."

Instead, there is Quality. Caring. Focus. Silence. Being ...

By design and nature, cars are logical machines. As logical as they are, the process of returning an old car to its original condition is anything but logical. Intuition and mindfulness must take over.

If the essence of Zen is attempting to understand the meaning of life directly, without being misled by logical thought or language, then we should consider the evidence in these factual car stories, evidence that may fail to convince or move us on a logical basis, but which succeeds in doing so, when our intuition is applied to unique, sometimes magical, circumstances.

Here, as you will recall from reading the stories, are several examples:

- Being offered a 1929 Packard Sport Phaeton for pocket change in a stranger's letter
- Finding the contact for a 1955 Chevrolet Cameo pickup in a box of old car address scraps twenty-five years after briefly glimpsing the truck in a garage
- Encountering a 1936 Cadillac V12 sedan, a decade after selling it in California, while picking up a new Cadillac at a Virginia dealership
- Selling a 1966 Pontiac GTO to a man driven to its purchase by an old magazine article which, unbeknownst to him, I'd authored years earlier
- Meeting a mechanical magus for the complex 1980s Mercedes Benz 560SL roadster in a postage-stamp town in backwoods New England
- Finding rare collectible vehicles such as the 1936 Cadillac V12, the 1958 Dodge Sweptside truck, and the only 1941 Alfa Romeo in the world in local newspapers

In life, things happen. Opportunities arise. Images are seen — or they're not. Sounds are heard — or they're not. "As long as one thinks about listening, one cannot hear clearly." For those who strive to see and hear, who slow down time and concentrate quietly, opportunities reveal themselves. They can be seized and acted upon. Zen's calm attentiveness, its reliance upon intuition rather than observation and logic, the very act of surrendering and being in the moment, can produce results beyond comprehension.

Every collector of old cars follows his or her elusive dreams. Most of us seek to re-create an earlier time or place, perhaps even an earlier version of ourselves. But there also exists in many of us a seeker of unique experience. We reach for that special moment of discovery that can elevate us beyond what passes for the normal, that instead grasps, if only briefly, for a higher plane, a higher truth, a place where other rules, largely unseen, apply.

Some of us, the very lucky or most persistent, are given to see such visions in our lives. For some, one brief glimpse might make the entire journey worthwhile. While for others, our dreams must serve in place of having such rarified experiences.

* * *

Years ago, a brief, humorous vignette in an automobile magazine caught, perhaps unintentionally, the very essence of what car collectors find most compelling in their hobby:

> After running out of gas on a remote country road, you hike over to a farmhouse, knock on the door and ask an old man with a weathered face if he has some gas you can buy.
>
> "Sure," he says. Out in the barn, as he sets to work with gas can and syphon, something in the shadows catches your eye.
>
> There, under a hay pile and covered in dust, canted sideways on a flat tire, is an early 1950s Corvette roadster. Left behind forty-five years earlier, you discover, by a son headed to Vietnam, who failed to return for his favorite car.

Nonchalantly, you walk around the vehicle, examining its details, and realize that, under the dust and straw, nothing is missing. It's all there.

"Never got around to selling it," the old man says.
"Oh?" You reply. "I might be interested."
"You would? Would $200 be okay?"

Then you wake up ...

* * *

Moments to cherish. Seeking, finding, and, if only now and then, coming to know something deeply and perfectly true, something well beyond the nature we once thought was understood.

The last car?

Some day, certainly.

About the Author

A former naval officer, test pilot, Washington speechwriter, and aerospace executive, Bruce Valley is the author of *Seahawk: Confessions of an Old Hockey Goalie* and *Rye Harbor: Poems of the New Hampshire Seacoast.* He lives in Rye, New Hampshire, and writes about commonplace matters in our lives, some unseen and unheard, those things which touch our hearts.

Acknowledgments

Seldom is a book brought to life only by the author whose name appears on its cover, and certainly not in this case. A great deal of help and support are required, ranging from critical suggestions by early readers to the practical skills of editing and copyediting, cover art, photographs, and captions, book design and assembly, printing and publishing. Of at least equal importance is the moral support furnished by family and friends, the latter contributions often the unmentioned but critically necessary ingredient that assures the book's completion.

In no particular order, these people together formed my vital underpinning for the creation of *Zen and the Art of Old Car Collecting*. My gratitude is without bound.

* * *

Nancy Valley, Noelle Valley Milam, Tom Milam, Christine Valley Marr, David Marr, Grace Peirce, Jay Leno, Michael Stansel, Rita Stansel, Robert Ross, Frank Mullinax, Carl Manofsky, Arsenio Valentim, Roger Soares, Bill Paweski, Steve Linden, Roger Byam Nold, Byron Dieckmann, Terry Eargle, Kay Ruma, Roy Gale, Bill Vivian, John Carberry, Eddie Ireland, Mike DiNola, Fred Miller, Henry Marsh, Paul Dentler, Mike Odening, Howard Vanderbilt, Dave Krolak, Richard Murray, Craig Wehde, Bob Broadbent, William Beebe, Kevin Supples, Gerry Dreschler, Chuck Roberts, Alves Reis, Nicholas Brower, King Bond, Larry Blose, Ed Hillebrand, Tom Moulton, Ron Lavoie, Brian Wilson, and Robert Pirsig.